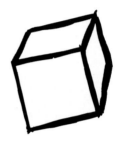

THE ART DIRECTORS CLUB
ANNUAL 90

EDITORIAL DIRECTOR
Jennifer Larkin Kuzler

EDITOR
Chelsea Temkin

EDITORIAL ASSISTANT
Kim Hanzich
Michael Waka

AWARDS STAFF
Jessica Alonso
Ana Benaroya
Kim Hanzich
Min Sun Kim
Jennifer McClelland
Michael Waka

COPY EDITOR
Anne Cherry

DESIGN
Paula Scher, Pentagram

**CALL FOR ENTRIES
AND GALA INVITA-
TION DESIGN BY
90TH CUBE PROJECT
PARTICIPANTS:**
Réne Clément
Marc Cozza
Paul Davis
Masashi Kawamura
Jeong Eun (Elle) Kim
Nosigner

JURY PHOTOGRAPHER
Geoff Green
geoffgreen.com

**PUBLISHED IN
ASSOCIATION WITH**
AVA Publishing SA
Rue des
Fontenailles 16
1000 Lausanne 6
Switzerland
Tel : +41 78 600 5109
enquiries@avabooks.com

**DISTRIBUTED IN USA
& CANADA BY**
Ingram Publishers
Services Inc.,
1 Ingram Blvd
La Vergne TN 37086
Tel: +1 866 400 5351
customer.services@
ingrampublisher
services.com

**DISTRIBUTED
EX-NORTH AMERICA**
Thames & Hudson
181a High Holborn
London WC1V 7QX
United Kingdom
Tel: +4420 7845 50000
sales@thameshudson.
co.uk

PRODUCTION BY
AVA Book Production
Pte. Ltd., Singapore
Tel ; +65 6334 8173
Email: production@
avabooks.com.sg
Library of Congress
Cataloging-in-
Publication Data
Art Directors Club
(New York, N.Y.).
The Art Directors Club
Annual. /
Art Directors Club
(New York, N.Y.). p. cm.
Includes index.
ISBN: 9782940411887
(pbk. : alk. paper)
1.Commercial art—
Exhibitions.
2.Art Directors Club
(New York, N.Y.)
—Exhibitions.
NC997.A1 A69

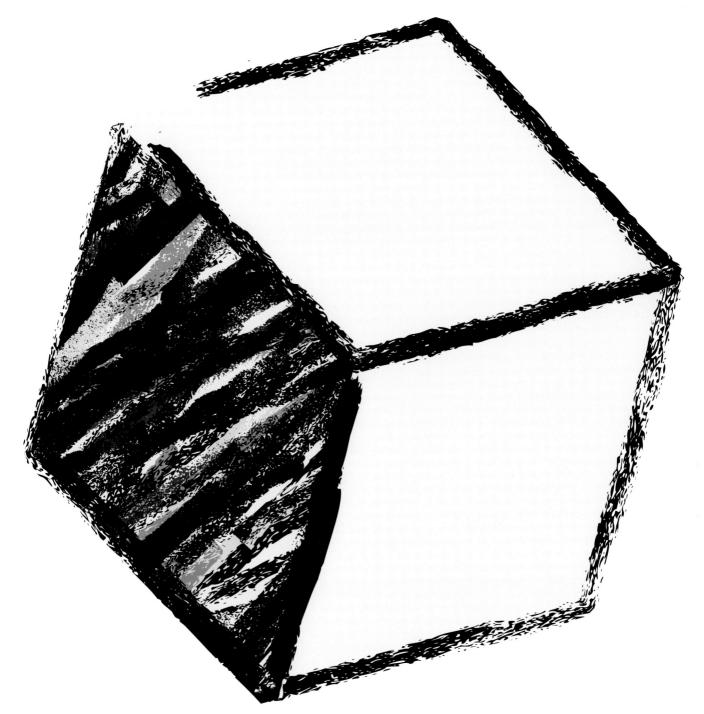

THE ART DIRECTORS CLUB
106 West 29th Street
New York, NY 10001
United States of America
www.adcglobal.org

ISBN 978-2-940411-88-7

Table of Contents

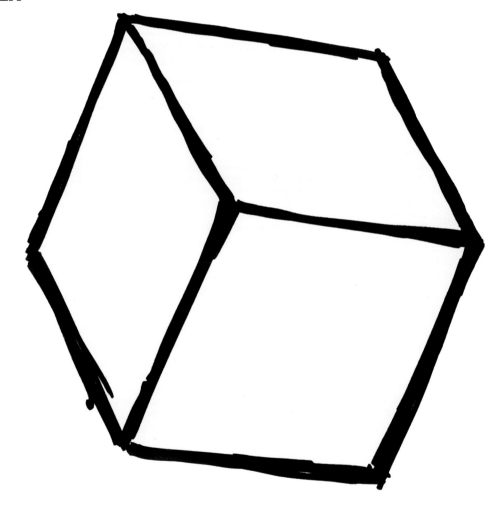

Welcome to 90. Since its inception in 1920, as a revolution led by artists moving into the commercial sphere, the Art Directors Club has been celebrating creativity. The club's purpose has been to teach the world that "great art leads to great commerce." Today we set the global standard for creative communications with our mission to connect, provoke and elevate the creative world. Every art director, artist, designer, creative director, illustrator, photographer or corporation that has entered this show has not only thrust their work in front of the brightest minds in the business, they fund high school workshops, programs to recognize young talent, and support the ADC Hall of Fame, which recognizes career excellence.

As a club, we continue to focus on new ways to engage, excite and further the careers of our community. This year I am proud to announce that our board has voted to provide a view of the winning work from the 90th in the form of a tablet application, as a companion to this Annual. In it, the work will come to life with sound, animation, video and dynamic content that will engage you and draw you closer to the works' creators. No matter what part of the world you find yourself in, I encourage you to become more involved with the Art Directors Club. It is an organization that at its core has the potential to change the world for the better, by connecting exceptional creative thinkers with mentors, rivals, collaborators and muses through its variety of programming, its physical space and digital presence online.

I feel it is important to thank Janet Froelich of Real Simple Magazine and Brian Collins of COLLINS:, both members of our board, who have volunteered their time to provide feedback to Paula Scher, Partner at Pentagram, designer of this 90th Annual. Paula, an artist and a designer whose involvement at the club as an educator, thought leader and ADC Hall of Fame Laureate is by definition a gold standard in moving our profession forward. This is my final year serving as Board President of the Art Directors Club, which has been an honor, working with a group of the most capable, talented, and inspiring people, whom I have come to know very well. It has been fantastic steering this organization with their support, and the help of our staff. Knowing and being part of its plans for the near future, I encourage you to stay tuned.

DOUG JAEGER
ART DIRECTORS CLUB
BOARD PRESIDENT
PARTNER, JAEGERSLOAN INC.

We are truly proud to have reached this extraordinary milestone—publication of the 90th (90th!) Art Directors Club Annual. And the opportunity to celebrate the occasion through the singular design of ADC Hall of Fame laureate Paula Scher is icing on the cake.

The very best work in the world is in here. And that is the happy result of having the very best people in the industry judging it. Steve Simpson generously oversaw stellar juror panels in six categories, each led by an industry luminary: advertising (Paul Lavoie), design (Michael Bierut), interactive (Will McGinness), hybrid (Wayne Best), photography (Kathy Ryan) and illustration (Marian Bantjes). I had the distinct pleasure of observing these juries during the review process, hearing them discuss, debate and ultimately defend the work you see here. I was struck by the pride the jurors took in their responsibility. I was moved by their dedication to the task. It was inspiring, like the work they selected.

Inspiration is what drives us here at the Art Directors Club. We seek to discover it and pass it along, across geographical and stylistic boundaries and from generation to generation. We've been at it for 90 years now. And because all the money we earn goes back into our programming—fueling scholarships, career workshops, portfolio reviews and more—we'll be here for the next generation of inspired professionals, too. We can't wait to be amazed by them, the way we are by the powerful work you now hold in your hands.

OLGA GRISAITIS
ART DIRECTORS CLUB
DIRECTOR

DESIGN

STEVE SIMPSON
OGILVY NORTH AMERICA

MICHAEL BIERUT
DESIGN CHAIR
PENTAGRAM

PETER ALFANO
TROLLBÄCK + COMPANY

THOMAS BARHAM
THOMAS BARHAM DESIGN

JAMIE CALIRI
DZED SYSTEMS

RENÉ CLÉMENT
PAPRIKA

PUM LEFEBURE
DESIGN ARMY

**SHEILA LEVRANT
DE BRETTEVILLE**
YALE UNIVERSITY

FRANCISCO LOPEZ
MOGOLLON

CHRISTY SHEPPARD
MARTHA STEWART LIVING

RYOSUKE UEHARA
DRAFT CO., LTD.

EDWIN VAN GELDER
MAINSTUDIO

ILLUSTRATION

HEATHER STEPHENS
WALL STREET JOURNAL

MARIAN BANTJES
ILLUSTRATION CHAIR
DESIGNER/WRITER

ANDRIO ABERO
ART DIRECTOR/DESIGNER

SEYMOUR CHWAST
PUSHPIN

PAUL DAVIS
ILLUSTRATOR

MAIA VALENZUELA
HEARST DIGITAL MEDIA

PAUL COLLINS
KIRSHENBAUM BOND
AND PARTNERS

CARLA ECHEVARRIA
R/GA

CORINNA FALUSI
STRAWBERRYFROG

PETE FAVAT
ARNOLD WORLDWIDE

MIKE GEIGER
GOODBY, SILVERSTEIN &
PARTNERS

JONATHAN HILLS
DOMANI STUDIOS

ADVERTISING

JEFFREY ZELDMAN
HAPPY COG

ANDREW ZOLTY
BREAKFAST NY

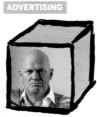

PAUL LAVOIE
ADVERTISING CHAIR
TAXI

WAYNE BEST
HYBRID CHAIR
COG NYC

JOE ALEXANDER
THE MARTIN AGENCY

SARAH BARCLAY
JWT NEW YORK

LINDA HONAN
BBDO NEW YORK

IVAN JOHNSON
NETWORK BBDO

MARGARET JOHNSON
GOODBY, SILVERSTEIN &
PARTNERS

ERIC KALLMAN
BARTON F. GRAF 9000 LLC

JEFF KLING
FREELANCE

IRIS LO
HK4A & DRAFTFCB

MANUEL DILONE
R/GA

CRAIG DUBITSKY
KIND

HITESH HAJARNAVIS
POPCORN, INDIANA

JUAN FRONTINI
MTV WDS

TIMOTHY GOODMAN
ART DIRECTOR/DESIGNER

STEFAN GUZY
ZWÖLF

JULIA HOFFMANN
MOMA

NICOLE JACEK
KARLSSONWILKER INC.

JEONG EUN (ELLE) KIM
ART DIRECTOR/DESIGNER

PHOTOGRAPHY

DANNY YOUNT
PROLOGUE FILMS

KATHY RYAN
PHOTOGRAPHY CHAIR
THE NEW YORK TIMES
MAGAZINE

KIERAN ANTILL
LEO BURNETT NEW YORK

HELOISE GOODMAN
MARTHA STEWART I LIVING

CHRISTOPHER LANE
PHOTOGRAPHER

LISA NAFTOLIN
NARS COSMETICS

INTERACTIVE

WILL MCGINNESS
INTERACTIVE CHAIR
VENABLES BELL &
PARTNERS

MATT ATKATZ
CP+B

KEMP ATTWOOD
AREA 17

VICTORIA AZARIAN
OGILVY NEW YORK

KRISTIN BERGEM
PEACOCK

**MEERA SHARATH
CHANDRA**
MOMENTUM WORLDWIDE

ALESSANDRA LARIU
SHE SAYS

DAN MALL
BIG SPACESHIP

KAREN MONAHAN
@RADICAL.MEDIA

VIVIAN ROSENTHAL
TRONIC

JOHN ROTHENBERG
SOSOLIMITED

RYSZARD SROKA
CHANGE INTEGRATED

MIGUEL BEMFICA
JWT MADRID

JEREMY CRAIGEN
DDB UK

CHRISTINE GIGNAC
MOTHER NEW YORK

AARON GRIFFITHS
TBWA\CHIAT\DAY

GRAEME HALL
Y&R NEW YORK

TOM HAUSER
CP+B

STUDENT BRIEF

DEBORAH MORRISON
UNIVERSITY OF OREGON

KALPESH PATANKAR
Y&R DUBAI

JAMES SPENCE
SYFY / NBC UNIVERSAL

ROB STRASBERG
DONER

TINA STRASBERG
ART DIRECTOR

SAMIRA ANSARI
TBWA\CHIAT\DAY

Jury Photographer: Geoff Green

Hall of Fame: In the four decades since it was established, the Art Directors Club Hall of Fame has become synonymous with excellence in visual communication. Its inductees represent a staggeringly wide-ranging set of creative endeavors, from advertising to design, from photography to filmmaking to the education of artists. More impressive still, as the roster of inductees grows, the scope of their collective accomplishments continues to expand. This isn't so much a sign of our changing times as an affirmation of the mission set out by the ADC Board of Directors when the Hall of Fame was inaugurated in 1971. From the beginning, it was understood that true achievement defies convention and pushes boundaries. As that year's Annual reads, "These men, and the people that will follow in the Hall of Fame, have lived their lives as art directors, salesmen, thinkers, innovators, but most of all, artists." As we honor this year's inductees, we are reminded that creative excellence is inherently cross-disciplinary. We are proud to recognize four individuals whose daring and generosity are as inspiring as their many outstanding achievements.

−Anthony P. Rhodes & Janet Froelich
Co-Chairs, 2011 Hall of Fame Selection Committee

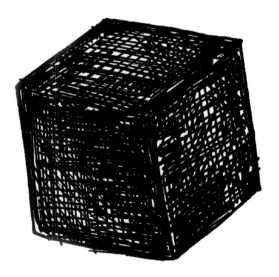

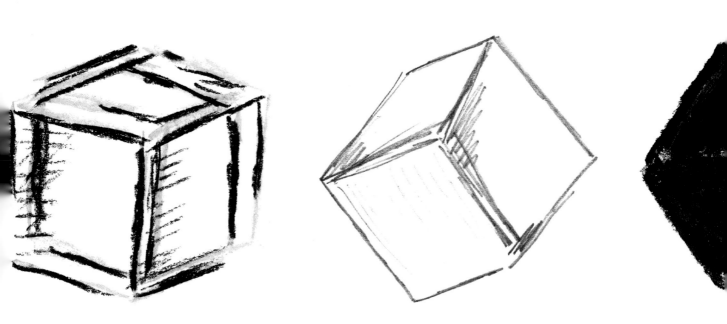

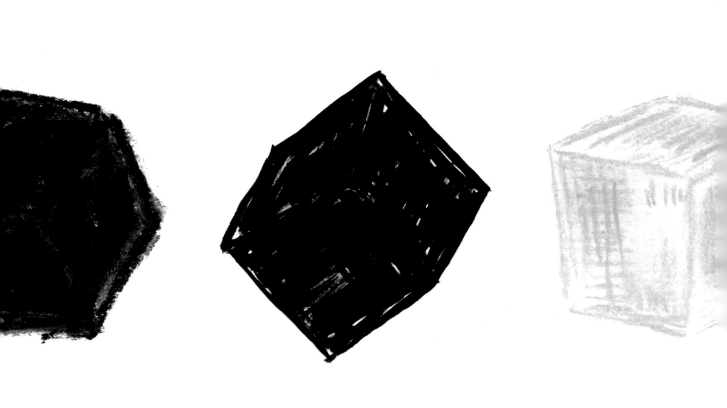

RUTH ANSEL is an art director, designer, and lecturer who has collaborated for over four decades with photographers, illustrators and artists such as Richard Avedon, Andy Warhol, Peter Beard, Bruce Weber, and Annie Leibovitz. She was the youngest co-art director of *Harper's Bazaar* magazine in the '60s. She then went on to art direct *The New York Times Magazine* in the '70s, *House & Garden* and *Vanity Fair* in the '80s, and *Vogue*. During that period she created film titles for the cult film *My Dinner with Andre* directed by Louis Malle.

While art directing magazines she also designed the celebrated books *Alice in Wonderland*, a book about a play, photographed by Richard Avedon, and the 1974 edition of *The End of the Game* by Peter Beard. In the early '90s she formed her own design studio, where she continued to design other notable book projects including, *Dark Odyssey* by Phillip Jones Griffiths, *The Sixties* by Richard Avedon, *Women and The White Oak Dance Project* by Annie Leibovitz, as well as a master monograph for Taschen by Peter Beard. She continued to work closely with Richard Avedon and designed significant portfolios of his work for The New Yorker including his photographs for *Egoiste* magazine in Paris. Her studio has also designed ad campaigns for Versace, Club Monaco, and Karl Lagerfeld.

Ansel has received the Art Directors Club's highest individual annual award for her work, the Gold Cube for Design in 1970, as well as being honored with a special tribute in 1994 from the Society of Publication Design. Award for Continuing Excellence in Publication Design. She has been a guest lecturer at Cranbrook Academy in Michigan,and been on fashion and design panels at The School of Visual Arts in New York. In the fall of 2010 Rizzoli published a book she art directed on the fashion work of photographer Jerry Schatzberg. An ongoing project that she has been deeply committed to is an extensive monograph on the life and work of the extraordinary jewelry designer Elsa Peretti, to be published in the near future.

In October 2009 she was invited to present her work and lecture at the prestigious Moderna Museet in Stockholm, Sweden. A book called *Hall Of Femmes* about Ruth and her celebrated forty-year career was published in 2010. This book consists of an extensive interview with her, including examples of her work in both editorial and advertising design. Personal pictures featuring many of her close colleagues will be published for the first time, together with her views on everything from photography to the business of image-making.

She is presently designing the first major monograph of the work of photographer Denis Piel for Rizzoli, as well as a book about Gary Cooper's enduring style for Powerhouse Books, featuring family photographs from the private collection of Maria Cooper. Currently she has just completed the design of a limited-edition large-scale portfolio of photographs of Kate Moss, for Danziger Projects. And most recently Ruth is thrilled and honored to be the recipient of the Art Directors Club prestigious 2011 Hall of Fame Award.

Ruth Ansel Photo by: Alexandra Catiere

APRIL 1965   HARPER'S   75

BAZAAR

WHAT'S
HAPPENING?
OP
and
TOP
FASHION
FRUG
THAT
FAT
AWAY:
Death
of
the
Diet
BEAUTY
BLAST-OFF:
Lunar
Glow

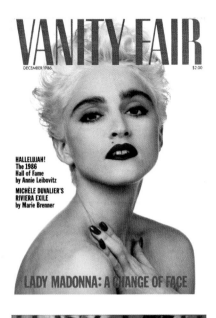

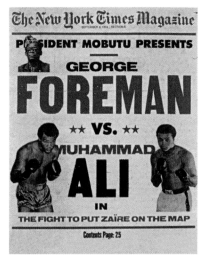

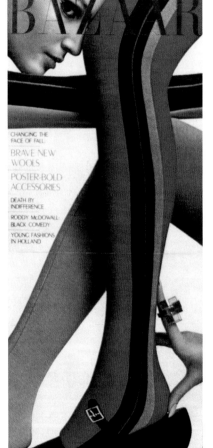

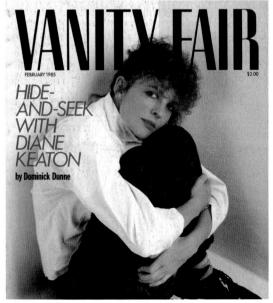

EGOÏSTE

Le Cirque du Soleil   *Nº 13 - Tome II*

Richard Avedon

AUSTRALIA : 54 AUD / BAHAMAS : 40 BSD / CAYMAN ISLANDS : 50 KYD / DENMARK : 230 DKK / EGYPT : 132 EGP / ESTONIA : 475 EEK / HONG KONG : 315 HKD / ISRAËL : 100 ILS / LIECHTENSTEIN : 52 FS
MONGOLIA : 8 000 MNT / MYANNAR : 240 MMK / NEPAL : 500 NPR / NEW GUINEA PAPOUASIA : 38 PGK / RUSSIA : 6 450 SUR / SEYCHELLES : 200 SCR / TAÏWAN : 1 000 TWD / VATICAN : 59 700 L

VERSACE

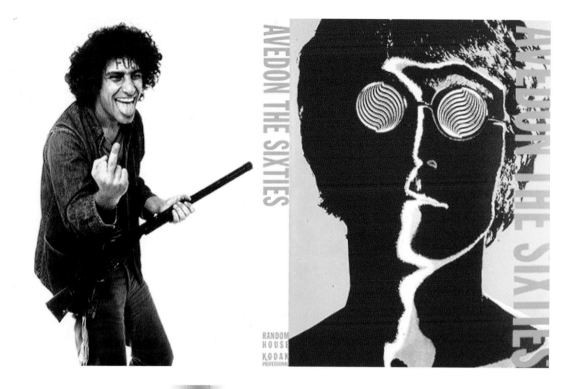

RANDOM
HOUSE
KODAK
PROFESSIONAL

The new Lenny Bruce is somewhat different.
She's black.
And she's making a splash.
JANET COLEMAN sees the Whoopi Goldberg variations

Making
Whoopi

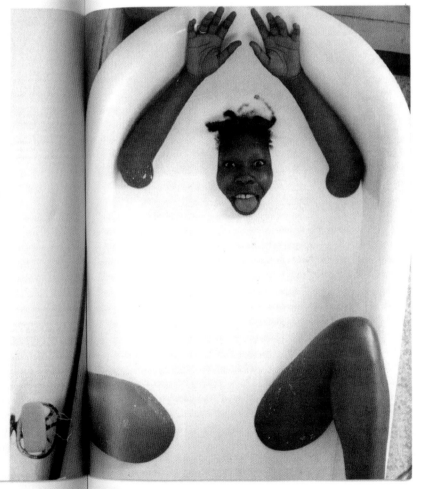

The bombilation started in New York on February 3, 1984, when the headline WHOOPI GOLDBERG DOES ''THE SPOOK SHOW'' exploded in the ''Weekend'' section of the *Times* above a picture of a grinning black woman and Mel Gussow's rave review. Whoopi Goldberg was described as a cross between Lily Tomlin and Richard Pryor, ''not simply a stand-up comedian but a satirist with a cutting edge and an actress with a wry attitude toward life and public performance.''

At the Dance Theater Workshop, in Chelsea, early the following Saturday night, the lines on the staircase included college kids, agents, middle-aged black men in tweed sport coats, old women in minks, and sisters in cornrows. To a dignified experimental theater like D.T.W., *The Spook Show* was obviously more than just a mild sensation. Twenty minutes before curtain, the only seats were on the floor.

For her New York debut, Whoopi Goldberg selected four haunting characters—''spooks''—to appear as a quartet: a dope fiend, a knocked-up surfer chick, a cripple, and a little girl. The dope fiend, Fontaine, opened the show, singing, ''Around the world in ay-tee muh 'fuckin' days.'' Scratching his

crotch, Fontaine moved into the audience and at once put the crowd at ease and on edge: ''How you doin', mama. That's a bad ring you're wearin'. Want me to hold it for you?''

Back in the spotlight, Fontaine blithely discussed every conceivable controversial subject, from legalized marijuana and Abraham Lincoln to Mr. T (''A guy with a Mohawk I'm supposed to relate to. This motherfucker is a throwback, man'') and AIDS (''A government conspiracy—they put germs in the discos''). He panned *The Big Chill* as ''a lot of motherfuckers sitting around crying about the sixties. I could have saved them a whole lot of money, Jack. 'Cause I know what happened in the sixties. CETA. You could get a CETA job and learn to part your hair. I see you had one of those jobs.''

Next, this funky Don Quixote ran down a European trip. His spiel was accompanied by a series of eye-popping physical transformations: into a stewardess steering a quivering beverage cart; a microwaved airplane string bean; a German burgher ogling ''the *Schwarze*'' making his way down narrow Amsterdam streets and thanking God for legal hashish.

The anxiety in the theater was tangi-

36   Photographs by ANNIE LEIBOVITZ

MARSHALL ARISMAN's paintings and drawings have been widely exhibited both internationally and nationally and his work may be seen in the permanent collections of the Metropolitan Museum of Art, Brooklyn Museum, the New York Historical Society and the National Museum of American Art, Smithsonian Institution, the Guang Dong Museum of Art, Telfair Museum of Art, as well as many private and corporate collections.

His illustrations have appeared on the covers of *Time*, *U.S. News and World Report*, *The Nation*, *The Progressive*, *The New York Times Book Review*. His editorial work has appeared in every national publication including *Esquire*, *Rolling Stone*, *Playboy*, *The New York Times* Op-Ed page, *The Village Voice* and *BusinessWeek*.

His original graphic essay *Heaven Departed* explores the emotional and spiritual impact of nuclear war on society. The essay was published in book form by Vision Publishers (Tokyo, 1988).

Among his other books are *The Cat Who Invented Bebop* (winner of the bronze medal by ForeWard magazine Book of the Year Award) published by Creative Editions. He has co-authored four books with Steven Heller: *The Education of an Illustrator*, *Inside the Business of Illustration*, *Teaching Illustration* and *Marketing Illustration* (all published by Allworth Press).

Arisman was the first American invited to exhibit in mainland China in 1999. The exhibition, *Sacred Monkeys*, appeared at the Guang Dong Museum of Art.

He is the subject of a full-length documentary film directed by Tony Silver titled *Facing the Audience, The Arts of Marshall Arisman*. The film received the Creative Achievement Award from the 2002 Santa Barbara Film Festival.

Arisman joined the faculty at the School of Visual Arts in 1965. In 1968 he was appointed chair of the Journalistic Art department and in 1970 became co-chair, with Richard Wilde, of the newly formed Media Department.

In 1984 Arisman created a Master of Fine Arts degree program under the title Illustration as Visual Journalism. Two years later the name was changed to Illustration as Visual Essay. He is currently the chair and faculty member of the department.

He has received two honorary doctorate degrees from Maryland Institute College of Art and Cincinnati Academy of Art. Among his other awards are Distinguished Educator awards from the School Art League of New York, Society of Illustrators, National Association of School of Art and Design and American Artist.

Marshall Arisman Photo by: Dan Wagner

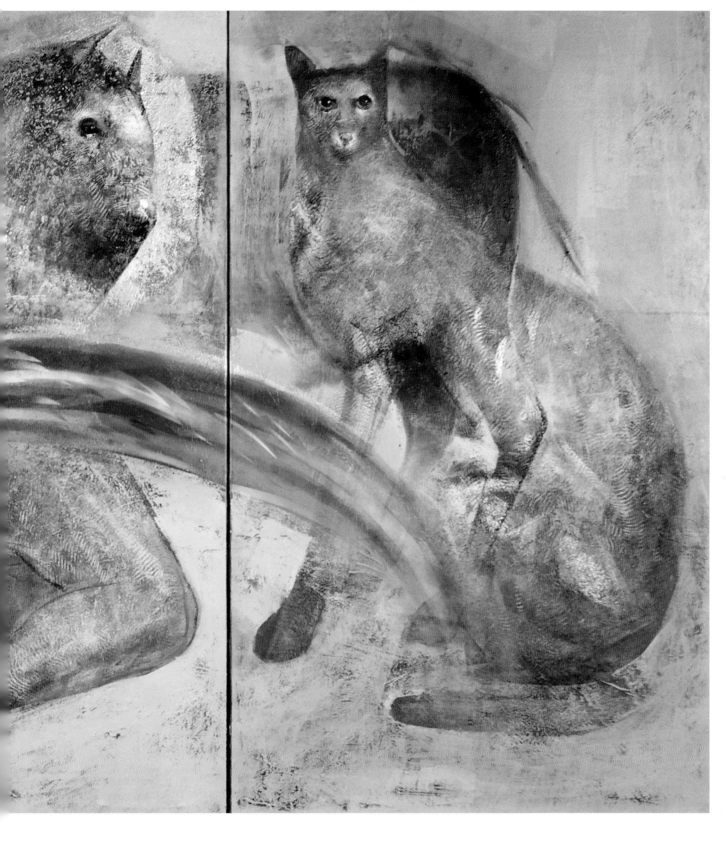

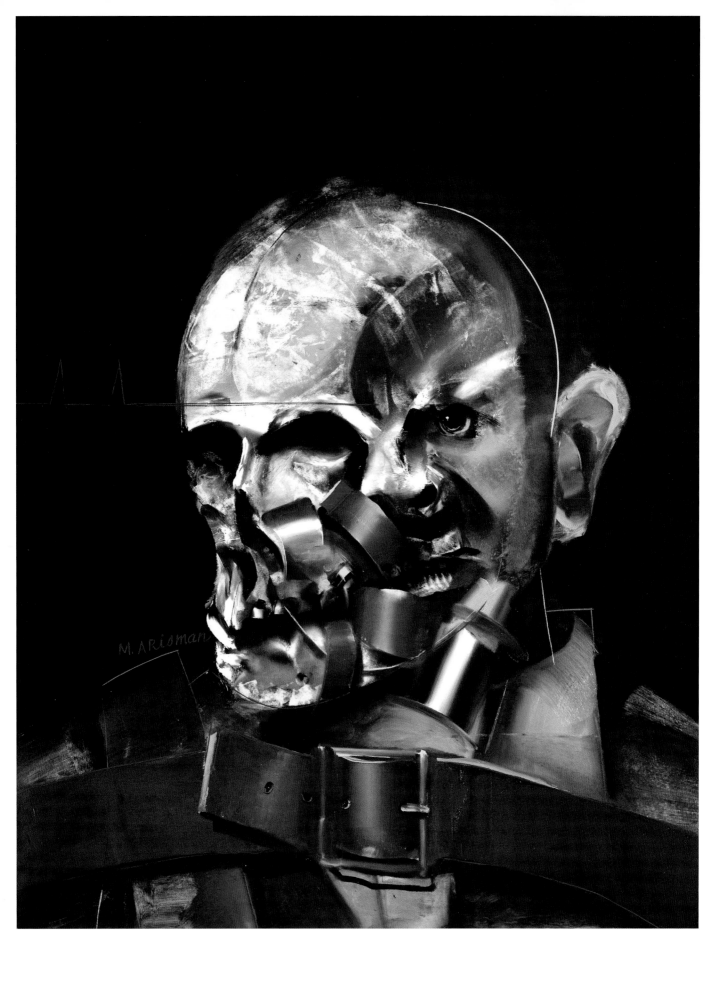

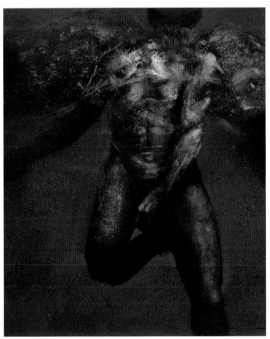

JOHN C JAY serves as the Global Executive Director for the independent creative agency, Wieden+Kennedy, headquartered in Portland Oregon with offices in New York City, London, Amsterdam, Tokyo, Shanghai, New Delhi and São Paolo. He teams with founder Dan Wieden to oversee all of the agency's global creative work and travels extensively for the agency. In Portland, Jay served as Co-Creative Director on the Nike Global account and also worked on the Coca-Cola and Microsoft accounts. In 1996, three years upon his arrival from New York City, he was named a partner in the agency.

Later, Jay helped to open the agency's Tokyo, Shanghai and New Delhi offices. He lived in Japan for six years while overseeing the W+K Tokyo office as Executive Creative Director. In Japan, he launched W+K Tokyo Lab, the independent music label featuring new Japanese music talent with innovative visual concepts and package designs. W+K Tokyo Lab has since received many awards for its creativity in the music industry.

Throughout his career, Jay's pursuit of innovation and cultural authenticity consistently took him to new cultures and experiences, allowing him to work across disciplines and in a diverse mix of industries. Starting in New York in editorial design, to fashion and retail marketing and then to an advertising agency; he continues his learning and creative process today.

His passion to avoid the status-quo inspires his professional and personal activities. Jay's work has received recognition from around the world, while participating in exhibitions with museums and galleries in major cities including New York, Boston, Chicago, London, Paris, Tokyo and St. Petersburg. His book *Soul of the Game* received the Gold Medal at the Leipzig Book Fair in 1997 and was also named one of the 14 Most Beautiful Books in the World by the Copenhagen Museum. *I.D.* magazine in NYC once named him as one of the 40 Most Influential in design. Similarly, *American Photographer* magazine named Jay as one of their 80 Most Influential in photography. In 2009, *GQ* honored PING in Portland, co-owned and designed by Jay, as one of the Top Ten New Restaurants in America. In 2010, Jay was a finalist for the National Design Award by the Cooper-Hewitt Museum of Design.

In 2011, *Fast Company* magazine named Jay as one of the 100 Most Creative People in Business. Prior to Wieden+Kennedy, Jay served for 12 years as Creative Director and Marketing Director for Bloomingdale's in New York City, overseeing the creative marketing of all stores including New York, Washington, D.C., Chicago and Boston. The store's international campaigns gave Jay the opportunity to direct creative campaigns in collaboration with the most influential global creative talent including those from France, Italy, Ireland, China, Japan, India and America.

Jay is the co-founder and director of Studio J, a creative consultancy designing and investing in new products, retail, digital concepts as well as real estate development. PING, co-owned and designed by Studio J, opened in 2009. The Grove, a 70-room creative hostel and retail concept, will also be co-owned and designed by Studio J. It will have its premiere in early 2011. New art, film and digital creative projects are included in 2011. Studio J also produces exclusive products for the Ace Hotel. His support for young creative talent continues to be a focus at Wieden+Kennedy. The Jay Scholarship at The Ohio State University's College of the Arts was created by Jay to encourage students of Asian descent to pursue a career in the arts. He teaches a Masters Class in design and advertising at The School of Visual Arts in New York City and lectures frequently in Japan, India, China and the U.S. Jay also writes on creativity and culture for a variety of international magazines and blogs.

John C Jay serves on the Board of Directors for The Smithsonian Institution in Washington, D.C., and Caldera, a non-profit organization founded by Dan Wieden to help unleash the potential of at-risk youth.

John C Jay Photo by: Ben Clark

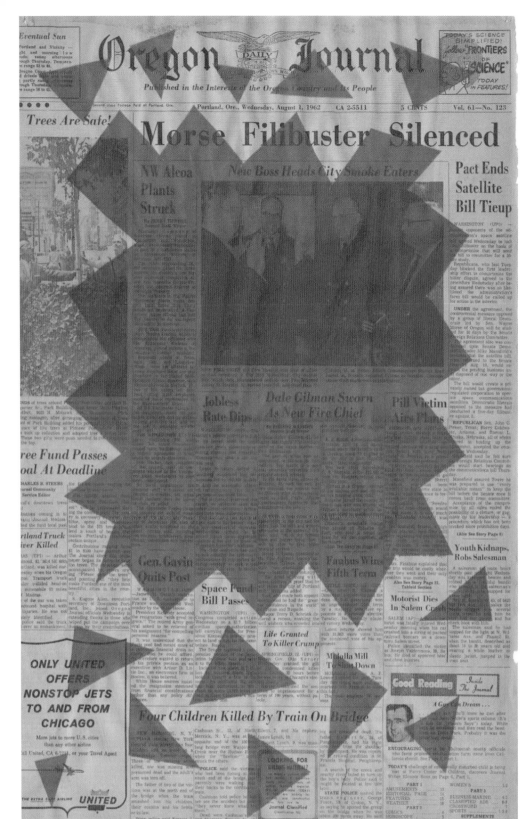

Studio J is a creative consultancy in Portland's Chinatown; designing and investing in product, business, retail and digital concepts. studioj-pdx.com

studioJ

JOE PYTKA was born in Braddock, Pennsylvania. He studied fine arts at Carnegie Institute, Carnegie Tech (now Carnegie Mellon University) then briefly, Chemical Engineering at the University of Pittsburgh. During this period he began working evenings at WRS Motion Pictures, a small industrial film company. After a brief sojourn to New York, running a post production department for MGM Telestudios, he returned to Pittsburgh to film a number of documentary and dramatic films for WQED, a National Educational Network (this was pre-*PBS*). These films and programs won numerous awards and one, *A View of the Sky*, was chosen as an official United States entry in the Montreal World's Fair.

He then partnered with Rift Fournier to form a production company, Fournier/ Pytka, to produce documentaries independently with an occasional foray into commercials. Disenchanted by the lack of formality in the pure documentary form, Pytka turned his attention more to commercials. At the same time, he experimented with an early music video format in his documentary *Maggie's Farm*, and in a short film with Steve McQueen, music by Richie Havens. The latter brought some notoriety and attention and his commercial career began to flourish.

Pytka brought documentary realism to his work, especially for Iron City Beer, in his hometown. This brought him to the attention of Ed McCabe and Hal Riney, who were also interested in this form. His work with the legendary McCabe and Riney won many international awards. After breaking with Fournier he formed an association with Rick Levine and then went out on his own.

Pytka's work with Riney included work for Blitz Weinhard Brewery, Gallo Winery's Bartles & Jaymes, and Perrier. This work is considered some of the greatest work in advertising history. At this time, Pytka began working extensively with Phil Dusenberry for Pepsi, General Electric, DuPont, FedEx. The Pepsi work, especially is also considered historic and garnered many awards, including the Grand Prix at the Cannes Film Festival. That commercial "Archaeology", also forced Coca-Cola to change its famous formula and introduce "new" Coke. Pytka teamed with writer Bill Heater to film work for John Hancock that broke new ground in naturalism, and it's conceded that this work has never been equaled. It also received a controversial Grand Prix at Cannes. His work with Wieden+Kennedy for Nike has also been called groundbreaking, especially the work with Jim Riswold and Stacy Wall.

Pytka has become known for his work with celebrities and athletes, including the Beatles, Madonna, Michael Jordan, Tiger Woods, Tom Hanks, George C. Scott, Marlon Brando, Wayne Gretzky, LeBron James, Dwayne Wade, and President Obama, among many others. In addition to commercials, Pytka has done two films, *Let It Ride*, a critical and commercial mess—although it became a Siskel and Ebert "guilty pleasure"—and *Space Jam*, a hugely profitable movie based in a commercial he did for Nike. This movie was the first successful animated film not done by Disney. He has also done videos for Michael Jackson, The Beatles, and John Lennon. Pytka's industry awards include two Cannes Grand Prix, seven Palmes d'Or, three Directors Guild of America Awards, hundreds of Clios and Cannes Lions, a Grammy, an Emmy, a Lifetime Achievement Award from the Clios, a Lifetime Achievement Award from Cannes, a Directors Guild of America Honors award, and a Wrangler Award from the National Cowboy Hall of Fame. He has been called a "genius" (by *Advertising Age*), and likened to Wolf Larson, the monstrous villain of Jack London's *The Sea-Wolf* (by Steve Hayden, the writer of Apple's "1984"). Pytka scoffs at the genius observations and points out that he and Hayden have worked together for 25 years. In that time their work for IBM took that brand from a negative worth of $50 million to a positive somewhere north of $60 *billion* today and isn't that what advertising is all about?

Joe Pytka Photo by: Joachim Ladefoged

ADC MANSHIP MEDALLION

has been awarded to Paola Antonelli in special recognition of her curatorial excellence.

PAOLA ANTONELLI is the Senior Curator of the Department of Architecture & Design of The Museum of Modern Art, where she has worked since 1994. Through her exhibitions—among them Design and the Elastic Mind in 2008—teachings and writing, Paola strives to promote a deeper understanding of design's transformative and constructive influence on the world. She is very proud of a recent acquisition into MoMA's Collection: the @ sign. She is working on several exhibition ideas—most recently Talk to Me— and on the book *Design Bites*, about basic foods taken as examples of outstanding design.

Paola Antonelli Photo by: Robin Holland

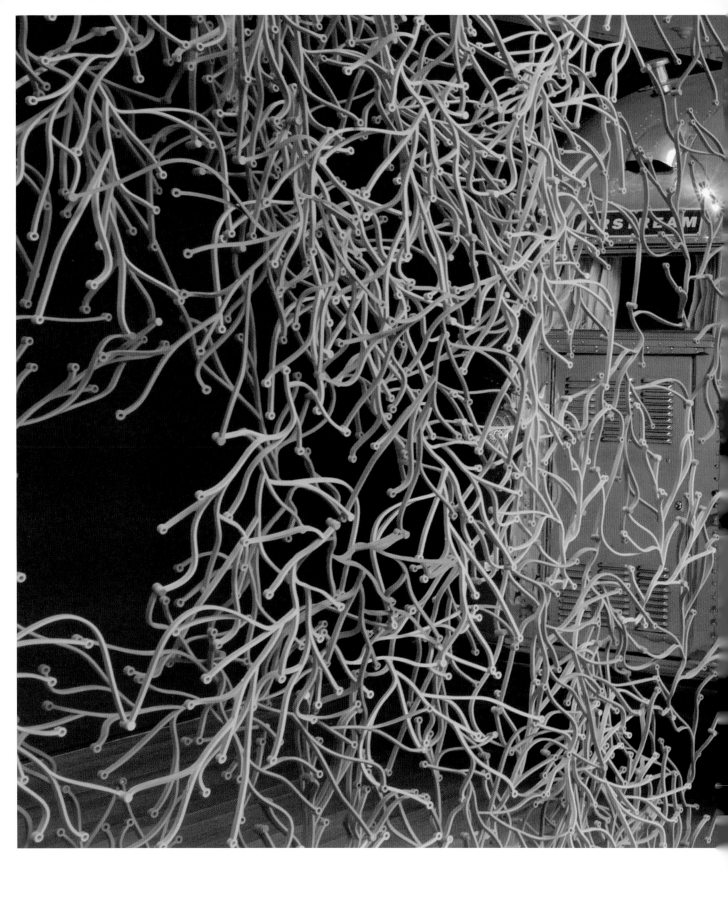

Black Cube: This was the year the work came back. Advertisers and their partners really seemed to have regained their confidence after a couple of years that gave everyone vertigo. The design work, which the ADC always showcases so well, felt rich and wonderfully global—designers from Asia-Pacific were especially dominant. But the real indication that the work had come roaring back was the awarding of the Black Cube—not once but twice. The Black Cube is given out rarely, and only to work that is *hors de catégorie*. This year, two pieces of work deserved it. In fact, it proved impossible to favor one over the other— a dilemma you face only in a very good year.

–Steve Simpson, Chief Creative Officer, Ogilvy North America, 90th Annual Awards Chair

WRITE THE FUTURE

WIEDEN+KENNEDY AMSTERDAM
Broadcast Media
Television Commercial

Executive Creative Director Jeff Kling
Creative Director Mark Bernath, Eric Quennoy
Art Director Freddie Powell, Stuart Harkness
Copywriter Stuart Harkness, Freddie Powell
Director Alejandro Gonzalez Inarritu
Editor Work Post London, Rich Orrick, Ben Jordan
Additional Editing Stephen Mirrione, Los Angeles
Producer Elissa Singstock, Olivier Klonhammer
Production Company Independent Films / Anonymous Content
Head of Broadcast Erik Verheijen
Account Team Gene Willis, Jordi Pont, David Anson, Marco Palermo
Planner Dan Hill, Graeme Douglas
Nike Clients Enrico Balleri, Colin Leary, Todd Pendleton
Visual Effects The Mill, London and New York
Sound Design Grand Central London, Raja Sehgal, Phaze UK
Music Hocus Pocus by Focus
Music Remix Massive Music Amsterdam
Mix Company Grand Central Studios London, Raja Sehgal
Agency Wieden+Kennedy Amsterdam
Client Nike
Country Netherlands

How could Nike dominate the world's biggest football tournament without being a sponsor? Every four years, the keys to football heaven are dangled in front of the international elite. One goal, one pass, one game-saving tackle can be the difference between fame and forgotten. What happens on the pitch in that split second has a ripple effect that goes beyond the match and the tournament. "Write the Future" was a messaging platform that allowed Nike to show how football creates this ripple effect. It gave us a glimpse into

WRITE YOUR FUTURE

Experience life at the top of the game and see how you can handle the pressure from signing a contract to making the big plays. The spotlight's on you. Time to shine.

the future to see what the players were really playing for, in their own lives and the lives of those who follow them. Our goal was to weave the brand into the conversations around this major tournament in a way that celebrated the participating teams and athletes and engaged football fans around the world.

Multiple Winner

Advertising Gold | Broadcast Media
Television Commercial

Advertising Gold | Broadcast Craft
Art Direction

Advertising Silver | Integrated

RESPONSE CAMPAIGN
WIEDEN+KENNEDY
Online Content | Branded
Short Films

**Executive Creative
Director** Mark Fitzloff,
Susan Hoffman
**Global Interactive
Creative Director**
Iain Tait
Creative Director
Jason Bagley,
Eric Baldwin
Art Director
Craig Allen, Eric
Kallman, Jason Bagley
Eric Baldwin
Copywriter
Craig Allen, Eric Kallman,
Jason Bagley, Eric Baldwin
Programmer
Trent Johnson,
John Cohoon
Editor Kamp Grizzly
Executive Producer
Emily Fincher
Interactive Producer
Ann-Marie Harbour
Production Company
Don't Act Big
**Digital Strategist/
Community Manager**
Dean McBeth
Digital Strategist
Josh Millrod
Interactive Studio Artist
Matthew Carroll
Agency Wieden+Kennedy
Client Old Spice
Country United States

"The Man Your Man Could
Smell Like" made a big
splash in early 2010. But
how could this character
engage with fans on a
more personal level? The
result was the "Response"
campaign, an experiment
in real-time branding in
which "The Man Your
Man Could Smell Like"
recorded 186 personal-
ized YouTube messages
over the course of 2 1/2
days. The work would go
to record more than 60
millions views, making it
one of the fastest growing
and most popular interac-
tive campaigns in history.

Multiple Winner
Hybrid Cube | Online Content |
Branded Short Films

Interactive Gold | Online Content |
Branded Short Films

Designism: When I conceived Designism as a speaker series in 2005, I wanted to start a dialogue to acknowledge that there's a big difference between using design to make the world look better and using design to make the world better. I believe that the two recipients of this year's first annual Designism award have done the latter brilliantly. They have turned design into action, and what is more, that action has garnered significant results. Since JWT New York helped Human Rights Watch create a campaign calling for the release of innocent political prisoners in advance of Burma's 2010 election, concerned citizens signed petitions, leaders from around the world paid attention, and more than 150 prisoners have been released. And when Cargo Collective created a line of undergarments printed with the text of the Fourth Amendment and readable by airport scanners, they empowered people to protest unwarranted search and seizure. Both of these efforts achieved something remarkable: they reminded citizens that they have a voice and gave them the tools to use it.

–Brian Collins, Chairman and Chief Creative Officer, Collins, ADC Board Member

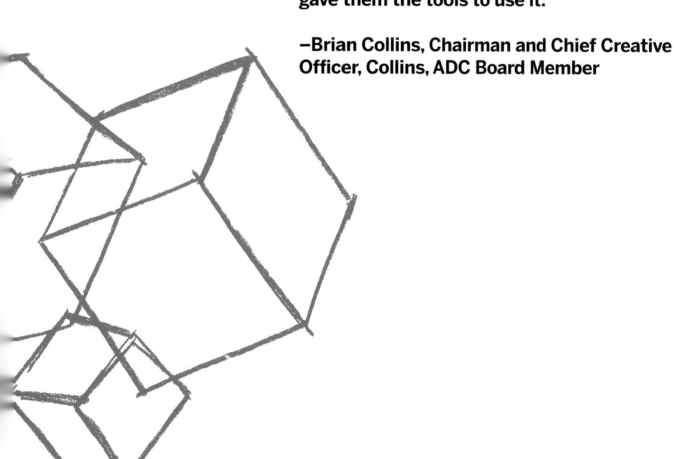

BURMA
JWT NEW YORK
Environmental | Retail, Restaurant,
Office, Outdoor, or Vehicle

**Executive Creative
Director** Andrew Clarke
Chief Creative Officer
Harvey Marco,
Peter Nicholson
Art Director Roy Wisnu
Copywriter Chris Swift
Head of Art Aaron Padin
Director of Photography
Izzy Levine
Photographer Izzy Levine,
Bill Bramswig, Platon
**Director of Integrated
Production** Clair Grupp
Director of Production
Nick Scotting, Kit Liset
Producer Paul Charbonnier,
John Minze, Tadd Ryan
Production Company
Cigar Box Studios Inc.,
Graphic Technology,
Uni-Graphic, Print
International, Circle
Graphics, C2 Graphics
Editing House JWTwo
Project Manager
Elaine Barker, Jessie Hoyt
Art Buyer Elizabeth Corkery,
Sara Levi
Account Executive
Lindsay Gash
Agency JWT New York
Client Human Rights Watch
Country United States

In 2010, Burma held its
first elections in 20 years.
These elections would
have been meaningless
when more than 2,100
political prisoners
remained locked up in
Burma's squalid prisons.
Human Rights Watch
created a campaign calling
for the release of these
innocent prisoners. A giant
installation was built at
New York's Grand Central
Terminal, consisting of
hundreds of prison cells.
A closer look reveals that
the cell bars were actually
pens. Visitors could remove
the pens to symbolically
free the prisoners, and
then use the pen to sign
a petition. Thousands of
signatures were collected
from people of 86 coun-
tries. The event attracted
media from around the
globe. The petition book
was sent to the United
Nations Secretary-General
and leaders of countries
that maintain close ties
with Burma. More than
150 political prisoners
have since been released,
including opposition
leader Aung San Suu Kyi.

Multiple Winner
Design Gold | Environmental |
Retail, Restaurant, Office, Outdoor,
or Vehicle

4TH AMENDMENT WEAR–METALLIC WEAR–INK PRINTED UNDERCLOTHES

4TH AMENDMENT WEAR
Collateral | Promotional

Founder Matthew Ryan
Creative Director
Matthew Ryan,
Tim Geoghegan
Art Director
Matthew Ryan
Copywriter
Tim Geoghegan
Designer Matthew Ryan
Illustrator
Matthew Ryan
Photo Editor
Matthew Ryan
Agency
4th Amendment Wear
Client
4th Amendment Wear
Country United States

Now there's a way to protest those intrusive TSA X-ray body scanners without speaking a word. Underclothes printed with the 4th Amendment in Metallic Ink. Let them know they're spying on the privates of a private citizen. The Fourth Amendment to the Constitution of the United States, meant to prevent unwarranted search and seizure, is readable on TSA body scanners. 4th Amendment Wear is specifically designed to broadcast messages to TSA X-ray officers just when they are peeking at your privates. We invented a proprietary metallic ink that displays any designed image or message on the TSA scanner screens, thus creating the only clothing that will display the Fourth Amendment when passed through airport security scans. The clothes are designed as a silent protest against the new reality—being searched to the point where we're basically naked.

Multiple Winner
Hybrid Cube | Collateral
Promotional

Advertising Gold | Collateral
Promotional

Design Silver | Corporate/
Promo | Promotional Apparel

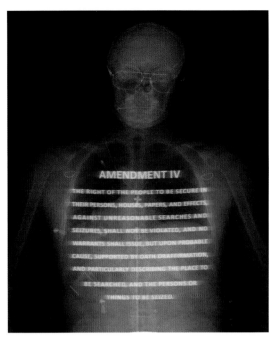

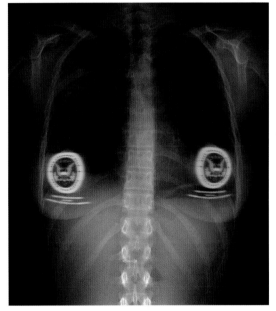

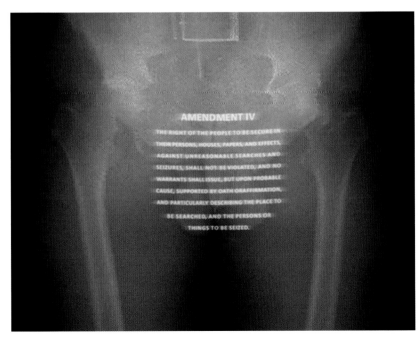

Design: Judging a competition like the Art Directors Club is—if you take it seriously— a lot of work. Books must be examined from cover to cover. Motion graphics must be watched from beginning to end. There are so many entries to look at. If you cut corners, you might miss a gem. What stood out this year? First, designers are thinking broadly, clearly exceeding the clients' initial briefs by stepping over and around disciplinary borders. Some of the most interesting entries were environmental pieces. Second, print is not dead, far from it. Is it the ubiquity of the Internet that seems to have provoked designers to transform what might have been disposable books and publications into memorable, desirable objects? Third, the line between personal work and commercial work, and student work and professional work, is so blurred that it's hard to see. All of us have access to the same tools, the same methods of reproduction, and the same channels of distribution. From the resulting confusion may emerge a new renaissance. Is it time to redefine the categories?

—Michael Bierut, Partner, Pentagram, Design Chair

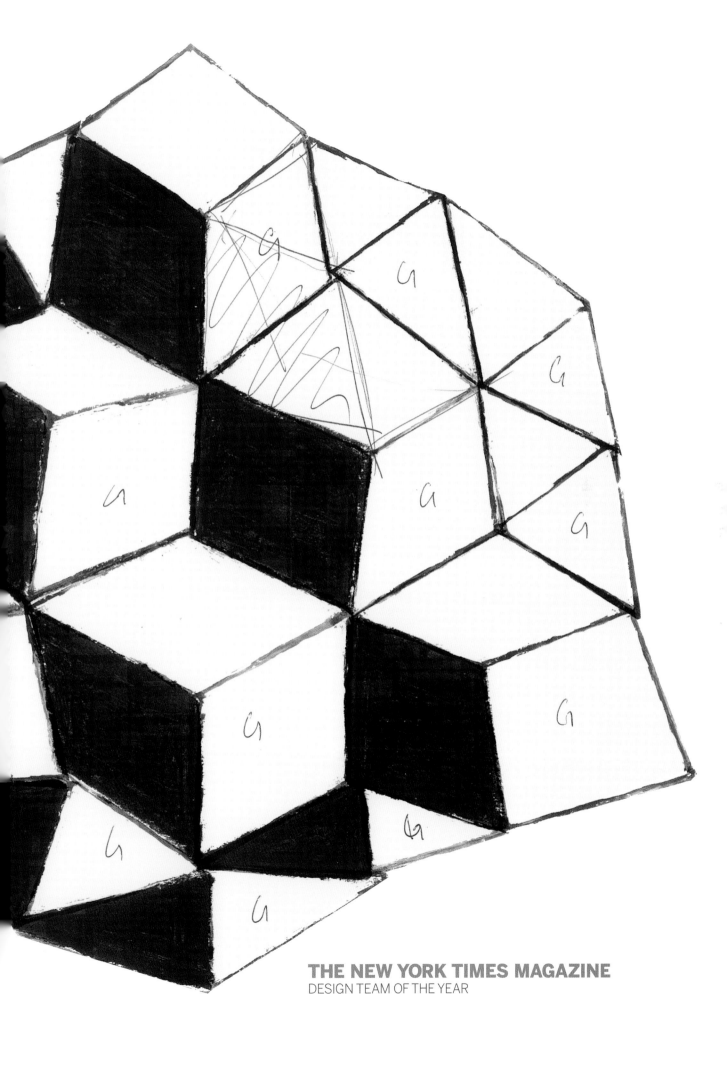

BURMA
JWT NEW YORK
Environmental | Retail, Restaurant,
Office, Outdoor, or Vehicle

**Executive Creative
Director** Andrew Clarke
Chief Creative Officer
Harvey Marco,
Peter Nicholson
Art Director Roy Wisnu
Copywriter Chris Swift
Head of Art Aaron Padin
Director of Photography
Izzy Levine
Photographer Izzy Levine,
Bill Bramswig, Platon
**Director of Integrated
Production** Clair Grupp
Director of Production
Nick Scotting, Kit Liset
Producer Paul Charbonnier,
John Minze, Tadd Ryan
Production Company
Cigar Box Studios Inc.,
Graphic Technology,
Uni-Graphic, Print
International, Circle
Graphics, C2 Graphics
Editing House JWTwo
Project Manager
Elaine Barker, Jessie Hoyt
Art Buyer Elizabeth Corkery,
Sara Levi
Account Executive
Lindsay Gash
Agency JWT New York
Client Human Rights Watch
Country United States

In 2010, Burma held its
first elections in 20 years.
These elections would
have been meaningless
when more than 2,100
political prisoners
remained locked up in
Burma's squalid prisons.
Human Rights Watch
created a campaign calling
for the release of these
innocent prisoners. A giant
installation was built at
New York's Grand Central
Terminal, consisting of
hundreds of prison cells.
A closer look reveals that
the cell bars were actually
pens. Visitors could remove
the pens to symbolically
free the prisoners, and
then use the pen to sign
a petition. Thousands of
signatures were collected
from people of 86 coun-
tries. The event attracted
media from around the
globe. The petition book
was sent to the United
Nations Secretary-General
and leaders of countries
that maintain close ties
with Burma. More than
150 political prisoners
have since been released,
including opposition
leader Aung San Suu Kyi.

Multiple Winner
Designism Cube | Environmental
Retail, Restaurant, Office, Outdoor,
or Vehicle

YEAR IN REVIEW
BLOOMBERG
BUSINESSWEEK
Editorial Design | Magazine Full Issue

Creative Director
Richard Turley
Design Director
Cynthia Hoffman
Art Director
Robert Vargas
Designer
Evan Applegate,
Jennifer Daniel,
Patricia Kim,
Gina Maniscalco,
Maayan Pearl,
Kenton Powell,
Lee Wilson
Illustrator
Tim McDonagh
Director of Photography
David Carthas
Photographer
Sarah Illenberger,
Stefan Ruiz
Senior Photo Editor
Karen Frank
Photo Editor
Donna Cohen,
Emily Keegin,
Myles Little,
Tania Pirozzi,
Diana Suryakusuma
Publisher Bloomberg LP
Agency Bloomberg
Businessweek
Client Bloomberg
Businessweek
Country United States

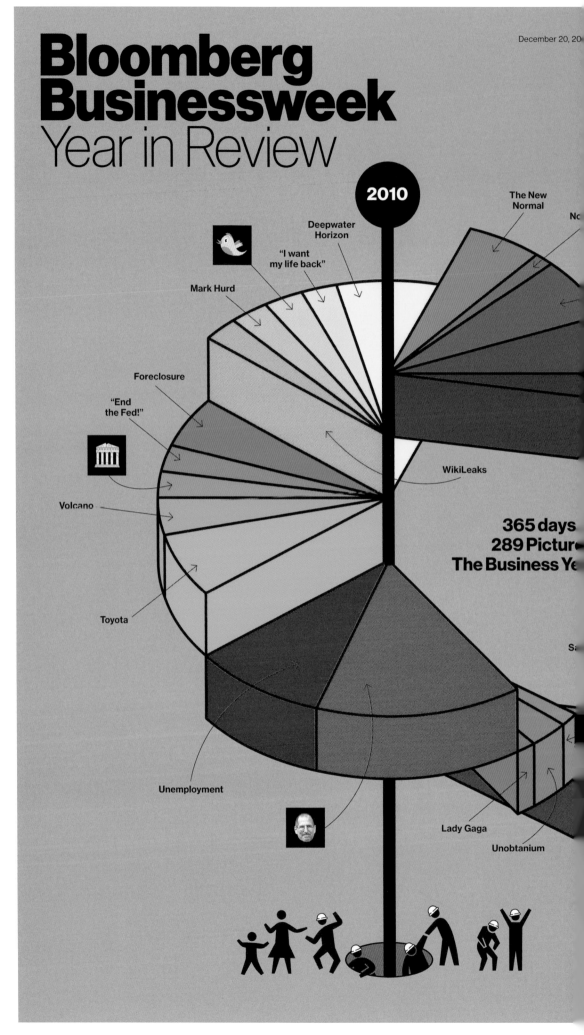

uary 2, 2011 | businessweek.com

Barack Obama

8-inch Hailstones

harts,
ssays.
Perspective

Gold

Euro

Bacon

Gaga

Miracle Whip   PlentyOfFish

PAID

PRODUCT PLACEMENT IN GAGA'S TELEPHONE VIDEO

Wonder Bread

UNPAID

Diet Coke

BUSINESS PARTNERS

HP   Polaroid

Heartbeats headphones

90

pounds of beef are consumed by the average American each year

Lady Gaga wore a meat dress —made mostly from flank steak— to the MTV Video Music Awards on Sept. 12

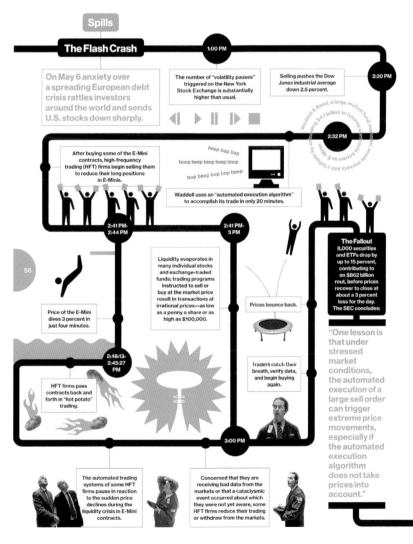

Spills

The Flash Crash

1:00 PM

2:30 PM

On May 6 anxiety over a spreading European debt crisis rattles investors around the world and sends U.S. stocks down sharply.

The number of "volatility pauses" triggered on the New York Stock Exchange is substantially higher than usual.

Selling pushes the Dow Jones industrial average down 2.5 percent.

Waddell & Reed, a large mutual fund manager, sends markets into a tailspin by unloading $4.1 billion in futures contracts known as e-Minis.

2:32 PM

After buying some of the E-Mini contracts, high-frequency trading (HFT) firms begin selling them to reduce their long positions in E-Minis.

beep bop bop
boop beep beep beep boop
bop beep bop bop beep

Waddell uses an "automated execution algorithm" to accomplish its trade in only 20 minutes.

2:41 PM-2:44 PM

2:41 PM-3 PM

The Fallout
8,000 securities and ETFs drop by up to 15 percent, contributing to an $862 billion rout, before prices recover to close at about a 3 percent loss for the day. The SEC concludes:

Liquidity evaporates in many individual stocks and exchange-traded funds; trading programs instructed to sell or buy at the market price result in transactions at irrational prices—as low as a penny a share or as high as $100,000.

Prices bounce back.

Price of the E-Mini dives 3 percent in just four minutes.

"One lesson is that under stressed market conditions, the automated execution of a large sell order can trigger extreme price movements, especially if the automated execution algorithm does not take prices into account."

2:45:13-2:45:27 PM

HFT firms pass contracts back and forth in "hot potato" trading.

Traders catch their breath, verify data, and begin buying again.

3:00 PM

The automated trading systems of some HFT firms pause in reaction to the sudden price declines during the liquidity crisis in E-Mini contracts.

Concerned that they are receiving bad data from the markets or that a cataclysmic event occurred about which they were not yet aware, some HFT firms reduce their trading or withdraw from the markets.

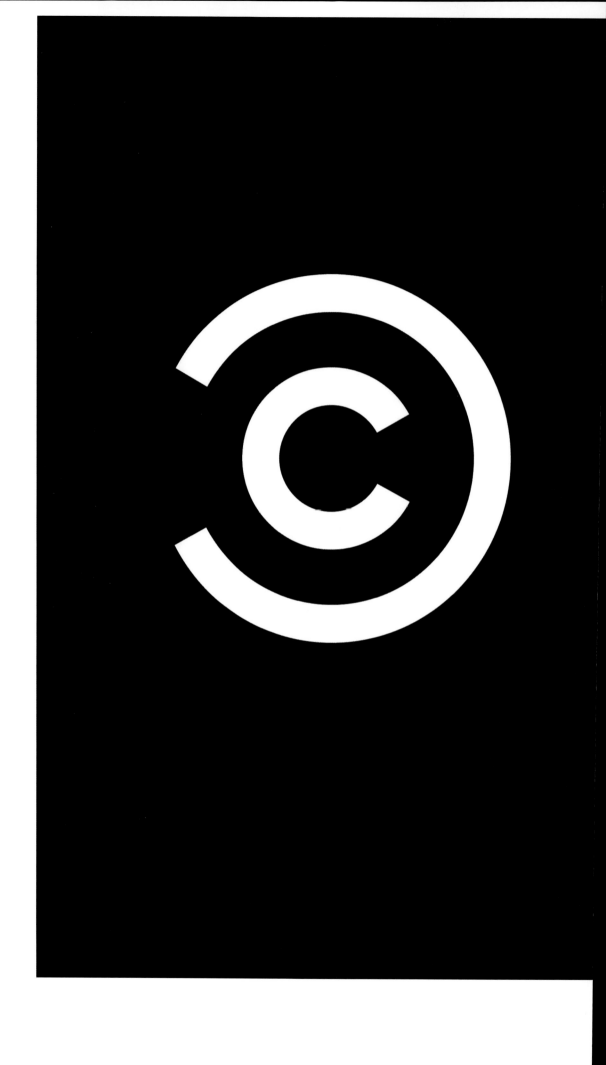

COMEDY CENTRAL
THE LAB
Branding | Branding Campaign

Creative Director
Alicia Johnson,
Hal Wolverton
Art Director Kiffer Keegan,
Keira Alexandra,
Adam McIsaac
Copywriter
Kyle Barron-Cohen,
Adam McIsaac,
Kiffer Keegan
Animator Daniel Pernikoff,
Brian McGee,Chris West,
Kiffer Keegan,
Joe Lawrence
Animation Director
Kiffer Keegan,
Catherine Chesters
Editor Eron Otcasek,
Roberto Serrini
Producer Allison Pickard,
Susie Shuttleworth
Production Company
thelab
Sound Design
Joe Johnson,
Eron Otcasek
Agency thelab
Client Comedy Central
Country United States

Comedy Central needed a branding solution that more firmly attached the network to their programming while reaching a younger audience. We began with the insights that (1) comedy is inherently social, and (2) the content needed to travel in a branded way across platforms. Challenges revolved around issues of scale and transportability that the branding needed to address. Because a network is a brand that houses other brands —shows, content, personalities—we needed to create a system that celebrated the rich content (the programming) without abandoning the providers (the network). This led to the idea of creating a new logo to "tag" content. We recommended that Comedy Central sanction funny content, not seek to be funny. The brand plays a larger role in culture, the arbiter of funny, and that's what the rebrand communicated. The arbiter of funny was considered for each adaptation of the brand, creating a next generation media brand.

**ELANDERS ON VERY
IMPORTANT MATTERS**
HAPPY F&B
Poster Design | Promotional

Art Director
Oskar Andersson,
Anderas Kittel,
Maria Glansèn
Illustrator Moa Pårup
Agency Happy F&B
Client Elanders
Country Sweden

Apollo 11
2/0/0/2

Spirit of St. Louis
5/0/0/9

Tears of Joy
3/0/0/3

Profit Warning
0/100/80/0

Dark Horse
50/0/0/85

Surrender
4/0/0/5

Olympic Black
0/0/0/100

Silver Platter
0/0/0/30

Defeat
100/0/0/90

Scoreboard
20/0/0/92

Fly in the Ointment
0/0/0/95

Checkmate
20/0/0/95

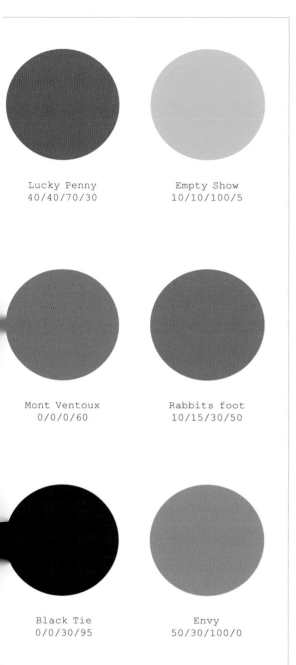

Lucky Penny
40/40/70/30

Empty Show
10/10/100/5

Mont Ventoux
0/0/0/60

Rabbits foot
10/15/30/50

Black Tie
0/0/30/95

Envy
50/30/100/0

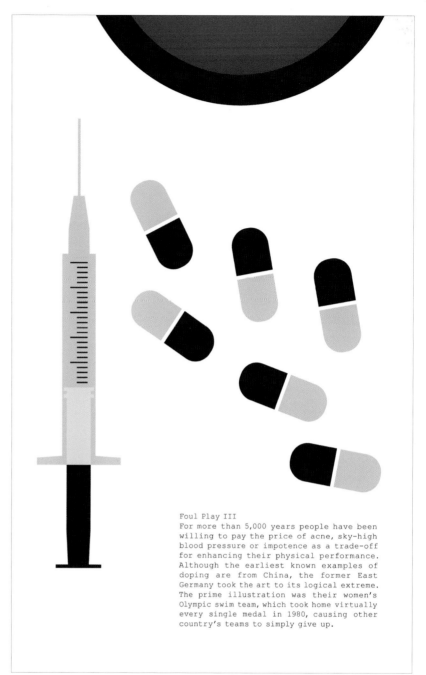

Foul Play III
For more than 5,000 years people have been
willing to pay the price of acne, sky-high
blood pressure or impotence as a trade-off
for enhancing their physical performance.
Although the earliest known examples of
doping are from China, the former East
Germany took the art to its logical extreme.
The prime illustration was their women's
Olympic swim team, which took home virtually
every single medal in 1980, causing other
country's teams to simply give up.

**GALLERIES OF
MODERN LONDON**
NB
Branding | Branding Campaign

Creative Director
Alan Dye,
Nick Finney
Designer Ed Wright
Agency NB
Client
Museum of London
Country
United Kingdom

The spectacular new Galleries of Modern London, opened on May 28, 2010, refurbished at a cost of £20 million, tell the story of London and its people from 1666 to the present day. Three years in the making, five new galleries show how the vibrant and unflagging energy of Londoners has shaped this global city. "You Are Here" is a bold cross-London campaign to launch the new Galleries of Modern London and to relaunch Museum of London as a relevant and exciting destination for Londoners and tourists. At the heart of our idea was the thrill of being on the same physical spot as something or someone historic and was encompassed in our campaign's "You Are Here" tagline.

PIN-UP
FEBU PUBLISHING
Editorial Design | Magazine Full Issue

Designer
Dylan Fracareta
Editor Felix Burrichter
Publisher
FEBU Publishing LLC
Agency FEBU Publishing
Client FEBU Publishing
Country United States

Since its launch in November 2006, *PIN-UP* has set new standards in independent publishing, conveying a fresh, international, and thoroughly contemporary vision of the world of architecture and design. The magazine casts a refreshingly playful eye on rare architectural gems, amazing interiors, smart design and the fascinating nexus where those areas connect with contemporary art. Rather than focusing on technical design details, *PIN-UP* captures an architectural spirit, featuring interviews with architects, designers and artists, and presenting content as an informal work-in-progress. In short, *PIN-UP* is pure architectural entertainment!

PIN-U

USD 15.00

Issue
Spring

MAGAZINE FOR
ARCHITECTURAL
ENTERTAINMENT

ISSN 19339755

9 771933 975000

**Featuring
DANIEL L
CHARLES
JACQUES
BARRY B
and
MARTINO**

ummer 2010

INTERVIEW BY
BROOKE HODGE

JOHNSTON MARKLEE

PHOTOGRAPHY BY
TODD COLE

Not only are Sharon Johnston and Mark Lee of Johnston Marklee & Associates considered the best-dressed architects in Los Angeles, they are also responsible for some of the most interesting new architecture in the city, not to say around the world. Since founding their practice just over ten years ago, the well-traveled duo has forged a reputation for sophisticated, inventive work that includes a number of residential projects from Pacific Palisades to Palm Springs, a double boutique far Maison Martin Margiela and Marneg in Beverly Hills, a holiday home in Rosario, Argentina, and the extension and renovation of a 1978 Thom Mayne classic in Venice Beach. They are currently working on several commissions in Europe, including an art complex and winery in Italy, and a housing project in Switzerland. During a recent conversation over Californian Shiraz and some excellent cheese, Mark and Sharon spilled about everything from their humble beginnings and their love of fashion, to apertures, L.A., and the beauty of constraints in architecture.

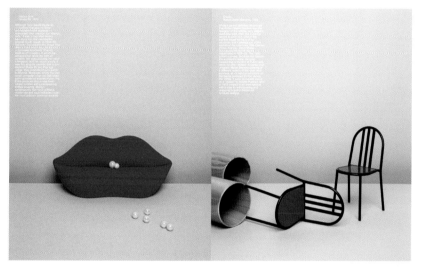

ESKIND
ENFRO
ERZOG
GDOLL

AMPER

PHOTOGRAPHY
BY
MAURICE SCHELTENS
& LIESBETH ABBENES

DUTCH GLAZE

Text by
Alec de Lussairet de la Sablonière

THE BMW LIGHT WALL "REFLECTION"

SERVICEPLAN
Poster Design | Outdoor/Billboard

Chief Creative Officer
Alexander Schill
Creative Director
Maik Kaehler,
Christoph Nann
Art Director
Roman Becker,
Manuel Wolff
Copywriter
Andreas Schriewer
Agency serviceplan
Client BMW AG
Deutschland
Country Germany

BMW asked us to develop
an idea for the BMW M3
Coupe for a very special
billboard at the Hamburg
airport; a 50 x 2 meter
light wall in the middle
of the arrivals hall. For a
car that exceeds limits,
we created a billboard
that exceeds limits. We
designed a headline
out of half letters. To
complete them we used
their reflection on the
shiny floor. The result: we
doubled the media space
for free, we doubled the
attention for free.

UNCHOP A TREE
@RADICAL.MEDIA
Environmental | Gallery/Museum
Exhibit or Installation

Creative Director
James Spindler
Art Director
Kristen Cahill
Copywriter
Ben Hieger
Editor Paul Bastin
Executive Producer
Jon Kamen,
Maggie Meade
Producer
Kathleen Russell
Production Company
@radical.media LLC
Agency
@radical.media
Client
Maya Lin
Country United States

To make the effects of rain
forest destruction more
immediate and personal
for the world leaders at the
15th UN Climate Change
Conference (COP-15),
we worked with artist,
architect and environ-
mentalist Maya Lin to
write and produce a short
film, which debuted at the
conference.Inspiration
came from the staggering
fact that one acre of rain
forest is destroyed every
90 seconds, and that the
carbon emissions produced
by deforestation outweighs
the emissions from all
the world's cars, boats
and trains combined. After
Copenhagen, the film was
distributed digitally to
further localize the impacts
of a global issue, and to
inspire change among an
international audience of
online viewers. *Unchop
a Tree* also served as a
highly targeted piece of
communication that helped
create awareness for
Maya Lin's final memorial,
What Is Missing?, a work
that exists in several
forms and in multiple sites
around the world.

UENO PARK, TOKYO, JAPAN
DESTROYED IN 2 MINUTES

CENTRAL PARK NEW YORK CITY, USA
DESTROYED IN 9 MINUTES

HYDE PARK LONDON, ENGLAND
DESTROYED IN 4 MINUTES

Options shown.

**SWAGGER WAGON
MUSIC VIDEO**
SAATCHI & SAATCHI LA
Motion | Music Video

**Executive Creative
Director** Mike McKay
Creative Director
Erich Funke
Art Director
Stephen Baik
Copywriter
Donnell Johnson,
David J. Evans V
Director Jody Hill
Editor Teddy Gersten
Editing Company
Butcher Edit
Producer Gil DeCuir
Production Company
Caviar Los Angeles
Agency Saatchi &
Saatchi LA
Client Toyota
Country United States

Traditionally the idea of owning a minivan would illict such responses as: "I'd rather have my tubes tied than drive a minivan!" We flipped the script on this thinking. We showed today's parents that owning the Sienna doesn't mean they need to be fitted for mom jeans (or immediately banned from Facebook). We showed them its the first minivan made with parents in mind. (Its not just for kids). To do this we created the Sienna parents. Parents who, in several episodes on TV and online, sum up the everyday struggles of Mom and Dad, but with swagger. Creating a music video seemed a natural extension and gave us the license to "up the attitude." It also fit with the sexier styling of the SE model. (It's all about Swagger.) With over 8.3 million views, the Sienna Parents hit single, "Swagger Wagon" brought the beat back to the burbs."

Multiple Winner
Advertising Silver | Broadcast Craft
Television Music/Sound Design

THE WILDERNESS DOWNTOWN

@RADICAL.MEDIA/
MILK+KOBLIN/GOOGLE
CREATIVE LAB
Motion | Music Video

Creative Director
Chris Milk, Aaron Koblin
Art Director
Ben Tricklebank
Copywriter Chris Milk
Director Chris Milk
Editor Livio Sanchez
Producer
Jennifer Heath,
Nicole Muniz
Production Company
@radical.media LLC,
B-Reel
Account Director
Thomas Gayno
Agency @radical.media/
Milk+Koblin/Google
Creative Lab
Client Arcade Fire
Country United States

The Wilderness Downtown
is an interactive film using
HTML5 programming and
Google Maps and Street-
view to create startling
individualized videos to
the Arcade Fire song "We
Used to Wait." The com-
plete work can be viewed
at www.TheWildernes
Downtown.com.

Multiple Winner
Hybrid Cube | Motion | Music Video

**OKGO-THIS TOO
SHALL PASS**
ZOO FILM PRODUCTIONS
Motion | Music Video

Director James Frost
with OK Go & Syyn Labs
Editor
Nicholas Wayman-Harris
Producer Shirley Moyers
Production Company
OKGo Partnership
Agency Zoo Film
Productions
Client OKGO
Country United States

2010'S FAIREST ANNUAL REPORT
JUNG VON MATT AG
Corporate/Promo | Annual Report

Executive Creative Director Wolf Heumann
Creative Director Peter Kirchhoff
Art Director Annika Frey
Copywriter Christina Drescher, Peter Kirchhoff
Designer Katja Kirchner
Illustrator Annika Frey
Photographer Stefanie Buetow, Johann Cohrs
Producer Christian Will
Agency Jung von Matt AG
Client Lemonaid Beverages GmbH
Country Germany

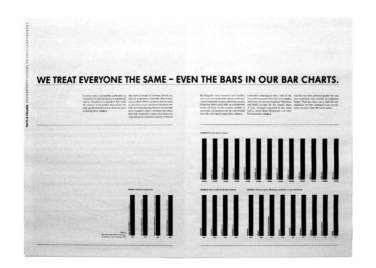

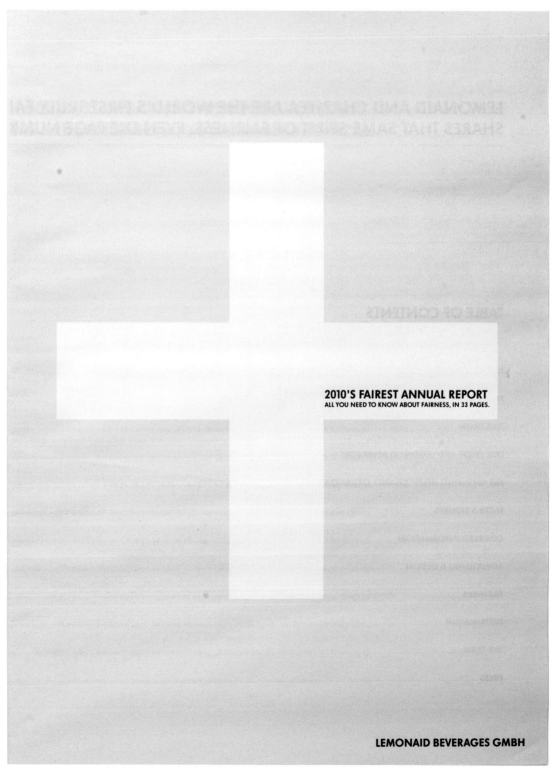

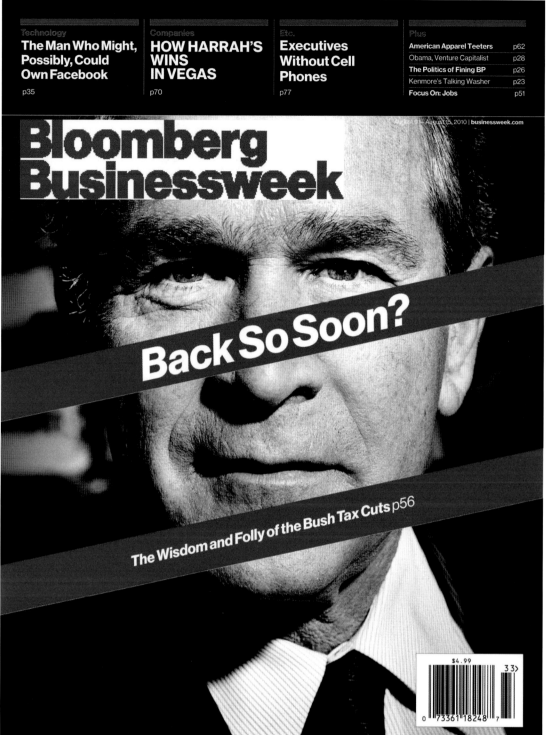

Technology
**The Man Who Might,
Possibly, Could
Own Facebook**
p35

Companies
**HOW HARRAH'S
WINS
IN VEGAS**
p70

Etc.
**Executives
Without Cell
Phones**
p77

Plus

Bloomberg
Businessweek

August 9 — August 15, 2010 | **businessweek.com**

Back So Soon?

The Wisdom and Folly of the Bush Tax Cuts p56

$4.99

3>

0 73361 18248 7

COVER SERIES
BLOOMBERG
BUSINESSWEEK
Editorial Design | Magazine Cover

Creative Director
Richard Turley
Design Director
Cynthia Hoffman
Art Director
Robert Vargas
Illustrator Steve Caplin,
Nishant Choksi,
Craig Robinson
Director of Photography
David Carthas
Photo Editor
Richard Turley
Publisher Bloomberg LP
Agency Bloomberg
Businessweek
Client Bloomberg
Businessweek
Country United States

**BLACK AND
WHITE DIAMOND**
HAKUHODO INC.
Book Design | Limited Edition,
Private Press or Special Format Book

Art Director
Rikako Nagashima
Designer
Rikako Nagashima
Photographer
Kazuhiro Fujita
Hair/Makeup
Akihiro Sugiyama
Stylist Mana Yamamoto
Agency Hakuhodo Inc.
Client Dictionary
Country Japan

Catalog for a fashion
brand called Dictionary.

I took this season's theme,
Black and White Diamond,
and expressed it as an
overlap of a variety of
graphics and photos
based on the diamond
shape using textile.

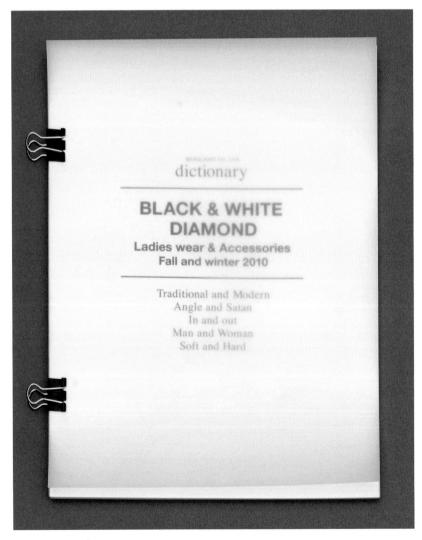

CENAKOVSKI
COSSETTE
Poster Design | Promotional

Creative Director
Michel De Lauw,
Barbara Jacques
Art Director
Marc-Andre Rioux
Copywriter
Francois Forget
Designer Daniel Cartier,
Nathalie Boucher,
Marc-Andre Rioux,
Isabelle Allard
Illustrator
Marc-Andre Rioux
Agency Cossette
Client Théâtre du
Nouveau Monde
Country Canada

This spring, Théâtre du Nouveau Monde hosted a Russian-flavored gastronomic event entitled Cenakovski. The posters, in red and white, used strong symbols: Russian dolls, vodka and the space shuttle.

Creative Director
Mike Dempsey
Designer
Mike Dempsey
Photographer
Andy Seymour
Publisher Royal Mail
Agency Studio Dempsey
Client Royal Mail
Country
United Kingdom

**MOBILITY—
REFLECTIVE
KINEMATRONIC**
ART+COM
Environmental | Gallery/Museum
Exhibit or Installation

Creative Director
Joachim Sauter
Art Director
Hermann Klöckner
Designer
Susanne Traeger,
Simon Haecker
Motion Design
Hermann Klöckner
Programming
David Siegel
Agency ART+COM
Client Otto Bock
Healthcare GmbH
Country Germany

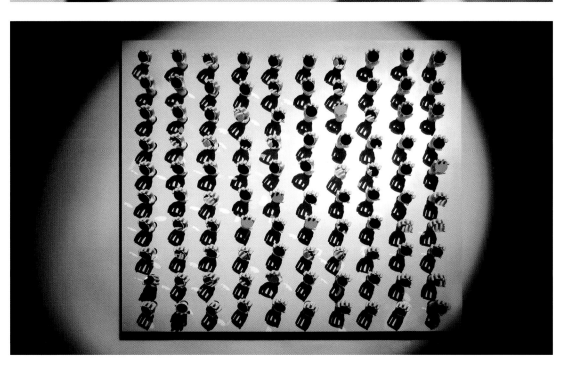

AMA DABLAM—A JOURNEY OF ASCENT
BROWNS
Book Design | Image Driven Book

Creative Director
Jonathan Ellery,
Nick Jones
Designer Sabrina Grill
Photographer Donovan
Wylie (Magnum)
Agency Browns
Client Invesco Perpetual
Country United Kingdom

In 2007, Ama Dablam in
Nepal became the visual
icon for the entire Invesco
global organization, using
their identity, designed by
Browns, in 20 countries
around the world. As an
ongoing commitment
to visualizing the brand,
Browns set up a photo
shoot in Nepal with
Magnum photographer
Donovan Wylie, to capture
images of the mountain.
Browns also proposed
producing a book that
would document this
expedition, demonstrate
the analogy between
mountaineering and fund
management while at the
same time reinforcing the
brand globally.

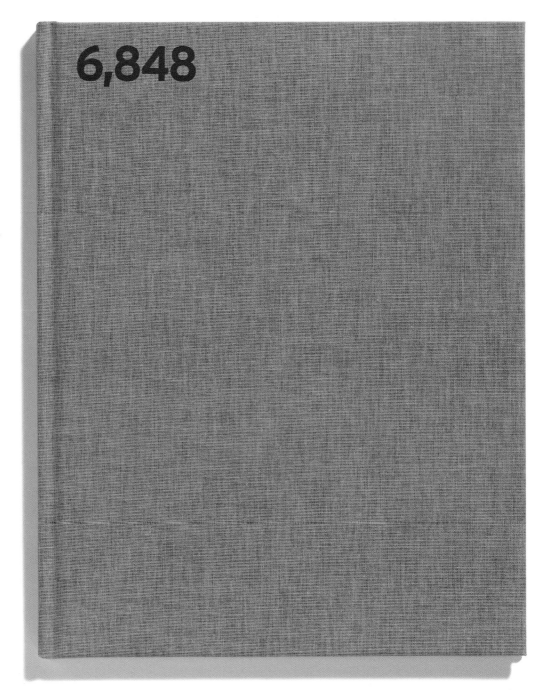

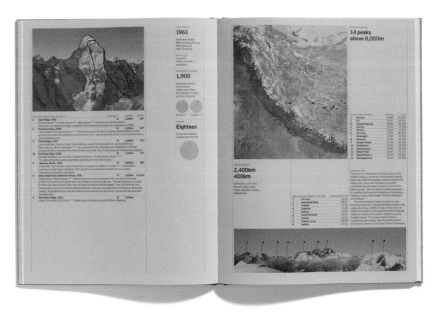

TED TALKS
THE PARTNERS
Poster Design | Promotional

Creative Director
Greg Quinton
Designer Dave Wood
Photographer
Dave Wood
Agency The Partners
Client The Partners
Country United Kingdom

A poster series was created to promote monthly screenings of selected talks from TED.com. An innocent teddy bear was ripped, frozen, baked, stitched, squashed, painted and dissected, all in the name of visually unifying a diverse series of talks.

DESIGN MUSEUM HOLON SIGNAGE SYSTEM

ADI STERN DESIGN
Environmental | Wayfinding Systems /Signage

Creative Director
Adi Stern
Designer Adi Stern
Agency Adi Stern Design
Client
Design Museum Holon
Country Israel

The signage and way-finding system of the Design Musem Holon challenges common approaches by using white arrows on white walls. The arrows, which are primarily discernible due to the shadow they cast on the wall, emerge from the museum walls and become fully three-dimensional forms. The shape of the arrows echoes the flow and movement of the Corten weathering steel bands that surround the museum building, creating a unity of design throughout the museum. The challenge in this project was to create a system that will be visible and easy to use, while not competing with Ron Arad's dynamic architecture. The system holds three scripts: Hebrew, Arabic and Latin, and includes a custom proprietary Hebrew font, designed specifically for the project.

גלריה תחתונה
Lower Gallery
صالة العرض السفلى

גלריה עליונה
Upper Gallery
صالة العرض العليا

מעבדת עיצוב
Design Lab
مختبر تصميم

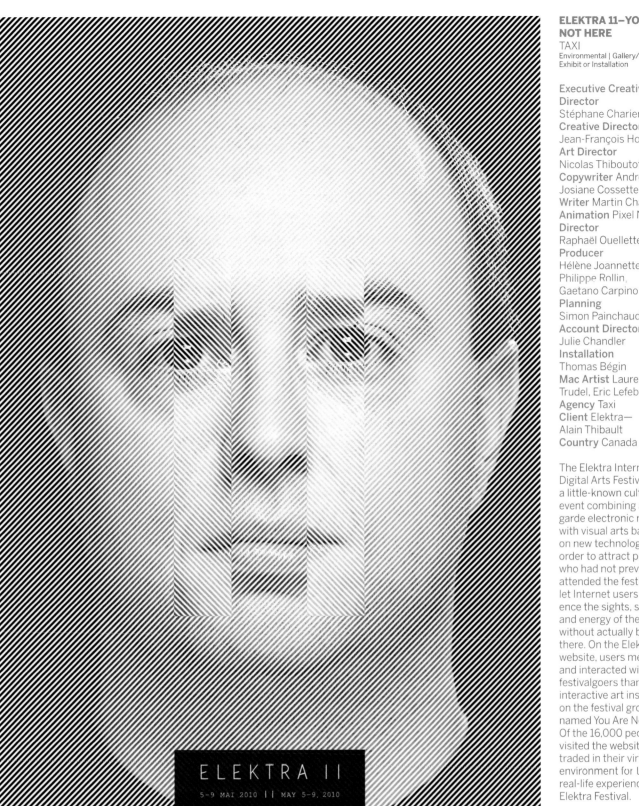

ELEKTRA II

5-9 MAI 2010 || MAY 5-9, 2010

ELEKTRA 11—YOU ARE
NOT HERE
TAXI
Environmental | Gallery/Museum
Exhibit or Installation

Executive Creative
Director
Stéphane Charier
Creative Director
Jean-François Houle
Art Director
Nicolas Thiboutot
Copywriter Andrew Lord,
Josiane Cossette
Writer Martin Charron
Animation Pixel Nickel
Director
Raphaël Ouellette
Producer
Hélène Joannette,
Philippe Rollin,
Gaetano Carpino
Planning
Simon Painchaud
Account Director
Julie Chandler
Installation
Thomas Bégin
Mac Artist Laurent
Trudel, Eric Lefebvre
Agency Taxi
Client Elektra—
Alain Thibault
Country Canada

The Elektra International
Digital Arts Festival is
a little-known cultural
event combining avant-
garde electronic music
with visual arts based
on new technologies. In
order to attract people
who had not previously
attended the festival, we
let Internet users experience the sights, sounds
and energy of the event's
without actually being
there. On the Elektra
website, users met, talked
and interacted with
festivalgoers thanks to an
interactive art installation
on the festival grounds,
named You Are Not Here.
Of the 16,000 people who
visited the website, 6,000
traded in their virtual
environment for the
real-life experience of the
Elektra Festival.

**SMART BUY WINES
BRAND IDENTITY**
MOHALLEM/ARTPLAN
Corporate/Promo | Corporate
Identity Program

Creative Director
Eugênio Mohallem,
Marcus Kawamura
Art Director
Marcus Kawamura,
Rodrigo Moraes
Copywriter
Ana Carolina Reis,
Julio D'Alfonso
Illustrator
Ellyson Lifante,
Ariê Magalhães,
Albino Camargo,
Estudio Onze
Photographer
Caio Miranda,
(Getty Images)
Producer Bruno Werner,
Vivian Tomaz
Agency
Mohallem/Artplan
Client Smart Buy Wines
Country Brazil

SmartBuy Wines is an
online store selling quality
wines at incredibly low
prices. As such, we cre-
ated the tagline "Great
wines at (barely) legal
prices," which guided the
brand positioning, based
on the underground
world. We used prohibi-
tion Days as a reference
to the brand identity,
starting by the logo. The
SmartBuy Wines graphic
material was in keeping
with the brand concept:
from business cards to
direct mailing, everything
was disguised. Trans-
portation packaging, for
instance, appeared to
have nothing to do with
SmartBuy Wines. Dis-
guised wine accessories
such as bottle openers,
wineglasses and thermal
wrapping for bottles were
disguised and put up for
sale on the website. From
the outside, they looked
like other products,
such as a bar of soap, a
lightbulb or a bottle of
ketchup. They were just
another way of saying
that SmartBuy Wines
sells wines at (barely)
legal prices.

**SIGNAGE FOR
MUSASHINO ART
UNIVERSITY MUSEUM
AND LIBRARY**
TAKU SATOH
DESIGN OFFICE
Environmental | Wayfinding Systems
/Signage

Art Director Taku Satoh
Designer Shingo Noma
Photographer
Satoshi Asakawa
Production Company
Inoue Industries Co.,Ltd.
Agency Taku Satoh
Design Office Inc.
Client Musashino Art
University
Country Japan

This is a design work for an academic library in an art university. We designed applications such as the logo, envelope, and the letterhead, as well as the signs, furnishings and the interface for the electronic media. We have selected the chairs for each of the floors, and almost everything except for the architecture itself and the lighting were designed by us. The concept "The Forest of Books," conceived by architect Sousuke Fujimoto, was implemented into this library, thus creating a space where one is guided by the numeric signs to the books they are looking for. The numbers of the signs represent the content of the classification: the number 7 is made from the letters spelling ART, and the number for the industrial category 6 is made of recycled plastic bottle caps painted white, collected from within the school.

**SVA UNDERGRADUATE
CATALOG 2011/12**
VISUAL ARTS PRESS, LTD.
Book Design | Limited Edition,
Private Press or Special Format Book

Creative Director
Anthony P. Rhodes
Art Director
Michael J. Walsh
Designer
E. Patrick Tobin,
Brian E. Smith,
Suck Zoo Han
Photographer
David Corio,
Paulo Barcellos,
Carolyn Deriso,
Deborah Farber,
June Young Lim,
Michelle Mecurio,
Joe Sinnott,
Michael Visconti,
Laura Yeffeth,
Harry Zernike
Editor Sheilah Ledwidge
Agency
Visual Arts Press, Ltd.
Client School of Visual
Arts
Country United States

The objective of the
School of Visual Arts
undergraduate cata-
log, "Proof," is to show
prospective students
why SVA is the preemi-
nent training ground for
the next generations
of artists. We want to
prove that SVA, located
in New York City, is
the best art school to
attend. Our solution is
to present visual and
factual evidence, first by
giving dozens of facts
about NYC, SVA and
its students, and then
by presenting literally
hundreds of examples of
student work throughout
the book. We also employ
a unique, heat-responsive
ink on the cover, so that
with the application of
heat (such as from one's
hand), a map of the
school is revealed.

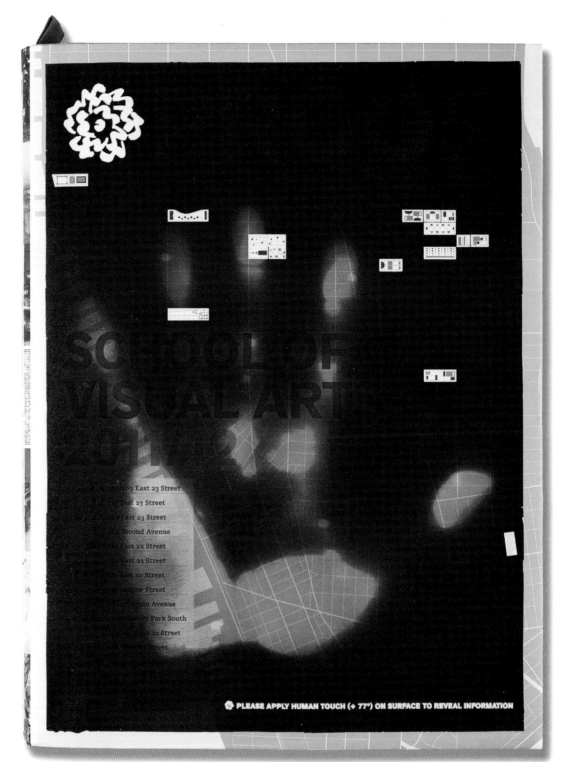

LAFORET 2010
A/W–'I WEAR TABOO'
HAKUHODO INC.
Poster Design | Promotional

Art Director
Rikako Nagashima
Copywriter
Rikako Nagashima
Designer
Rikako Nagashima,
Naonori Yago
Photographer
Yasutomo Ebisu
Production Company
Amana inc.
Publisher
Kazuhiro Hashimoto
Printing Director
Koichiro Kawabata
Hair/Makeup
Katsuya Kamo
Stylist Tsuyoshi Noguchi
Model Casting HYPE
Set ENZ
Agency Hakuhodo Inc.
Client Laforet
Country Japan

A poster for a fashion department store called Laforet Harajuku, which is at the center of Japanese fashion culture. Because of the fast-fashion trend, everyone can buy cheap clothes and end up all looking similar. Can this be called fashion? Is it such a taboo to wear what you want to wear and look different? Laforet Harajuku is a place where taboo is allowed and supported. This "taboo" is expressed by hiding the clothes models would ordinarily be wearing to pass on this message.

I WEAR TABOO. LAFORET

Never care about what you say, I wear the way I wanna do.

THE ARMOURY
IDENTITY
PURPOSE
Branding | Branding Campaign

Creative Director
Stuart Youngs
Designer Will Kinchin,
Paul Felton
Senior Project Manager
Alice Javor
Agency Purpose
Client The Armoury
Country
United Kingdom

ROCCA SPIELE
10 INC.
Product Design | Recreation:
Sports, Toys or Games

Creative Director
Trulie Okamocek
Art Director
Masahiro Kakinokihara
Designer
Masahiro Kakinokihara,
Noriko Inujima,
Shortreed Jessica
Game Designer
Trulie Okamocek
Photographer Shi No Go
Production Company
Rocca Spiele
Publisher 10 Inc.
Agency 10 Inc.
Client Rocca Spiele
Country Japan

In 1995, Trulie Okamocek (1969–) met Mr. and Mrs. Randolph by chance in Venice and made friends with them. Alex Randolph (1922–2004) was a famous table game designer. (Trulie visited his grave in 2005.) The day before getting on board a plane to Venice, an idea for a game flashed into his mind. He made a prototype and contacted his friend Masahiro Kakinokihara (1970–) and they made the game together. The name Rocca is derived from the Japanese word *Rokkaku*, which means hexagon. The cards of Rocca & Rocca Book are the same as ordinary playing cards, so you can play Poker, Sevens or other traditional games, or use the face and the back as two-dimensional building blocks to make geometric patterns. And, sure, you can play the original games. Rocca Card Blocks look like wooden bricks, and you can play color-matching games.

COPY ON CAMPAIGN
OGILVY FRANKFURT
Poster Design | Point-of-Purchase

Creative Director
Dr. Stephan Vogel,
Helmut Meyer
Art Director
Eva Stetefeld
Copywriter
Dr. Stephan Vogel,
Taner Ercan
Art Buyer
Christina Hufgard
Consultant
Peter Heinlein,
Georg Fechner
Agency Ogilvy Frankfurt
Client Rolling Stone
Magazine
Country Germany

Today, for every legal
music download, there
are six illegal downloads.
Internet piracy and
illegal copying are
destroying musicians'
livelihoods and those of a
whole branch of creative
expression. Especially
young artists are con-
cerned about the impact
on their revenue
streams and not least
their entire existence as
artists. In order to sup-
port musicians, *Rolling
Stone magazine* asked us
to come up with a cam-
paign to make this point
very clear.

Multiple Winner
Advertising Merit | Poster or
Billboard | Point-of-Purchase

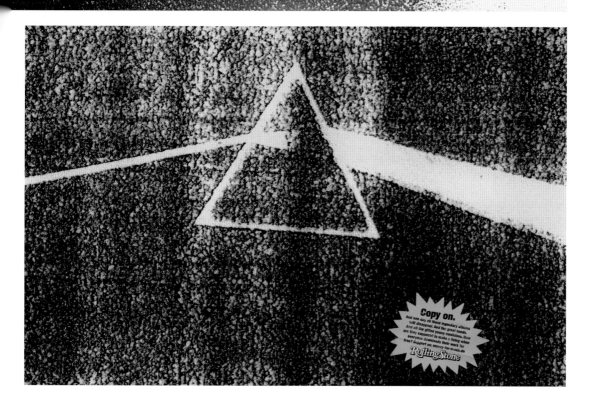

COLORS COLLECTOR
FABRICA S.P.A.
Editorial Design | Magazine Full Issue

Creative Director
Sam Baron
Art Director
Magdalena Czarnecki,
Brian Wood
Copywriter
Benjamin Joffe Walt
Editor Carlos Mustienes
Producer Erica Fusaro
Photo Editor
Mauro Bedoni
Publisher Fabrica
Agency Fabrica S.p.A.
Client Colors
Country Italy

Collector has a double
meaning, someone who
collects as well as an
adjective that qualifies
a memorable object
produced for a special
event. In the year of its
20th anniversary, *Colors*
has decided to dedicate
the winter 2010–2011 edi-
tion to collectors: those
who amass, categorize
and catalog objects of
the same type. They may
be collectors of nature,
works of art or, in most
cases, everyday objects
which, because they are
rare, distinctive or represent something special,
become extraordinary
cult objects, steeped
in memories that feed
passions and obsessions.
These objects of desire,
refined, coveted and
exchanged, thus become
the pretext for a journey
into the history of design,
graphics and industrial
production, and at the
same time, into the hab-
its, interests and needs of
human beings.

COLORS LECTOR

NO 79 / 147 234

WINTER 2010 / 2011
WWW.COLORSMAGAZINE.COM
QUARTERLY EDITION / PUBLICATION TRIMESTRIELLE
Poste Italiane Spa - Sped. in abb. post. D.L. 353/03 (conv. in L. 27.02.04, n° 46), art. 1, c. 1, DCB Milano.
Belgique € 6 / Canada $ 10.95 CA / Deutschland € 7 / España € 6 / France € 9 / Italia € 4,90 / Korea 23,000 KRW / Luxembourg € 8 /
Nederland € 7,50 / Österreich € 7,99 / Portugal Cont. € 6 / Schweiz 9.50 CHF / USA $ 8.95 US / UK £ 6.50

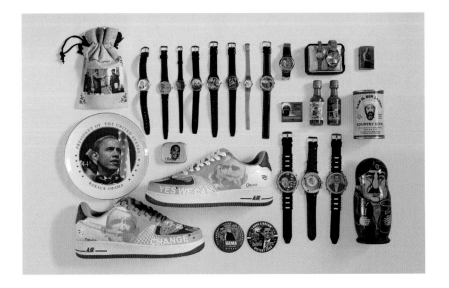

THE REJECTED BREAD EXHIBIT
DRAFTFCB+SHIMONI FINKELSTEIN BARKI
Environmental | Gallery/Museum
Exhibit or Installation

Executive Creative Director Kobi Barki
Creative Director Kobi Barki, Reuven Givati
Art Director Liat Tsur
Copywriter Kobi Barki
Industrial Designer Reuven Givati
Flash Designer Shimi Kuperly
Producer Eti Naaman, Reuven Givati
Curator Ifat Zvirin
Interactive Manager Maria Knigin
Account Director Mira Finkelstein
Account Supervisor Yael Nizan
Agency Draftfcb+Shimoni Finkelstein Barki
Client Arla Foods: Lurpak—Butter Spreads
Country Israel

When Lurpak premium spreadable butter asked us to strengthen the brand's connection to bread, we decided to prove that 'Lurpak loves all bread—even the rejects'. We discovered that every week many challah breads (traditional Jewish bread) are taken off the production line for aesthetic reasons only—a fact we decided to bring to the public's attention. We collected rejected challah breads from major bakeries and curated them into an exhibition at a leading art gallery. The exhibition celebrated the bizarre, weird and wonderful challah breads no one ever sees. Design was kept neutral and minimalistic to focus maximum attention on the bread, leaving viewers space for reflection and emotional response.

TILLY DEVINE
PARALLAX DESIGN
Package Design | Food/Beverage

Creative Director
Matthew Remphrey
Copywriter
Matthew Remphrey
Designer Kellie
Campbell-Illingworth
Typographer Kellie
Campbell-Illingworth
Agency Parallax Design
Client Antipodean
Vintners
Country Australia

Tilly Devine is a McLaren Vale Shiraz named after the notorious Sydney madam and bootlegger of the 1920's. So successful was Tilly's bootlegging operation that her name was adopted as Australian rhyming slang for wine. The design solution came out of the fact that in her heyday, Tilly could be found behind either prison bars or cocktail bars.

THE FIRST PAGE CALENDAR
SCHOLZ & FRIENDS BERLIN GMBH
Corporate/Promo | Calendar or Appointment Book

Executive Creative Director Martin Pross, Matthias Spaetgens
Creative Director Mathias Rebmann, Florian Schwalme
Art Director Johannes Stoll
Copywriter Nils Tscharnke, Felix Heine
Agency Producer Franziska Ibe
Account Manager Marie Toya Gaillard, Eva Verena Schmidt
Graphics Sebastian Haus
Agency Scholz & Friends Berlin GmbH
Client Frankfurter Allgemeine Zeitung GmbH
Country Germany

THE INJURED JOCKEYS FUND—HELP
THE PARTNERS
Poster Design | Poster Typography

Creative Director
Michael Paisley
Designer Leon Bahrani,
James Titterton
Fashion Designer
Lisa Menzel, Alice Speak
Photographer
Toby Edwards
Agency The Partners
Client The Injured
Jockey's Fund
Country
United Kingdom

Since 1964, the Injured Jockeys Fund has provided financial, medical and pastoral help to amateur and professional jockeys who are forced out of competition for long periods, or must end their racing career early, as a result of sustaining serious injury. Traditionally supported by the racing establishment and celebrities within the sport, the charity wanted to raise its profile amongst younger race-goers. We created a unique typeface of 26 letters, each composed from details found within UK regulation racing silk patterns. The new typeface gives the charity a distinct voice, allowing them to promote their cause to enthusiasts in a refreshingly bold and colourful way. The first example of the typeface in use is a series of four posters displayed at race meetings around the UK. When arranged together, they simply read, "HELP," identifying the charity as providers of assistance to injured jockeys whilst subtly appealing for support.

THE NATIONAL BAR AND DINING ROOMS
LOVE AND WAR
Branding | Branding Campaign

Creative Director
Eng San Kho,
Peter Tashjian
Art Director Katie Tully
Copywriter
Peter Tashjian
Designer
Minh Anh Vo,
Victor Schuft
Photographer
Michael Guenther
Producer
Cole Hernandez
Agency Love and War
Client Denihan
Hospitality Group
Country United States

Love and War's branding
for The National restau-
rant brings chef Geoffrey
Zakarian's vision of New
York grand café to life.
The design is intended to
be familiar and sophis-
ticated, but with quirky
touches and a dry wit
befitting the New York
City location and culture.
A key motif in the brand
design is a series of turn-
of-the-century etchings
that we reassembled into
unique scenes and cre-
ations. These creations
were incorporated into
the design sparingly,
and are often hidden
for patrons to discover
during their meal; tucked
away on the inside cover
of a matchbook, beneath
a glass on a drink coaster,
and so forth.

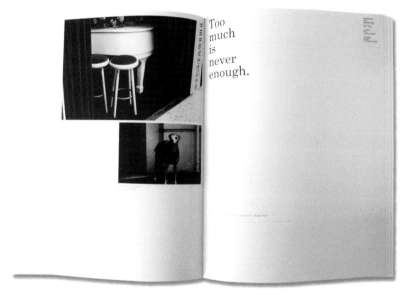

GESTÄNDNISSE EINES LABRADORRÜDEN
NORBERT HEROLD
Book Design | Limited Edition,
Private Press or Special Format Book

Creative Director
Sigi Mayer
Art Director Sigi Mayer
Copywriter
Janet Fox,
Lothar Hackethal,
Thorsten Hainke,
Peter Hirrlinger,
Felix Lott, Ono Mothwurf,
Sven Nagel
Designer Sigi Mayer
Photographer
Norbert Herold
Photo Editor Sigi Mayer
Publisher INSTANT
Corporate Culture
Agency Norbert Herold
Client Norbert Herold
Country Germany

VICTORE OR, WHO DIED AND MADE YOU BOSS?

OFFICE OF PAUL SAHRE
Book Design | Image Driven
Book

Creative Director
James Victore
Art Director Paul Sahre
Copywriter
James Victore,
Michael Bierut (intro)
Designer Paul Sahre
Illustrator Robert Hunt
Photographer
Tom Schierlitz
Editor
Deborah Aaronson
Publisher
Harry N. Abrams
Agency
Office of Paul Sahre
Client Abrams
Country United States

In his first book, icono-
clastic designer James
Victore gives fans a
survey of his work and
his no-holds-barred take
on the practice, business,
and teaching of graphic
design today. Known for
making vivid, memorable,
and often controversial
work, Victore has sought
comrades, not clients;
brave, smart collaborators
who have encouraged
him to reinterpret old
design solutions and to
pressure viewers to think
about issues in a new
way. Leading readers
through this collection
of "greatest hits," Victore
tells the stories behind his
inspirations, his process
and the lessons learned.
The result is an inspiring,
funny and honest book,
which showcases a body
of work that has been
plastered on the streets of
New York, hung at MoMA,
and featured in maga-
zines all over the world.

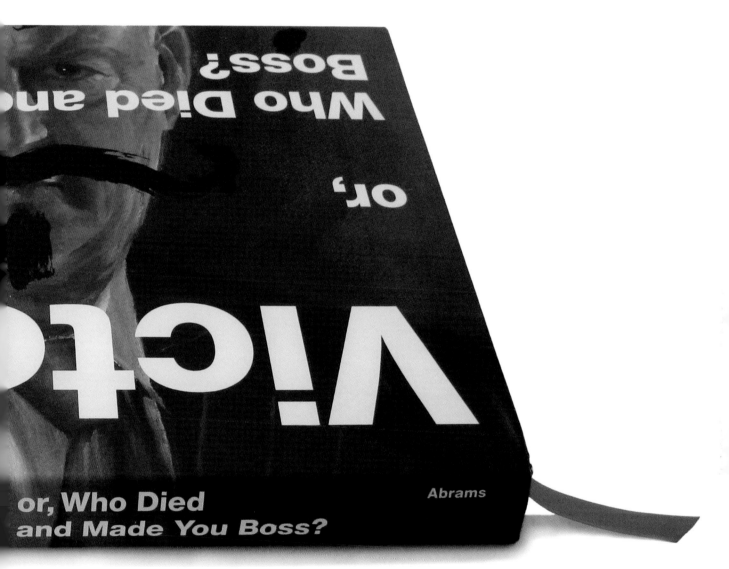

TYPOTRON-HEFT 28
TGG HAFEN SENN
STIEGER
Book Design | Image
Driven Book

Designer
TGG Hafen Senn Stieger
Copywriter
Liana Ruckstuhl
Photographer
das digitale bild GmbH
Publisher Typotron AG
Agency
TGG Hafen Senn Stieger
Client Typotron AG
Country Switzerland

The Typotron series is a
cultural contribution
by Typotron AG, a
printing factory in St.
Gallen. This year's topic
is the old locomotive
shed in St. Gallen. The
shape, color and weight
of the book resemble a
charcoal briquet.

VOL. 30 SPRING/ SUMMER 2010
KID'S WEAR VERLAG
Editorial Design | Magazine Full Issue

Art Director Mike Meiré
Photo Editor
Ann-Katrin Weiner
Publisher Achim Lippoth
Agency kid's wear Verlag
Client kid's wear
Magazine
Country Germany

Photo Viviane Sassen

kid's wear

Vol.30

FASHION, LIFE AND CULTURE

Spring/Summer 2010

Viviane Sassen, Nan Goldin, Ingar Krauss,
Achim Lippoth, Mike Meiré

Glossary/SubTEENAGE 2010

4 194596 412500   30

12,50 €

More feelings per minute:

longing,
stress,
happiness,
hate,
fear,
boredom,
anger,

joy,
melanch
love…

I AM ONE THOUSAND
COSSETTE
Corporate/Promo | Annual Report

Creative Director
Michel De Lauw,
Barbara Jacques
Art Director
Richard Belanger
Copywriter
Patricia Doiron
Designer
Daniel Cartier,
Nathalie Boucher,
Richard Belanger
Illustrator
Richard Belanger
Photographer Enablis
Account Manager
Emmanuelle Petit
Agency Cossette
Client Enablis
Country Canada

Enablis is a Canadian
non-profit organization
founded by Charles
Sirois, whose mission is
to provide financial and
professional support to
entrepreneurs in West
and South Africa, through
its member network. "I
am one thousand."
Strength in numbers and
the uniqueness of
everyone: each member
is important and brings
something unique and
different to the group.
To illustrate this point, we
put together a series of
various papers and
used different graphic
styles to communicate
a positive portrayal of
today's Africa.

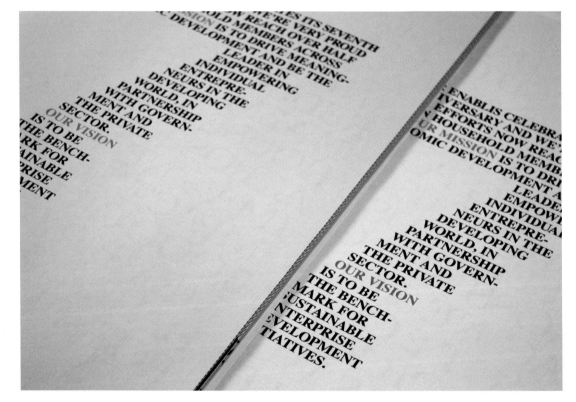

**TURBINE-FREE
WIND POWER**
BUCK
Motion | Motion Graphics

Creative Director
Orion Tait
Art Director
Gareth O'Brien,
Yker Moreno
Designer
Gareth O'Brien,
Yker Moreno
Animator
Gareth O'Brien,
Claudio Salas,
Daniel Oeffinger
Executive Producer
Anne Skopas
Producer Kitty Dillard
Production Company
Buck
**Executive Music
Producer**
Sean McGovern
Sound Designer
Wilson Brown
Original Music Antfood
Composer Wilson Brown
VO Talent Tristan Tait
Agency Buck
Client The New York
Times
Country United States

BIRTHDAY
BBDO NEW YORK
Motion | Special Effects

Executive Creative
Director Greg Hahn,
Ralph Watson
Chief Creative Officer
David Lubars
Art Director
Ralph Watson
Copywriter Greg Hahn
Director of Photography
Wally Pfister
Director Peter Thwaites
Editor Kirk Baxter
(Rock Paper Scissors)
Executive Producer
Grant Gill,
Amy Wertheimer
Assistant Producer
Becky Burkhard
Production Company
Gorgeous
Music Producer
Melissa Chester
Account Team
Julie Meyerson,
Heather Bell
Agency BBDO New York
Client AT&T
Country United States

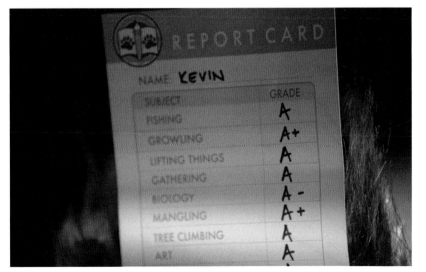

PROUD PAPA
LEO BURNETT
CHICAGO
Motion | Direction

Executive Creative Director
John Montgomery
Chief Creative Officer
Susan Credle
Creative Director
Reed Collins,
Bob Winter
Art Director
Reed Collins
Copywriter Bob Winter
Director Bryan Buckley
Editor Chris Franklin
Producer Denis Giroux,
Mino Jarjoura (Hungry
Man), Cheryl Panek (Big
Sky Editorial)
Production Company
Hungry Man
Sound Design
John Binder (Another
Country)
Visual Effects Big Sky
Editorial
Agency Leo Burnett
Chicago
Client McDonald's
Country United States

2010

WHITNEY MUSEUM OF
AMERICAN ARTS
Book Design | Museum, Gallery or
Library book

Designer
Project Projects
Editor Beth Huseman
Publisher Whitney
Museum of American Art,
New York, Rachel de
W. Wixom
Agency Whitney Museum
of American Art
Client Whitney Museum
of American Art
Country United States

The design for the 2010
Whitney Biennial, curated
by Francesco Bonami and
Gary Carrion-Murayari,
takes the subject of time
as one of its primary
organizing principles.
Building on the history
and logic of the Biennial's
history while reflecting
the current recessionary
climate of the country,
the catalog periodically
applies a set of related
frameworks as a means
of representing recent
contemporary American
art. In the middle of the
book, a series of textured,
glossy, awkwardly heavy
pages layer archival
photographs of the Whit-
ney's successively more
modern three buildings
with odd photographs
showing an American
president associated with
each decade. Serving
as both a transitionary
gesture and a physi-
cal barrier between the
catalog's present and
past, the pages create the
visceral sense of a paper-
and-ink time machine,
complete with the effect
of vertigo. Overall, the
catalog acknowledges the
weight of American
political realities asper-
vasive in the privileged
space of exhibition.

**ALL ABOUT TEA—
BRAND IDENTITY**
MOVING BRANDS
Corporate/Promo | Corporate
Identity Program

Creative Director
Ben Wolstenholme
Designer Marian Chiao
Project Manager
Graves Englund
Agency Moving Brands
Client All About Tea
Country United States

All About Tea is an expert manufacturing whole-saler and distributor of specialty teas. All About Tea engaged Moving Brands to develop an identity system that would work effectively across their existing wholesale market, and enable them to grow into retail channels. Our assessment of All About Tea brought to light the company's inherently metronomic delivery, the quality and rigor of their service and products, and their unparalleled passion for tea. The new identity has the straightforward approach necessary in the wholesale market, yet appeals to the retail audience by standing out in a landscape dominated by brown/green colors, tea leaves and tree hug-gers. The mark references the process of making tea—the blending and the straining. The symbol expresses a stamp of quality, representing the brand's confidence as an iconic industry standard. It is a moving world identity, designed to work across all platforms.

Creative Director
Michel De Lauw,
Barbara Jacques
Art Director
Richard Belanger
Designer
Nathalie Boucher,
Richard Belanger
Illustrator
Richard Belanger
Agency Cossette
Client McCord Museum
Country Canada

McCord Museum
invitation: Inspired by
traditional quilt designs,
we created an artisanal
typography that evoked
a party mood. This same
typography, shaped like
modern quilts, was used
to create invitation cards,
VIP invitations, posters
and wrapping paper for
the fair.

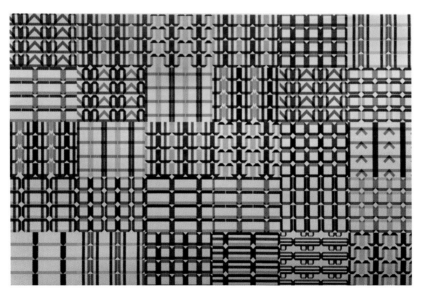

120 COLORS
ADK JAPAN
Poster Design | Transit

Creative Director
Tomotake Kawagoe
Art Director
Tetsufumi Takei
Copywriter
Atsushi Matsumoto
Designer
Kenichi Yamamoto,
Chika Shimizu
Other Hiroki Ishiyama,
Hirofumi Sato, JM Lopez
Agency ADK Japan
Client PENTAX
Country Japan

The posters advertised the launch of a digital SLR camera, which can be ordered to have a color combination chosen from 12 body colors and 10 grip colors. The objectives: to make available a camera with never-before-seen colors; to convey that this camera can have any color combinations from the palette available. All the visuals were prepared using photographs of actual product. Photographs were taken of each color combination to create 10 brilliantly patterned mosaics, each mosaic made into a poster consisting of 12 color combinations. Through advertising all 120 possible color combinations in such a manner, we appealed to the idea that a customer can choose any color combination from the 120 available.

524A—ARCHITYPO
524 ARCHITECTURE
Corporate/Promo | Stationery

Creative Director
Zhou Wenjun
Art Director
Zhou Wenjun
Designer Zhou Wenjun
Director Zhou Wenjun
Agency 524 Architecture
Client 524 Architecture
Design Studio
Country China

"Type Is Architecture"
took the integrated
modularized traditional
Chinese characters 5, 2,
4; Arabic numerals 5, 2,
4 and the English word
architecture, to construct
the logo image of 524
Architecture Studio.
The logo and several
materials are designed
to promote the value of
the studio. Envelopes
and business cards with
different styles can be
adapted for various users.
Scale sketching paper
is designed for multiple
uses in the sketch book
and tear off calendar.

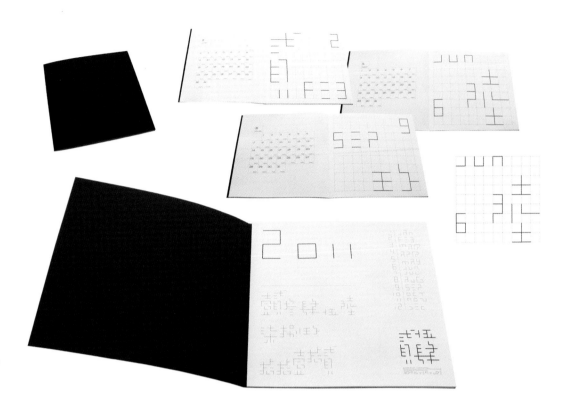

**ARS ELECTRONICA
NIGHTLINE POSTER**
VERENA PANHOLZER
Poster Design | Wild Postings

Art Director
Verena Panholzer
Photographer
Peter Garmusch
Agency
Verena Panholzer
Client Ars Electronica
Festival 2010
Country Austria

Electronic music that
goes under the skin.
Sense organs were pho-
tographed like art objects.
Using the words LISTEN,
WATCH, FEEL, THINK,
the viewer is invited to
sharpen his senses on the
music and visuals of this
year's "Nightline."

AT CUCULIC'S PLACE
SESNIC&TURKOVIC
Environmental | Gallery/Museum
Exhibit or Installation

Creative Director
Marko Sesnic,
Goran Turkovic
Art Director
Marko Sesnic,
Goran Turkovic
Designer Marko Sesnic,
Goran Turkovic
Illustrator
Marko Sesnic,
Goran Turkovic,
Stefano Katunar
Agency Sesnic&Turkovic
Client Museum of
Modern and
Contemporary
Art Rijeka
Country Croatia

Our friend and colleague
Vanja Cuculic asked us to
design the exhibition of
his work in his home-
town, Rijeka. It has been
conceived as paraphrases
of his own home. His
work is integrated into
classic apartment rooms
to make the exhibits
more accessible to the
audience as well as to
accentuate the ubiquity
of design in our everyday
life. Because there was
practically no budget,
we achieved the apart-
ment atmosphere by
drawing almost all the
elements of an apartment
on the walls.

WHAT IS I AM MAKING MOVIES?

I AM Making Movies is a competition launched by Auckland Museum as part of our eLearning strategy to support the new Digital Technologies curriculum.

The competition invites students to create a short movie based on exhibits throughout the Museum. Movies may be conceived as either documentaries or creative storytelling – like those featuring performance artist Mika in our current exhibition, *Wonderland—The Magic of the Rose*.

Competition finalists will be showcased online, and all contestants will be invited to attend a glittering awards evening on Sunday, 20 June. Entries will be judged and prizes presented on the night by stars of the New Zealand film industry.

School programmes are funded jointly by Auckland Museum and the Ministry of Education through their Learning Experiences Outside The Classroom programme (LEOTC).

www.aucklandmuseum.com/
iammakingmovies

A REAL LIFE LEARNING EXPERIENCE FOR DIGITAL MEDIA CREATIVITY

I AM MAKING MOVIES

TAMAKI PAENGA HIRA
AUCKLAND MUSEUM

AUCKLAND MUSEUM— I AM CAMPAIGN
ALT GROUP
Corporate/Promo | Corporate Identity Program

Creative Director Dean Poole
Copywriter Ben Corban, Dean Poole, Felicity Stevens
Designer Dean Poole, Toby Curnow, Shabnam Shiwan, Tony Proffit, Jinki Cambronero, Aaron Edwards, Sam Fieulaine
Photographer Toaki Okano
Agency Alt Group
Client Auckland Museum
Country New Zealand

Auckland Museum holds the world's largest Maori and Pacific collection and is also a natural history and a war memorial museum. The challenge was to develop a campaign identity and communications platform that aligned the team internally and repositioned the museum externally. The solution came from a fundamental questioning of what a museum is: AM was developed as the campaign mark in conjunction with a brand voice. AM is an acronym. I AM is an introduction and an affirmation. A pattern language was developed, referencing the traditions of Maori and Pacific carving and the building's architecture. A typographic language combined different typefaces with visual elements relating to the logo. A photographic portraiture approach was developed putting the people of Auckland at the center of communication. Core identity elements were applied across a broad range of comms including brandbooks, collateral, exhibition/ event campaigns, education program, signage, online, radio and television advertising.

CINEMATOGRAPHIES IN AFRICA—A MEETING WITH HIS PROTAGONISTS
ENA CARDENAL DE LA NUEZ
Book Design | Book Jacket

Designer
Ena Cardenal de la Nuez
Prepress Cromotex
Printer TF Artes Graficas
Publisher Casa África
Agency Ena Cardenal
de la Nuez
Client Casa África
Country Spain

This publication aims to bring the reality of African cinema and its protagonists to the Spanish audience by means of 30 articles and interviews with the most representative African filmmakers. The abstract language on the cover is used to highlight the encounter to which the title refers. The word *encuentro* (encounter) is in the middle of the intersection of two different-colored spotlights (focal points or worlds) that get together. Inside the book, each author is introduced with a page shorter than the rest. This graphic gesture helps us to give dynamism to a book about 400 pages long.

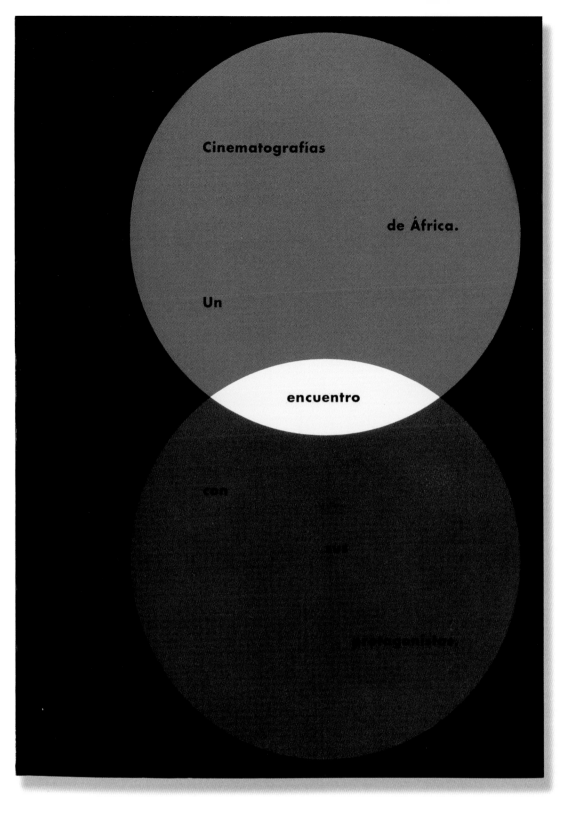

**BOLS GENEVER
CAMPAIGN**
Beattie McGuinness
Bungay New York, Staat
Creative Agency
Branding | Branding Campaign

Creative Director
Neil Powell
Copywriter
Peter Rosch
Designer
Neil Powell
Photographer
Neil Powell
Production Company
Robert Pyzocha
Agency
Beattie McGuinness
Bungay New York, Staat
Creative Agency
Client Bols Genever
Country United States

In 2010, Beattie McGuin-
ness Bungay New York
was tasked with a chal-
lenge: introduce Bols
Genever, an unknown
luxury spirits category
and brand in the clut-
tered US market. BMB
NY leveraged design and
innovation to approach
this project in a different
way. Through a series of
memorable experiences,
we revealed this magnetic
brand by challenging the
dated rules of trial and
awareness. We replaced
the typical red cocktail
straw with a polished
stainless steel one, and
the napkin we placed
the drink on encouraged
conversation as conden-
sation revealed hidden
messages. We also made
Bols Genever a fixture at
cocktail bars. From age-
distressed wooden boxes
that housed the straws
and napkins to a new spin
on the drink coaster, BMB
disrupted the traditional
promotional patterns.
The result was an alluring
campaign that increased
brand awareness and
trial, putting Bols Genever
on the map.

CARL*S CARS ISSUE 28
CARL'S CARS
Editorial Design | Magazine Full Issue

Creative Director
Stéphanie Dumont
Copywriter Lars Eriksen,
Bjørn Hatterud,
På Fröberg
Illustrator
Therese Mæhle
Photographer
Kimm Saatvedt, Marius
Ektvedt, Rob Hann
Editor Karl Eirik Haug
Production Company
Postproduksjon AS
Publisher Carl*s Cars
Other
Ruben Kristiansen, Siren
Lauvdal, Steffen Oftedal,
Jørn Tomter
Agency Carl*s Cars
Client Carl*s Cars
Magazine
Country Norway

Launched in 2001,
*Carl*s Cars* was the
first international "car
lifestyle" magazine with
a twist. *Carl*s Cars* 10
years old slogan, "A
Magazine about People,"
is more valid than ever
with this issue: Car talks
with David Lynch, Liam
Gallagher and others, and
an unashamed reportage
about the phenomenon of
mooning (showing one's
butt from a car window
when passing by) is typi-
cal. In addition, offbeat
and not too serious
presentations of green
transport, documenta-
tions of car culture and a
"signature" intimate tone
of voice make *Carl*s Cars*
stand out from the rest.

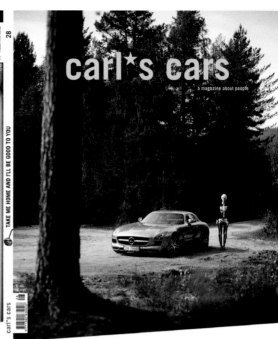

A CAR TALK WITH DAVID LYNCH

Interview: Karl Eirik Haug   Photo: Kimm Saatvedt

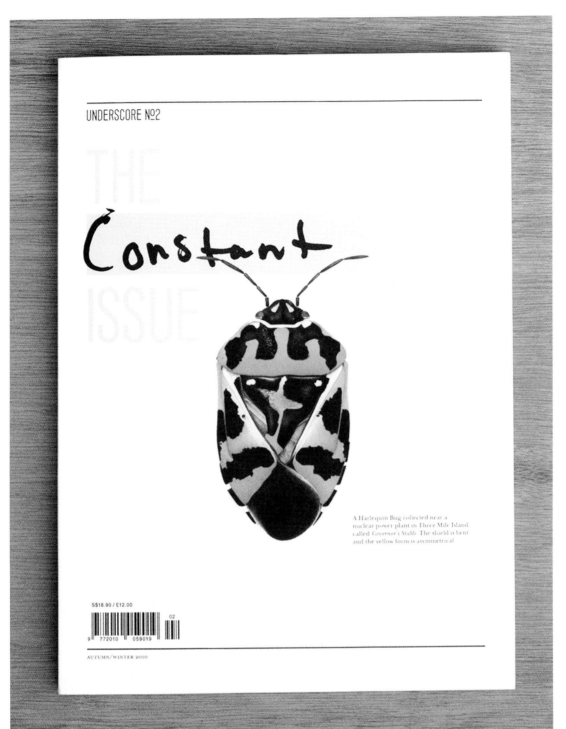

**UNDERSCORE N°2
THE CONSTANT ISSUE**
HJGHER
Editorial Design | Magazine Full Issue

Art Director Jerry Goh
Photographer
Jovian Lim
Editor Justin Long
Sub-editor
Stephanie Peh
Publisher H/Publishing
Agency HJGHER
Client Underscore
Country Singapore

Underscore is a magazine attuned to a simple rhythm; quality of life. *Underscore* N°2, The Constant Issue, begins with the notion that impermanence is the inevitable constant in the journey of life with all content curated to highlight meditations of the Constant theme. As another definition of *Underscore* is background music tracks were carefully selected to accompany articles to enhance, if not complete, the reading experience. The entire soundtrack is free for download online. The cover features an illustration of a mutated bug brought on by effects of a nuclear accident—a personal reminder of the possibility of survival and beauty in the event of devastation. The theme, "Constant", is by Jónsi Birgisson of Sigur Ros.

BIT.CODE

OGILVY FRANKFURT
Environmental | Gallery/Museum
Exhibit or Installation

Creative Director
Peter Strauss
Art Director
Christian Leithner
Copywriter
Peter Strauss
Director of Photography
Stephan Heinze,
Raphael Metz
Director
Thomas Bausenwein
Editor Raphael Metz
Producer
Thomas Bausenwein
Digital Artist
Julius Popp
Production Company
Filmmeisterei
Exhibiting Museum
Victoria and Albert
Museum
Agency Ogilvy Frankfurt
Client SAP Germany
Country Germany

In order to demonstrate
how innovative SAP
software is, the com-
pany commissioned an
unusual "product
demonstration." The
digital artist Julius Popp
created an interactive
installation entitled bit.
code. It uses SAP soft-
ware to identify and filter
key words from Internet
news sites in real time,
which then appear on
an oversize mechanical
display. The film follows
the creative process
from the artist's studio
in Leipzig to the start of
the exhibition "decode.
digital design sensations"
in the Victoria and Albert
Museum, London.

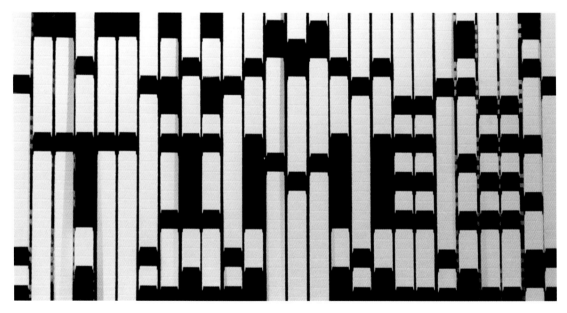

MIZUKAGAMI
HAKUHODO INC.
Book Design | Museum, Gallery
or Library Book

Art Director
Rikako Nagashima
Designer
Rikako Nagashima
Photographer
Kazuhiro Fujita
Printing Director
Koichiro Kawabata
Hair/Makeup
Akihiro Sugiyama
Stylist Mana Yamamoto
Agency Hakuhodo Inc.
Client Rocket Gallery
Country Japan

This is a catalog for
"Mizukagami," an exhibi-
tion for mirrors shaped
as water. Inside the white
envelope is a invitation
card for the exhibition.
The words are written
to reflect into the mir-
ror below so the card
receivers read it in the
mirror. The catalog book,
expressed the sight of
"Mizukagami" as a comi-
cal and poetic world.

BOOK WORM
HESIGN 2
Book Design | Limited Edition,
Private Press or Special Format Book

Designer Jianping He
Editor Jianping He
Publisher Hesign(Berlin/
Hangzhou)
Agency Hesign 2
Client Hesign (Berlin/
Hangzhou)
Country Germany

DISTRICT GRIFFIN
BLEUBLANCROUGE
Branding | Typography Systems

Creative Director
Daniel Fortin
Designer Joe Lapalme
Agency Bleublancrouge
Client Devimco & Groupe
Cholette
Country Canada

ROLL & HILL CATALOG
STUDIO LIN
Corporate/Promo | Booklet/
Brochure

Creative Director
Studio Lin and Roll & Hill
Art Director Alex Lin,
Jason Miller
Copywriter Andrew Yang
Designer Alex Lin
Director Jason Miller
Editor Andrew Yang
Producer Roll & Hill
Publisher Roll & Hill
Agency Studio Lin
Client Roll & Hill
Country United States

VISIONS AND FEARS
BRIAN REA
Environmental | Gallery/Museum
Exhibit or Installation

Designer Brian Rea
Curator Martina Millá
Agency Brian Rea
Client Joan Miró
Foundation
Country United States

Visions and Fears was
included in the exhibition
entitled "Murals" at the
Joan Miró Foundation
in Barcelona. Each list-
based mural measured
roughly 10 by 3.5 meters
and was installed in a
narrow hallway in the
museum. During his final
year in New York City, the
artist cataloged a year's
worth of worries and
fears into a visual inven-
tory of anxiety. *Visions*
expanded on one of those
fears. It contained some
of the most interesting
and unusual UFO sight-
ings over the last 50
years archiving the intersection between fear,
storytelling and drawing
with people's imagination.

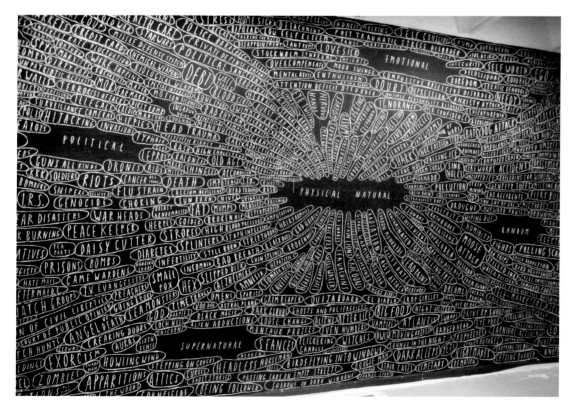

FILM NORTH
CONCRETE DESIGN
COMMUNICATIONS
Branding | Branding
Campaign

Creative Director
John Pylypczak,
Diti Katona
Designer Jordan Poirier,
Markus Uran
Illustrator Adrian Forrow
Editor Rene Ostetto
Agency Concrete Design
Communications
Client Film North
Country Canada

Film North is Canada's newest, and Muskoka's first, international film festival. Located two hours north of Toronto, scenic Muskoka is the country vacation get-away for nature-seeking urbanites, a kind of Hamptons of the north. The festival presents a unique opportunity for local residents and visitors to experience a wide range of emerging independent international and Canadian films, set against the backdrop of the region's renowned lakes, forests and picturesque towns. As a start-up venture, the branding needed to garner much attention on an extremely limited media budget. The branding presents the festival, and the host town of Huntsville, as an unpretentious, welcoming place for young talent from around the world. Concrete combined standard festival imagery—such as the Cannes laurel leaves—northern Canadian kitsch. This approach capitalizes both on the lore of the region, as well as the great part of the Canadian psyche—our ability to make fun of ourselves.

MURALS FOR QUEENS METROPOLITAN CAMPUS

PENTAGRAM DESIGN
Environmental | Retail, Restaurant, Office, Outdoor or Vehicle

Art Director Paula Scher
Designer Paula Scher, Andrew Freeman
Photographer Ian Roberts
Agency Pentagram Design
Client NYC Department of Education/NYC School Construction Authority /NYC Department of Cultural Affairs
Country United States

Paula Scher was commissioned to create a pair of murals at the new Queens Metropolitan Campus in Forest Hills, which includes Queens Metropolitan High School and the Metropolitan Expeditionary Learning School, a middle school. The murals are located in a pair of solariums at the campus and each covers approximately 2,430 square feet. One mural provides a view of the New York metropolitan region with a focus on Queens; the other depicts Metropolitan Avenue in 20 languages spoken by residents of Queens. The murals merge Scher's large-scale typographic map paintings and environmental supergraphics to create a dimensional painting in which the students' own community wraps around the walls in vibrant color. Some of the locations are misspelled or misidentified, and the artist seems to be figuring out the geography along with the students, creating a joyous sense of recognition that mirrors the learning process.

THE STATE OF THINGS
—DESIGN AND THE
21ST CENTURY
SHUAL.COM
Book Design | Museum, Gallery
or Library Book

Art Director
Guy Saggee, Adi Stern
Designer Guy Saggee,
Yotam Hadar
Agency Shual.com
Client Design Museum
Holon
Country Israel

A 208-page bilingual catalog for "The State of Things," the inaugural exhibition of the Design Museum Holon. While the common model for Hebrew and English bilingual publications is creating two opposite covers and two separate narratives uncomfortably meeting in the center of the book (because of the languages' opposite writing directions), in this catalog, Hebrew and English content was positioned to allow both languages to flow together, one alongside the other in the same direction, creating one, linear, unidirectional narrative, while sharing reference images. The objects in the exhibition were divided into eight thematic groups, each represented in the book in a separate signature, wrapped by the relevant cover pages and indices, printed on paper of different stock and size. The same dividers were also used as cover pages for the essays preceding the image section. The hardcover features a die cut of the exhibition's leading image.

מצב הדברים
עיצוב והמאה ה-21

The State of Things
Design and the 21ˢᵗ Century

NIKLAUS TROXLER & HIS STUDENTS
HESIGN 2
Poster Design | Outdoor/Billboard

Agency Hesign 2
Client Hesign International & Phoenix Creativ Park & FourZero Art Space
Country Germany

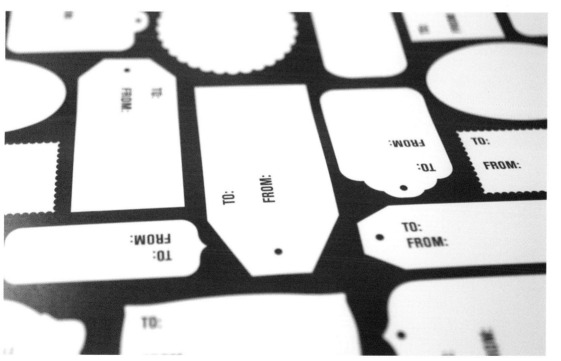

TO/FROM
DESIGN ARMY
Product Design | Gift/Specialty Product

Creative Director
Pum Lefebure,
Jake Lefebure
Art Director
Pum Lefebure
Designer
Taylor Buckholz
Agency Design Army
Client Design Army
Country United States

No tags required when you wrap your gifts in custom "To/From" wrapping paper. Festive shapes and medallions make it easy to give a gift (or re gift) without all the extra fuss. Perfect for those who are wrapping-challenged.

SCIENCE STORMS
EVIDENCE DESIGN
Environmental | Gallery/Museum
Exhibit or Installation

Art Director
Shari Berman
Exhibit Designer Len
Soccolich, Carlos Fierro
Designer
Laura Sheedy,
Ari Nakamura
Project Director
Jack Pascarosa, AIA
Content Specialist
Rondi Davies
Graphic Production
Josh Whitehead
Media Production
Cortina Productions
Engineering Consultant
The Wheel Thing
Lighting Design
Focus Lighting Media
AV Integration MAD
Systems
General Exhibit
Fabrication Lexington,
Chicago Scenic Studios
Specialty Fabrication
Advanced Entertainment
Technology, Production
Resource Group
Agency Evidence Design
Client Museum of
Science and Industry
Chicago
Country United States

THE SMOKER'S LUNG
SERVICEPLAN
Environmental | Retail, Restaurant, Office, Outdoor, or Vehicle

Chief Creative Officer
Alexander Schill
Creative Director
Maik Kaehler,
Christoph Nann
Art Director
Savina Mokreva,
Manuel Wolff
Agency serviceplan
Client BARMER GEK
Country Germany

The BARMER GEK insurance company wanted to highlight the risks of nicotine consumption at the turn of this year—the time to make New Year's resolutions. Idea: To drastically illustrate how smoking harms you, we chose a very significant, highly visible kind of lung: the city's green lung—a tree. One sycamore tree, 150 black balls, as a symbol for the harmful tar blebs, resembling the shape of a human lung. At the root of the tree, we placed a big sign, explaining the medical dangers of smoking. Now it became clearly visible to every passerby what cigarettes can do to one's lungs.

VIVE LA TARTE!
MARTHA STEWART
LIVING OMNIMEDIA
Editorial Design | Magazine Story
Multi-Page

Illustrator Miyuki Sakai
Director
James Dunlinson
Agency Martha Stewart
Living Omnimedia
Client
Martha Stewart Living
Country United States

144 | MARTHASTEWART.COM

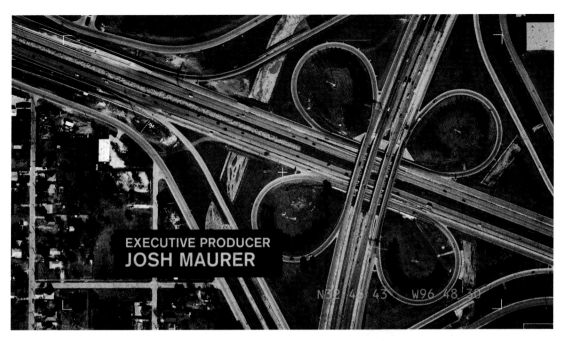

EXECUTIVE PRODUCER
JOSH MAURER

N32 42 43 W96 48 30

RUBICON
IMAGINARY FORCES
Motion | Title Design

Creative Director
Karin Fong
Designer Karin Fong,
Theodore Daley,
Jeremy Cox
Animator Jeremy Cox,
JJ Johnstone,
Andy Chung
Director Karin Fong
Editor Jordon Podos,
Caleb Woods,
Adam Spreng
Producer
Cara McKenney
Production Company
Imaginary Forces
Agency
Imaginary Forces
Client AMC
Country United States

For the main titles for
AMC's Rubicon, we
wanted to communicate
the feel of the show,
which is, "nothing is what
it seems." The challenge
was to engage the
audience into looking
closer and sensing that
something is not quite
right. The design process
involved looking at secret
codes and thinking of
ways to suggest conspir-
acy and connections. We
wanted to keep a
somewhat analog feel
—the show takes place in
the present but the
characters at the agency
are constantly moving
scraps of paper around in
their quest for patterns,
so we didn't want a purely
electronic feel. We used
elements such as
newspapers, numbers,
bar codes, and maps,
which are connected by
what appears to be a
hand-drawn yellow line, to
lead the audience to
perceive links that may or
not be there.

CREATED BY
JASON HORWITCH

19. 1. 38. 3. 41. 28. 29. 33. 49. 2. 22. 19. 38.

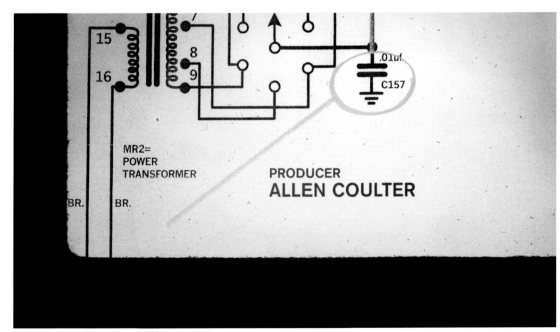

15
16
8
9
.01uf
C157
MR2=
POWER
TRANSFORMER
BR. BR.
PRODUCER
ALLEN COULTER

DISNEY LOGO
PROLOGUE FILMS
Motion | Animated Logo

Creative Director
Danny Yount
Art Director
Daniel Klöhn
Animator
Eric Demeusy,
Takayuki Sato, Joey Park
Producer Unjoo Byars
Design Company
Prologue Films
Agency Prologue Films
Client Walt Disney
Pictures/Joseph Kosinski
Country United States

We were commissioned
by director Joseph
Kosinski to create a new
look and animation of the
traditional Disney Studio
logo in celebration of its
film *Tron Legacy*. It
needed to be made in
stereoscopic 3-D and
designed in a way that
was connected to the
visual style of the film
while still maintaining the
integrity of the estab-
lished brand. To bring it
into a more futuristic
environment and style we
chose to light everything
up electronically—replac-
ing fireworks with laser
beams and incandescent
lighting with LED and
fluorescent lights. We also
altered the form of the
castle to match the
architecture of the city in
the film. *Tron* fans
received this extremely
well, and we were
commended by our
delighted client because
it "received an applause
every time" in early
audience screenings.

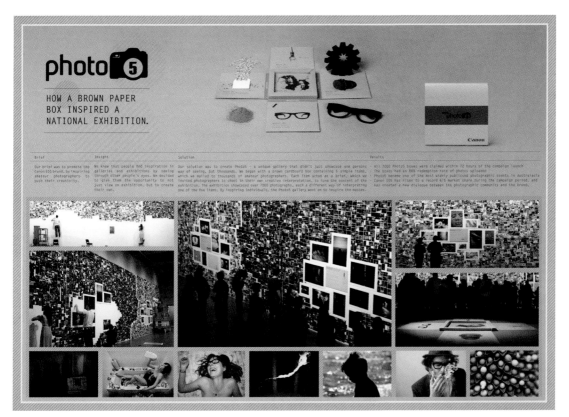

PHOTO 5 GALLERY
LEO BURNETT SYDNEY
Environmental | Gallery/Museum
Exhibit or Installation

Creative Director
Andy DiLallo,
Jay Benjamin
Art Director
Kieran Antill
Copywriter
Michael Canning
Designer
Masataka Kawano
Editor
Patrick Fileti
Agency
Leo Burnett Sydney
Client Canon Australia
Country Australia

Our objective was to inspire a wide range of photographer. We knew that people find inspiration in galleries and exhibitions by seeing through other people's eyes. We decided to give photographers the opportunity to not just view an exhibition, but to create their own. Our solution was to create,"PHOTO5." We began with a brown cardboard box containing five simple items. Each item acted as a brief, which we invited photographers to shoot in their own creative interpretation, to form the content of the exhibition. The "PHOTO5" exhibition showcased more than 7,000 photographs, each a different way of interpreting one of the five items. By inspiring individuals, the PHOTO5 Gallery went on to inspire the masses.

VAN BEEM & VAN HAAGEN STOP MOTION FILM
FABRIQUE
Motion | Animation

Art Director
Jeroen Van Erp
Designer Petr Skala
Editor Petr Skala
Project Manager
Kay Timmers
Agency Fabrique
Client Van Beem &
Van Haagen
Country Netherlands

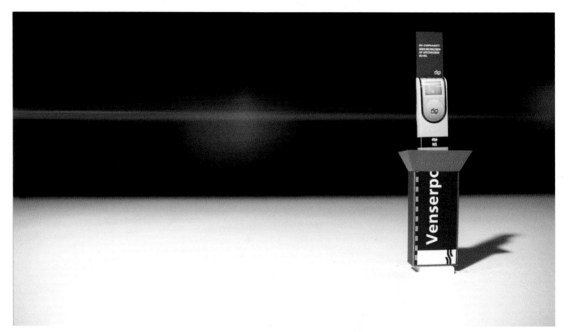

WINNIE THE POOH

WINNIE THE POOH
DRAFT CO.,LTD.
Corporate/Promo | Complete Press
/Promotional Kit

Creative Director
Ryosuke Uehara
Art Director
Ryosuke Uehara
Designer Aya Iida,
Daisuke Kokubo
Director
Ryosuke Uehara
Producer
Yoko Kawashima
Production Company
Walt Disney Japan +
Antipast
Agency Draft Co.,Ltd.
Client Walt Disney Japan
Country Japan

ART OF OUBEY
SAGMEISTER INC.
Book Design | Limited Edition Private
Press or Special Format Book

Creative Director
Stefan Sagmeister
Designer Roy Rub,
Seth Labenz
Photographer visuell
GmbH, Rheinstetten
Editor
Dagmar Woyde-Koehler
Production Laurence Ng
Production Company
Engelhardt und Bauer,
idN (Slipcase)
Publisher Deutscher
Kungstverlag Berlin
München
3-D Prototyping
Guz Gutman
Agency Sagmeister Inc.
Client Oubey
Country United States

This lavish publication
introducing the art of the
late German artist Oubey
was designed as five
distinct books. The books
are contained in a fractal
white slip case reflecting
Oubey's formal interest in
the sciences.

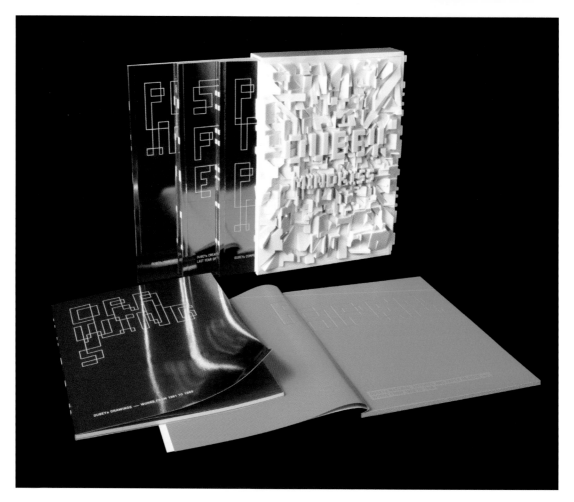

12 LETTERS
DRAFT CO.,LTD.
Product Design | Gift/Specialty/
Product

Creative Director
Satoru Miyata
Art Director
Yoshie Watanabe
Designer
Yoshie Watanabe
Illustrator
Yoshie Watanabe
Producer
Minako Nakaoka,
Takumi Goto
Production Company
Draft
Publisher D-Bros
Agency Draft Co., Ltd.
Client D-Bros
Country Japan

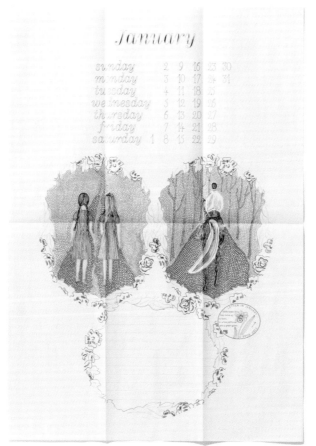

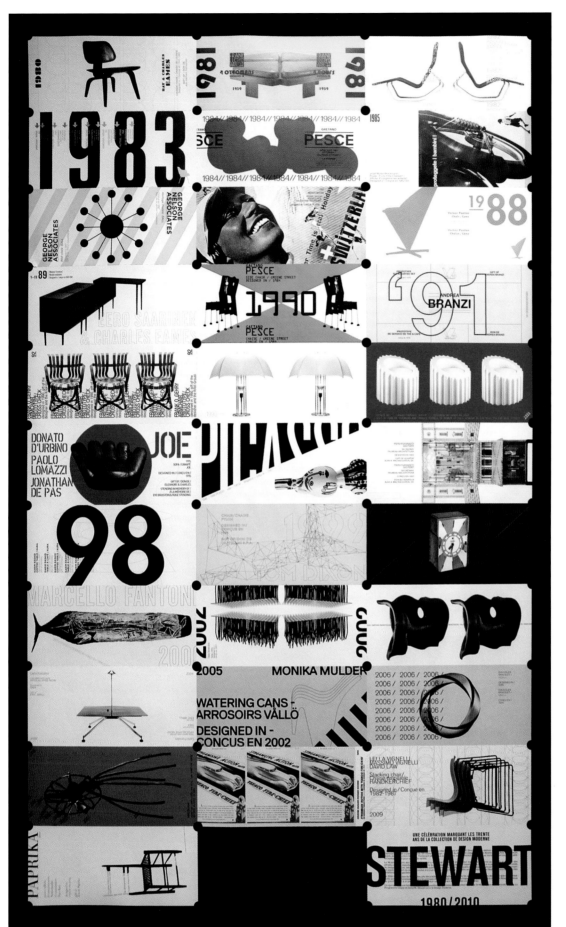

THE LILIANE AND DAVID M. STEWART PROGRAM FOR MODERN DESIGN 1980–2010
PAPRIKA
Corporate/Promo
Announcements

Creative Director
Louis Gagnon
Art Director
Daniel Robitaille
Designer
Daniel Robitaille
Production Company
Tanscontinental
Litho Acme
Agency Paprika
Client The Liliane
and David M. Stewart
Program for
Modern Design
Country Canada

Poster commemorating
the 30th anniversary of
the Collection Liliane and
David M. Stewart. This
poster shows a glimpse
of the exhibitions in which
we saw the Stewart col-
lection in its 30 years of
existence. It was given
to people during special
events organized by
the Stewart Program in
the fall of 2010 at the
Montreal Museum of Fine
Arts, at the Museum of
Modern Art of New York
and in Paris.

Creative Director
Alan Dye, Nick Finney
Copywriter
David Fowle, Ajab Samrai
Designer Ed Wright
Photographer
David Stewart
Agency NB
Client D&AD
Country
United Kingdom

D&AD New Blood is the most important graduate show for design and advertising, but its success is dependent on the presence of industry professionals. This year, NB produced a direct mailer targeting top creatives and designers. "Sorry old blood, the new blood has arrived" is a campaign that aims to provoke the insecurities of the, "blood" reminding them that the "New Blood" is hot on their tails. The 11 executions were printed onto Offenbach Bible paper as A1 posters that unfold to reveal the voyeuristic scene within and were sent to more than 3,000 recipients across design and advertising. As expected, the adverts shocked and entertained, and brought D&AD New Blood to the forefront of the minds of the industry's top creatives.

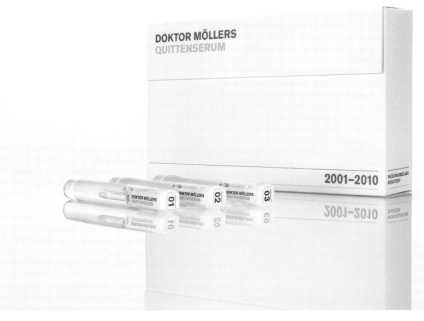

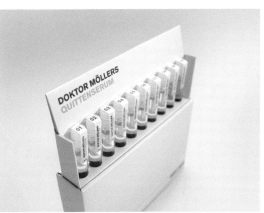

DR. MÖELLER´S QUINCE SERUM—THE DECADE EDITION
SERVICEPLAN
Package Design | Food/Beverage

Chief Creative Director
Alex Schill
Creative Director
Christoph Everke, Cosimo Möeller, Alexander Nagel
Art Director
Alexander Nagel, Elena Ressel, Matthias Nösel
Copywriter
Cosimo Möeller
Agency serviceplan
Client Schnapsbrennerei Dr. Thorsten Möeller
Country Germany

ESPOLÓN
LANDOR ASSOCIATES
Package Design | Food/Beverage

Creative Director
Nicolas Aparicio
Art Director
Cameron Imani
Designer
Anastasia Laksmi, Tony Rastatter
Insights Director
Kara McCartney
Client Associate
Kate Fisher
Agency Landor Associates
Client Espolón
Country United States

EATING TOGETHER
THE NEW YORK
TIMES MAGAZINE
Editorial Design | Magazine Story
Multi-Page

Design Director
Arem Duplessis
Art Director
Gail Bichler
Deputy Art Director
Leo Jung
Designer
Sara Cwynar, Leo Jung
Illustrator Kate Wilson,
Always With Honor,
Sacred Mountain,
Losiento
Photographer
Lucas Foglia
Production Company
The New York
Times Company
Photo Editor
Luise Stauss
Agency The New York
Times Magazine
Client The New York
Times Magazine
Country United States

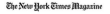

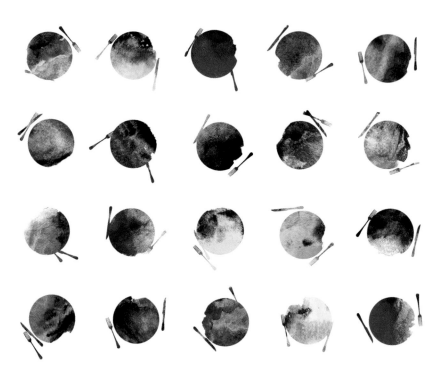

THE FOOD ISSUE

Eating Together

Over the centuries, we've moved from huddling around a fire to gathering around a hearth to sitting around a table to clustering on the Web. But food is what has always brought us together — for sustenance as well as for conversation. In the last decade, the movement toward buying locally has, perhaps inadvertently, resulted in the creation of new communities. Conversations are started when people ask questions of the men and women who grow, make, cook and serve their food, as they are when they seek out others with similar tastes. One result is a multitude of new — and often surprising — connections. Strangers are chipping in to buy a whole steer together. Orthodox Jews are eating wood-fired pizza next to West Indians and hipsters. Graphic designers are trying to revive an impoverished county with an all-butter crust. In one city, 100,000 people have converged to eat street food and learn how to butcher, pickle, home-roast coffee and brew beer. In this, our third annual food issue, the hunger to connect is stronger than ever.

CHARACTER ILLUSTRATIONS BY ROBERT SAMUEL HANSON

43

PLAY THE UNDERGROUND
JUNG VON MATT AG
Poster Design | Wild Postings

Creative Director
Jo Marie Farwick,
Jens Pfau,
Tobias Grimm
Art Director
Benjamin Busse
Copywriter
Florian Hoffmann
Producer
Christian Will
Agency
Jung von Matt AG
Client JEUDI
Country Germany

The varied event series "Jeudi" held in the Baal-saal (ranked 40th in the top "scene" clubs of the world) was looking for a way to attract attention in Hamburg's underground scene. Organizers of parties in Hamburg are permitted to put up posters—and these posters are huge, colorful and loud. Our goal was to create the poster that would attract everyone to our club, and away from other clubs. We also wanted our work to become the talk of the town among our design-oriented target group. Taking the colorful flyers on the city's walls as our basis, our outdoor campaign featured the internationally known PLAY symbol on a white background. It showed passersby that "Jeudi" unites the entire range of underground electro music on one evening of the week.

MT EX KYOTO
IYAMA DESIGN INC.
Environmental | Gallery/Museum
Exhibit or Installation

Creative Director
Koji Iyama
Art Director Koji Iyama
Designer Koji Iyama,
Mayuko Watanabe,
Chie Kai
Production Company
Iyama Design Inc.
Agency
Iyama Design Inc.
Client
Kamoi Kakoshi Co., Ltd.
Country Japan

HELP REBUILD HAITI!
POSTER DESIGNED BY JUSTUS OEHLER FOR
THE HAITI POSTER PROJECT

HELP REBUILD HAITI
PENTAGRAM DESIGN
Poster Design | Poster Typography

Designer Justus Oehler
Director of Photography
Haiti Poster Project
Senior Photo Editor
Pentagram Design
Agency
Pentagram Design
Client Haiti Poster Project
Country United States

**MAKE-UP
COLLECTION**
MARC ATLAN
DESIGN, INC.
Package Design | Cosmetics/
Perfume

Creative Director
Marc Atlan
Art Director Marc Atlan
Designer Marc Atlan
Agency Marc Atlan
Design, Inc.
Client Kjaer Weis
Country United States

Kjaer Weis gave us carte
blanche to design her
eponymous makeup
collection from scratch.
We were in charge of
creating every single
element, from the
logotype to the product
design to the packaging.
The design of the Kjaer
Weis cosmetics line
distills the fundamentals
of women's makeup to its
three essential areas of
application: lips, cheeks
and eyes. We designed
compacts shaped to
mirror the features they
will be used to enhance:
slim and long for the lips,
large and square for the
cheeks, small and round
for the eyes. Tangibly, the
compacts swivel open
with an innovative lateral
movement, fanning
out like the wings of a
butterfly. Entirely
refillable, these compacts
are purposely conserved
rather than recycled.
Highly polished in a white
bronze "Palladium"
finish, monogrammed in
glossy white enamel,
each object conveys the
substance and heft of a
valuable keepsake.

**MAH JONGG:
CRAK, BAM, DOT!**
PENTAGRAM DESIGN
Book Design | Museum, Gallery
or Library Book

Art Director
Abbott Miller
Designer Abbott Miller,
Kristen Spilman
Illustrator
Maira Kalman,
Bruce McCall,
Isaac Mizrahi,
Christoph Niemann
Photographer
James Shanks
Editor Patsy Tarr,
Abbott Miller
Publisher 2wice Arts
Foundation
Agency Pentagram
Design
Client Museum of
Jewish Heritage—A Living
Memorial to the
Holocaust/2wiceBooks
Country United States

*Mah Jongg: Crak, Bam,
Dot!* Was designed by
Abbott Miller and pub-
lished by 2wice to serve as
a companion to the exhibition Project "Mah Jongg"
at the Museum of Jewish
Heritage in New York,
also designed by Miller.
The book and exhibition
explore the connections
between mah jongg and
Jewish-and Chinese-
American cultures.
Portfolios feature imagery
from the mah jongg
craze of the early 20th
century and photographs
of vintage sets, tiles and
other ephemera. Miller
commissioned guest art-
ists to interpret the game
through their distinct sensibilities. Fashion designer
Isaac Mizrahi sketched
mah jongg–inspired
ensembles; Maira Kalman
illustrated a mah jongg
murder mystery; Bruce
McCall created Miami
Mah Jongg, juxtaposing
ancient Chinese figures
tutoring a group of Jewish
women; and Christoph
Neimann designed tile ico-
nography combining the
visual language of mah
jongg with symbols of
Jewish life. The book was
designed with the propor-
tions and rounded corners
of a mah jongg tile.

FIVE VODKA
THE BRAND UNION
Package Design | Food/Beverage

Creative Director
Glenn Tutssel
Art Director
Glenn Tutssel
Copywriter
Ian Crammond
Designer
Glenn Tutssel, Phil Dall
Director Glenn Tutssel
Publisher Welsh Whisky
Company
Agency The Brand Union
Client Welsh Whisky
Country United Kingdom

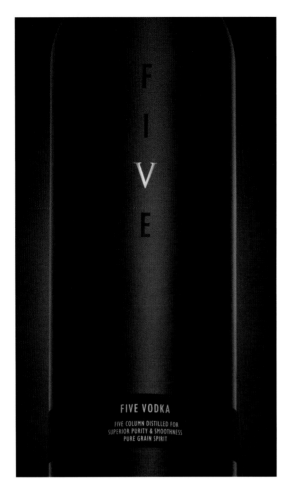

**ZWISCHEN KULTUR
UND POLITIK, PRO
HELVETIA 1939 BIS
2009**
RAFFINERIE AG FÜR
GESTALTUNG
Book Design |Text Driven Book

Designer Raffinerie AG
für Gestaltung
Production Company
Raffinerie AG für
Gestaltung
Publisher Pro Helvetia
und Verlag NZZ
Agency Raffinerie AG für
Gestaltung
Client Pro Helvetia
Country Switzerland

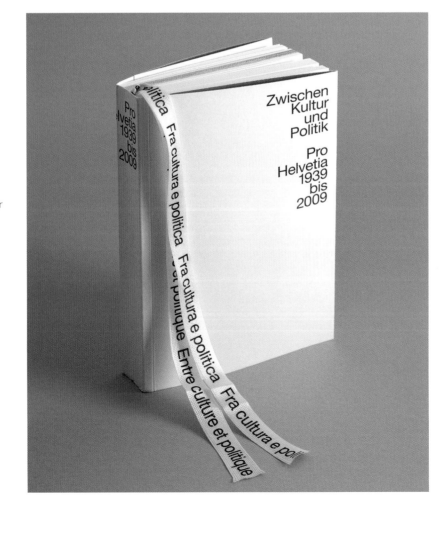

BOARDWALK EMPIRE
IMAGINARY FORCES
Motion | TV Identities, Openings,
Teasers

Designer Karin Fong,
Lauren Hartstone,
Michelle Dougherty
Director Karin Fong,
Michelle Dougherty
Editor Caleb Woods
Producer
Cara McKenney
Production Company
Imaginary Forces
Visual Effects
Supervisor Jeremy Cox
Agency
Imaginary Forces
Client HBO
Country United States

Boardwalk Empire is a
period drama set in the
1920s in Atlantic City. We
worked with the show's
creator, Terence Winter,
his team and HBO to
design and produce a
main title sequence that
introduces us to the
main character, Nucky
Thompson. Our visuals
set up Nucky's posi-
tion as the ruler of the
city—half gangster and
half politician. As he looks
to the ocean he sees
a sea of bottles, which
symbolize the influence
of Prohibition that would
come to color the entire
decade and his fortunes.
Throughout the changing
tides during this turbulent
time in history, Nucky is a
constant. We suggest his
invincibility by showing
him unchanged by the
storm and waves that
hit the shore. In the final
shot, Nucky walks away,
apparently unscathed.

Creative Director
Hoon Kim
Designer Hoon Kim
Agency Why Not Smile
Client Pratt Insititute
Country United States

More & Less is an event
poster informing of a
special lecture by Sulki &
Min at the Pratt Institute
in New York. Sulki & Min
is a graphic design studio
based in Seoul, Korea.
Their design is very bold,
simple, and metaphoric.
In order to represent
the pairs in their studio
name, Sulki & Min, and
also the lecture subject,
More & Less, the designer
created graphical blanks
on the two paired posters
which the audience may
easily fill in To emphasize
the concept, black and
white were applied on
both front and back of
the poster. It is a poster
having two faces without
an order.

SULKI & MIN
MORE & LESS

FEB 12
5:30 PM
PRATT MANHATTAN
ROOM 213

SULKI-MIN.COM

SULKI

SPRING 2010
DESIGN LECTURE SERIES
GRAD COMD

Pratt

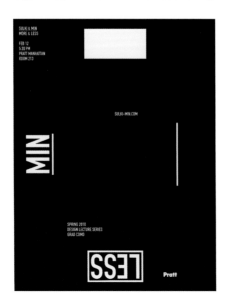

**RECEIVE DON'T
DECEIVE**
PAPRIKA
Corporate/Promo
Self-Promotion

Creative Director
Louis Gagnon
Art Director
Daniel Robitaille
Designer
Daniel Robitaille
Agency Paprika
Client Paprika
Country Canada

RECEIVE DON'T
DECEIVE! Placemats,
coasters, a Bristol
board and a notepad.
Add to this practical
and funny advice to
receive friends and the
night will be perfect!

MÉXICO CIUDAD FUTURA
BLOK DESIGN
Book Design | Reference or How-To Book

Creative Director
Vanessa Eckstein
Designer
Vanessa Eckstein,
Patricia Kleeberg
Editor DN3 Editores
Publisher BLOK/RM
Agency Blok Design
Client Alberto Kalach
Country Canada

Our challenge was to chronicle the bold, visionary plan to transform the environmental and social dynamics of Mexico City through the rescue of the dry Texcoco lakebed, just 10 kilometers from the city's historic center. Blok's challenge was to edit 50 boxes of archival documents into a meaningful book that would create understanding, inspire change and help raise funds for the project. We designed the book to be accessible yet weighty enough to instill in the reader a sense of the project's importance. The concept presents the book as though it were an X-ray of Mexico City, revealing all the layers that will be impacted by the plan. The information is laid out simply and clearly. In keeping with the project's environmental goals, it is a completely green book printed on recyclable paper using vegetable inks. Blok also served as publisher and helped in fund-raising.

RE-COLLECTION
ANNE BUSH DESIGN
Environmental | Gallery/Museum
Exhibit or Installation

Designer Anne Bush
Producer Anne Bush,
Allyn Bromley
Agency
Anne Bush Design
Client
The Contemporary
Museum
Country United States

Re-collection was a 9 x
30 foot installation that
brought together, in a
new form, 300 works
of "art" that had been
exhibited previously
by The Contemporary
Museum (TCM) in
Honolulu. Transformed
with a simple number 11
x-acto blade, images from
the museum's existing
exhibition catalogs were
remade into objects and
reinstalled in the gallery
where they were originally
shown. The resulting
design underscored the
ephemeral aspects of
TCM's exhibition pro-
grams, the reproductive
and unifying conditions of
print and how artworks,
which traditionally find
their ultimate form in
reproduction, can be
given new life.

SNOW VOICE—A MAN WHO LOVES SNOW
DENTSU INC. TOKYO
Corporate/Promo | Booklet/ Brochure

Art Director
Yoshihiro Yagi
Copywriter
Haruko Tsutsui,
Nae Mikuni
Designer Yoshihiro Yagi,
Yo Kimura,
Katsutoshi Hanada,
Eri Kotani
Photographer
Shingo Fujimoto
Production Company
Katachi Co., Ltd.
Printing Producer
Takeshi Arimoto
Photo Producer
Fukutaro Inadome
Agency
Dentsu Inc. Tokyo
Client Mitsubishi
Estate Co.,Ltd & Idee
Co.,Ltd
Country Japan

Brief: Create a promotional tool for the "Snow Voice" winter haiku reading event that will change and create a new image for haiku, part of Japan's traditional culture. The target was people not familiar with haiku, particularly young women who work in the business district of Tokyo, where the event was to be held. Solution: Using the Abominable Snowman as the artwork theme, each page of the book communicates emotions evoked by the purity of white snow, such as tranquility, solitude and excitement. The 60-page B4-sized book includes, among other things, what a snowman eats and how he spends his time, the composition of snow, and a poem of love for the Snow Woman.

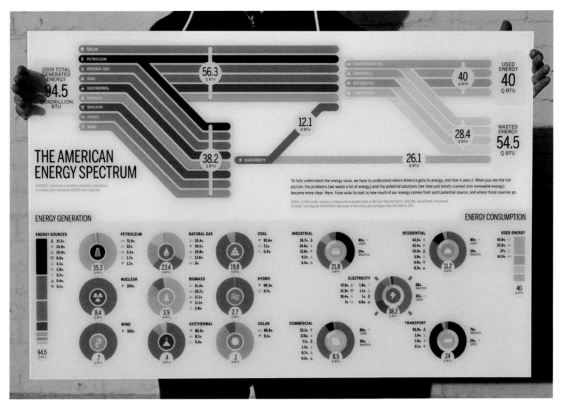

**THE AMERICAN
ENERGY SPECTRUM**
HYPERAKT
Editorial Design | Magazine
Infographic

Creative Director
Deroy Peraza
Copywriter
Morgan Clendaniel
(GOOD)
Designer Deroy Peraza,
Eric Fensterheim
Agency Hyperakt
Client GOOD Magazine
Country United States

How do Americans use
their energy, and where
does it all come from
in the first place? We
teamed up with *GOOD*
magazine to design an
infographic that tells the
story of energy use (and
misuse) in America. The
infographic was cre-
ated as a full spread for
the January 2011 issue
of *GOOD* Magazine. An
interactive version of the
infographic was created
for *GOOD*'s website.

THE GREAT CYBERCROOK
THE NEW YORK TIMES
Editorial Design | Magazine Cover

Design Director
Arem Duplessis
Art Director Gail Bichler
Production Company
The New York Times
Company
Agency The New York
Times Magazine
Client The New York
Times Magazine
Country United States

The New York Times Magazine
NOVEMBER 14, 2010

```
void HttpSniffer::foundPacket (const struct pcktHdr
*hdr,const u_char*packet){constchar*payload;const
struct netSniffer *ethernet=(struct netSniffer*)(packet
); u_short type=ntohs (ethernet→type); switch (type) {
caseETHERNET_IP:ip=(structipSniff*)(ETHERNET_
SIZE +packet ); ipLength = ip→length; if ( IP_HL(ip)*4
< 20) throw runtimeError (str ('I've been asking myself,
Why did I do it? At first I did it for monetary reasons. ...
Then I'd already created the snowball and had to keep
doing it. I wanted to quit but couldn't. ... Whatever
morality I should have been feeling was trumped by
the thrill.' ) ); payload = (u_char *) (ETHERNET_SIZE
+ipSize+tcpSize+pckt);intpayloadSize=ipLength-
(ipSize + sizeTcp); HttpPacket *httpPacket = new
HttpPacket(fromHere,toThere); break; default: return
;}if(httpPacket→parse(payload,payloadSize)){device
= lookupDevice( errorBuffer ) ; if ( device == NULL
) handle = openStream(device, buffer Size, 1, 1000,
errorBuffer ); if (handle != NULL && isReady) fprintf(
stderr, The Great Cybercrook );cout<<Inside the mind
of America's most notorious computer hacker.<<endl;
By James Verini if(httpPacket→complete()) { readCtnt(
httpPacket); delete httpPacket; iterator→next( ); return; }
```

THE DESIGN SOCIETY JOURNAL NO. 1
— DESIGN LITERACY —

MICA (P) No. 217/12/2009

THE DESIGN SOCIETY JOURNAL #1
H55
Editorial Design | Magazine Full Issue

Creative Director
Hanson Ho
Designer Hanson Ho
Illustrator Tan Zi Xi
Photographer
Ming, Justin Zhuang
Editor Hanson Ho,
Caroline
Nagulendran-Mowe
Publisher
The Design Society
Showcase Editor
Yanda
Printer Dominie Press
Agency H55
Client The Design Society
Country Singapore

The Design Society Journal is a means for the newly founded The Design Society to document and create awareness for the graphic design scene in Singapore. It is sent to all members and sold in major bookstores. Our intention is for the journal to be a reference point for future generations, and therefore we wanted the design to be bold and timeless, very much inspired by newsprint but with a twist to engage our audience.

THE BOOK OF TAPAS
GRAFICA
Book Design | Reference or
How-To Book

Creative Director
Pablo Martin
Art Director
Pablo Martin
Designer
Oscar Germade,
Marianne Noble
Photographer
Mauricio Salinas
Editor Laura Gladwin
Producer
Karen Farquhar,
Nerissa Dominguez Vales
Publisher
Phaidon Press Ltd.
Agency Grafica
Client Phaidon Press Ltd.
Country Spain

The design of the book is
based on the way people
eat tapas in Spain and
how they are served.
The photography tries to
reproduce a real Spanish
bar full of dishes, wine,
bread, toothpicks, paper
napkins, etc. Red and
yellow add an obvious
Spanish flavor. The main
typefaces are also Span-
ish: a wood type from
my personal collection
and Hidalgo, a revival of a
17th-century font.

The New York Times Magazine

APRIL 11, 2010

BUILDING A GREEN ECONOMY

BY PAUL KRUGMAN

NEW YORK TIMES MAGAZINE COVER, APRIL 2010 ISSUE
MICHAEL FREIMUTH
Editorial Design | Magazine Cover

Creative Director Arem Duplessis
Art Director Gail Bichler
Copywriter Paul Krugman
Designer Michael Freimuth, Kyle Poff
Publisher New York Times
Agency Michael Freimuth
Client The New York Times Magazine
Country United States

The New York Times Magazine is the weekly standard for editorial excellence in journalism. The April 11th, 2010, issue featured an extensive piece by *Times* columnist Paul Krugman, entitled "Building a Green Economy." The article outlines the need and opportunity for international cooperation to resolve the impasse between Western and developing nations' environmental policies. The cover design strives to visually capture the content of the article while providing a provocative entry point to the entire magazine. More specifically, the cover is an interplay between the graphic articulation of a number of monetary currencies juxtaposed with a more literal, typographic "building" of the feature's title. Additionally, the magazine has an international circulation of 1.5 million in more than 340 markets around the world.

THE INVISIBLE POSTER
BBDO GERMANY GMBH,
DÜSSELDORF
Poster Design | Outdoor/Billboard

Creative Director
Ton Hollander,
Jens Ringena
Art Director
Claudia Janus
Copywriter
Dominique Becker
Managing Director
Sebastian Hardieck
Agency BBDO Germany
GmbH, Düsseldorf
Client Daimler AG,
Mercedes-Benz Vertrieb
Deutschland
Country Germany

The smart-for-two electric
drive makes harmful
emissions disappear in
urban traffic. The objec-
tive was to communicate
this fact to sophisticated,
ecology-minded urban
drivers. Idea: the first
invisible poster. Special
labeling on the inside of an
inner-city fence— bound-
ary of a well-known city
park—made the image of
a smart-for-two electric
drive become invisible to
the eyes of people passing
by and almost invisible
to the environment.

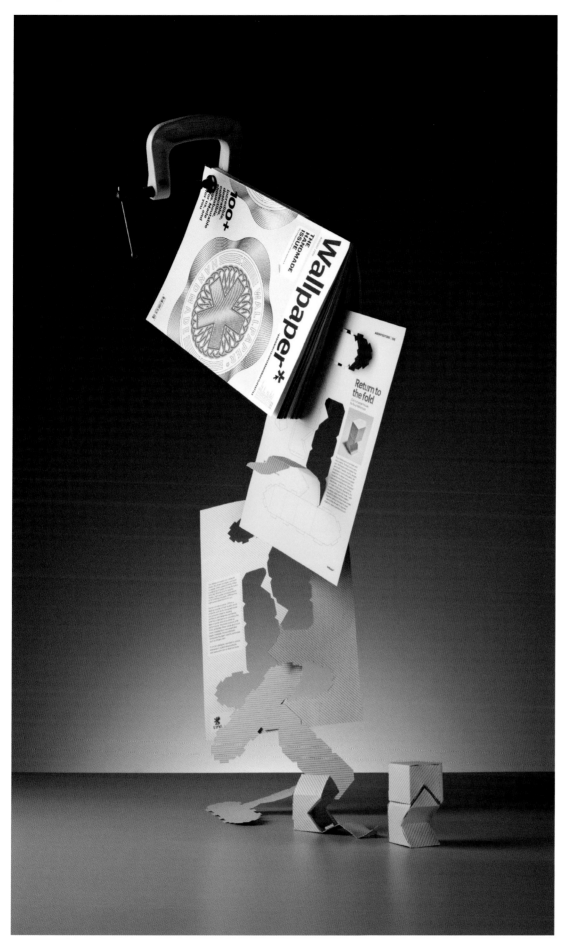

WALLPAPER* HANDMADE
INTERACTIVE DESIGN BY KIN
Editorial Design | Magazine Full Issue

Art Director
Meirion Pritchard
Designer
Sarah Douglas,
Lee Belcher,
Dominic Bell
Illustrator
Anthony Burrill,
James Joyce, Kam Tang
Photo Editor James Reid
Publisher IPC Media
Agency Interactive
design by Kin
Client Wallpaper*
Country
United Kingdom

THEM—AND—US
DISTURBANCE/THE
DISTILLERY
Corporate/Promo | Booklet/
Brochure

Art Director
Richard Hart,
Noel Pretorius
Copywriter
Adrian Shaughnessy
Designer Noel Pretorius,
Richard Hart
Illustrator
20 African and 20
European Illustrators
Other Roger Jardine,
Matt Kay, Jenna Turpin,
Greg Darrol, David Drew
Agency Disturbance/The
Distillery
Client Amnesty
International
Country Sweden

Them—and—Us brings
together 20 European
and 20 African visual
artists, designers,
illustrators and photog-
raphers to explore the
similarities and differ-
ences between their
respective worldviews
and visual sensibilities.
The 20 European and
20 African artists were
paired—one from Europe
with one from Africa.
Each pairing selected a
theme from our online
forum such as "heal-
and-hurt, more-and-less,
reason-and-madness,"
and then designed a
double-sided poster: one
side European, the other
African. Communica-
tion, discussion and the
cross-pollination of ideas,
opinions and styles were
actively encouraged, and
the resulting posters form
a vivid dialogue centred
on the notion of Them—
and—Us, and the broader
themes of tolerance and
intolerance, as seen from
the respective cultural
viewpoints. The catalog
contains all 20 double-
sided posters. It also
houses a 56-page booklet
profiling all the artists
involved and detailing the
purpose and processes of
the project.

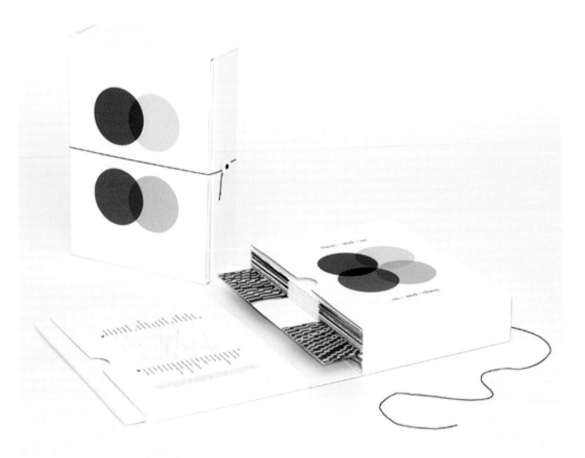

**REDU LAUNCH
ANIMATION**
CAA MARKETING/
HUNTERGATHERER
Motion | Animation

Creative Director Todd
St. John
Designer Todd St. John,
Gary Benzel
Director Todd St. John
Production Company
HunterGatherer
CAA Jay Brooker,
Jesse Coulter,
Todd Hunter,
Jae Goodman,
Ricardo Viramontes
Agency CAA Marketing/
HunterGatherer
Client REDU/Bing
Country United States

This animation was
created to announce
the launch of REDU and
letsredu.com: an online
community and resource
for education reform.
It is a stop-motion animation, created in camera
from more than 1,000
hand-made wood blocks.

BOTTLES AND JARS
MARTHA STEWART
LIVING OMNIMEDIA
Editorial Design | Magazine Story
Multi-Page

Art Director
James Dunlinson
Editor Fritz Karch
Agency Martha Stewart
Living Omnimedia
Client
Martha Stewart Living
Country United States

Fortunately, because the shape of a bottle is bound to its function, with neck length and height dictated by the contents, standardized production has never bred conformity. There are as many colors and silhouettes as there are things that need bottling: stout ink pots, bulbous wine jugs, whimsical log cabins of maple syrup. This also means there is no shortage of options for collection, from the 20th-century soda bottles going for $5 apiece at thrift shops to a delicate $2,500 1820s Pitkin flask in mint condition coveted by experts. Arranged on a sunlit windowsill, a grouping of bottles and jars is simultaneously a visual glossary of packaging history and an incandescent sculptural display.

SEEING GREEN
Bottles in a variety of greens are common, because the raw materials needed to make the color have historically been affordable and widely available. Shades include celery (the gargantuan demijohn), deep teal (the tall 1880s bottle of German or French origin, which was used for Reisling wine), and emerald (the little square apothecary jar).

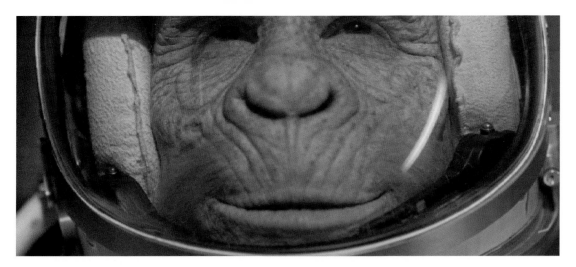

IT'S NOT A PLANET, ▪ IT'S OUR HOME▪

MONKEY
LEO BURNETT SYDNEY
Motion | Cinematography

Creative Director
Andy DiLallo,
Jay Benjamin
Art Director
Kieran Antill,
Andy DiLallo,
Jay Benjamin
Copywriter
Michael Canning,
Andy DiLallo,
Jay Benjamin
Designer
Masataka Kawano
Director Steve Rogers
Editor Jack Hutchings
(The Butchery)
Agency Producer
Adrian Shapiro
Producer
Michael Ritchie,
Georgina Wilson
Production Company
Revolver Films
Agency
Leo Burnett Sydney
Client WWF
Country Australia

Our objective was to
create a new brand spot
for the World Wildlife
Fund (WWF) that did not
focus on one specific
environmental issue, but
the future of our planet
as a whole. With people
growing increasingly
jaded by environmental
messages, we wanted to
reconnect with people on
an emotional level, and
change the way people
think about the environ-
ment. Our solution came
in the unique story of an
original "space mon-
key" from the US space
exploration program, who
returns to Earth after
65 years lost in space.
The film features a new
music track by musician
Ben Lee called "Song for
the Divine Mother of the
Universe," and "Space
Monkey" will air as both a
music video to launch
the single, and a long
format spot.

Multiple Winner
Interactive Merit | Online Content
Branded Short Films

IN THE LAND OF TALKING
LEO BURNETT WARSAW
Motion | Animation

Creative Director
Heinze Iwinski
Art Director
Mateusz Goll
Copywriter
Natalia Dudek
Designer Mateusz Goll
Director Pawel Borowski
Producer
Ewelina Zawadzka,
Janusz Wlodarski
Production Company
Opus Film, Platige Image
Agency Leo Burnett
Warsaw
Client Orange, PTK
Centertel
Country Poland

In the Land of Talking,
time is a hero. We gave
it shape and personal-
ity. Inspired by primitive
painting, full of orna-
ments, second after
second, we created a rich,
spectacular 3-D world, in
which time and conver-
sations take the form of
various friendly creatures
you can play with.

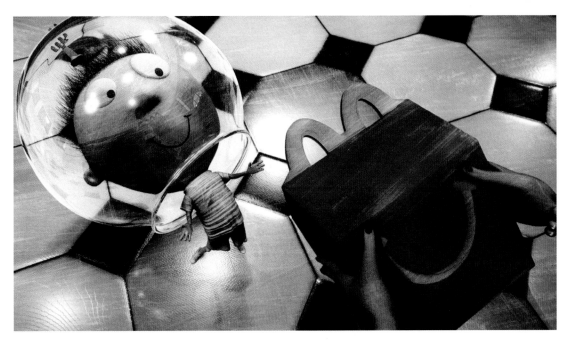

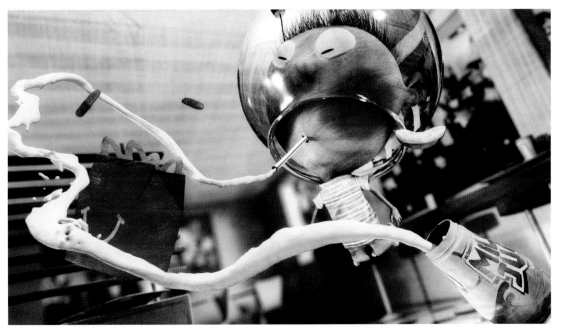

SPACEMAN STU
LEO BURNETT CHICAGO
Motion | Animation

Creative Director
Susan Credle,
John Montgomery,
Keith Hughes
Art Director
Keith Hughes
Copywriter
Susan Credle,
John Montgomery
Animator
Christian Semczuk,
Lazlo Nyikos
Director Oliver Conrad
Producer Eric Faber
Production Company
Duck Studios
Music Producer
Bonny Dolan
Composer Pete Schmidt
Music Company
Comma
Agency Leo Burnett
Chicago
Client McDonald's
Country United States

A handcrafted marriage
of 2-D/3-D paper-cut
animation tells the story
of Spaceman Stu as if it
were a children's book.
Space-helmeted hero
Stu is precariously bent
back, looking at the stars
whether walking outside
or gazing through a car
moon roof. He and his
mom stop when they see
the golden arches in the
heavens. Inside McDon-
ald's Stu looks up to see
a bright red Happy Meal
Box and he goes zero-g
with delight as he enjoys
his favorite foods like milk
and apple dippers. Stu's
imagination is captioned
by a simple original piece
of music to underscore
his sense of wonder.

Photography:

A picture speaks a thousand words, but which words? That was the ultimate question asked of each jury member when confronted with varying styles of photography. It's important to remember that an image with an unclear purpose is very difficult to judge. This was not a technical forum determining the proper ISO, aperture, or even composition, for that matter. It was about photography that spoke a thousand of the right words for the concept it was communicating.

—Kieran Antill, Creative Director, SVP Leo Burnett, New York, Photography Jury Member

In Charac
of 'Biutiful' al
nearly b

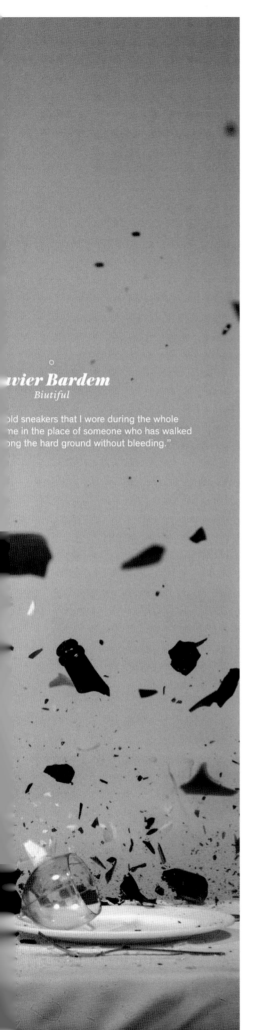

Javier Bardem
Biutiful

"...old sneakers that I wore during the whole
...me in the place of someone who has walked
...ong the hard ground without bleeding."

**FIFTEEN ACTORS
ACTING**
THE NEW YORK
TIMES MAGAZINE
Magazine Editorial | Miscellaneous

Design Director
Arem Duplessis
Art Director Gail Bichler
Designer Gail Bichler,
Caleb Bennett
Director of Photography
Kathy Ryan
Photographer
Solve Sundsbo
Photo Editor
Joanna Milter
Production Company
The New York
Times Company
Agency The New York
Times Magazine
Client The New York
Times Magazine
Country United States

Lesley Manville

Jesse Eisenberg

**DUMPING ACROSS
THE DIGITAL DIVIDE**
THE NEW YORK
TIMES MAGAZINE
Magazine Editorial | Miscellaneous

Design Director
Arem Duplessis
Art Director Gail Bichler
Designer Caleb Bennett
Director of Photography
Kathy Ryan
Photographer
Pieter Hugo
Production Company
The New York
Times Company
Photo Editor
Joanna Milter
Agency The New York
Times Magazine
Client The New York
Times Magazine
Country United States

Dumping Across The Digital Divide

The unexpected consequences
of shipping computers to the developing world.

The Basel Convention on the Control of Transboundary
Movements of Hazardous Wastes and Their Disposal, agreed to in 1989 and now adopted
by a majority of nations, was meant to stop the dumping of toxic waste in poor
countries. But what if the waste arrives as a gift? ● In Agbogbloshie, a slum in Accra, the
capital of Ghana, adults and children tear away at computers from abroad
to get at the precious metals inside. The computers and other equipment in this digital
cemetery come mainly from Europe and the United States, sometimes as secondhand donations
meant to reduce the "digital divide" — the disparity in computer access between poor
nations and rich. As Pieter Hugo shows in these haunting photographs, the equipment often
becomes part of a particularly toxic recycling business. In 2008, Greenpeace
sampled the burned soil at Agbogbloshie and found high levels of lead, cadmium, antimony, PCBs
and chlorinated dioxins. ● At the dump, the machines are dismantled and often burned to
extract metals for resale. Copper is perhaps the most desirable, then brass, then aluminum, then
zinc. Prices in Agbogbloshie are about four times below the international market
price, but for the scavengers of the dump, the income is incentive enough. Many of the workers
there are boys, sent by their families in the impoverished north of the country
to work at the dump and send back what money they can.

Photographs by PIETER HUGO

MAKESHIFT METALLURGY David Akore, 18, and other foragers in the Agbogbloshie dump in Accra.

176 | PHOTOGRAPHY | GOLD

FASHION SHOW
INSTITUTE
Magazine Editorial | Fashion

Photographer
Lauren Greenfield
Editor Adam Moss
Producer
Lauren Greenfield,
New York Magazine
Production Company
Evergreen Pictures
Photo Editor Jody Quon
Publisher New York
Magazine
Agency Institute
Client New York
Magazine
Country United States

Lauren Greenfield
documents a face of
fashion where grit and
glamour coexist fabulously.
The body of empathic
photographs teases
open the seams of an
oft-airbrushed world to
reveal detailed stitching,
elaborate machinations,
and delicate incisions.
Her signature investigative
style captures the New
York, Milan, and Paris
collections, alongside
the pathos and process,
creating a critically
sympathetic portrait
of powerful posturing,
vulnerable moments, and
striking beauty. Greenfield
pairs photographs of
models emerging in
runway perfection, with
various stages of the
assembly line. A full
visual deconstruction of
the industry shows the
sacrifices: stumbling
models, anxious dressers,
revealing moments of pain
and vulnerability behind
the facade; but also the
reward: frenzied flashes,
preeminent designers,
and applauding critics. By
including the methodical
process and the stunning
show, the essay's, gestalt
is in the intoxicating power
held by fashion, and the
very human participants
who perform on its stage.

THE HOLLYWOOD ISSUE
THE NEW YORK
TIMES MAGAZINE
Magazine Editorial | Cover

Design Director
Arem Duplessis
Art Director Gail Bichler
Director of Photography
Kathy Ryan
Photographer
Solve Sundsbo
Production Company
The New York Times
Company
Agency
The New York Times
Magazine
Client The New York
Times Magazine
Country United States

THE HOLLYWOOD ISSUE

The New York Times Magazine

DECEMBER 12, 2010

Javier Bardem
Lesley Manville
Jesse Eisenberg
James Franco
Chloë Moretz
Jennifer Lawrence
○ Natalie Portman
Robert Duvall
Annette Bening
Anthony Mackie
Noomi Rapace
Tilda Swinton
Matt Damon
Vincent Cassel
Michael Douglas

The Scene Makers : Actors Who Defined Cinema in 2010

Photographs by Solve Sundsbo. Introduction by A.O. Scott.

BODIES WE WANT
ESPN THE MAGAZINE
Magazine Editorial | Miscellaneous

Creative Director
Siung Tjia
Copywriter Morty Ain
Photographer Various
Editor Gary Belsky
Photo Editor Catriona Ni Aolain
Publisher Walt Disney Company
Agency ESPN The Magazine
Client ESPN The Magazine
Country United States

AUGUST 2010:
FLEXIBILITY FEATURE
REAL SIMPLE MAGAZINE
Magazine Editorial | Healthcare

Creative Director
Janet Froelich
Art Director
Cybele Grandjean
Designer Joele Cuyler
Photographer
Robert Maxwell
Photo Editor
Casey Tierney
Associate Photo Editor
Lindsay
Dougherty-Rogers
Agency
Real Simple Magazine
Client Real Simple
Country United States

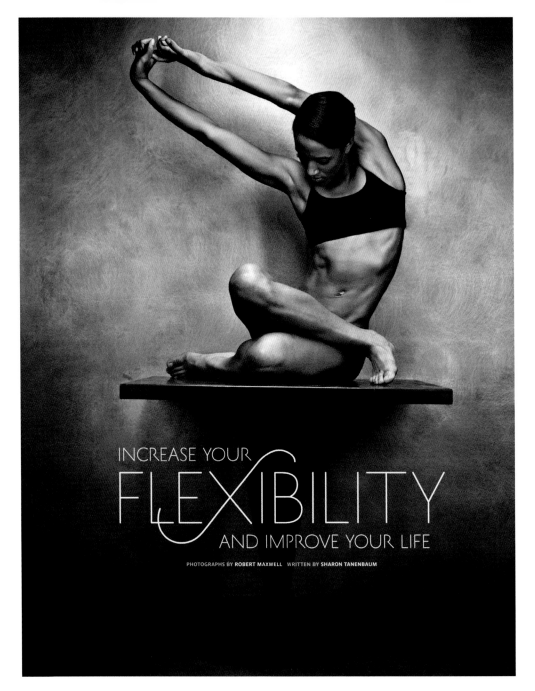

INCREASE YOUR

FLEXIBILITY

AND IMPROVE YOUR LIFE

PHOTOGRAPHS BY **ROBERT MAXWELL**   WRITTEN BY **SHARON TANENBAUM**

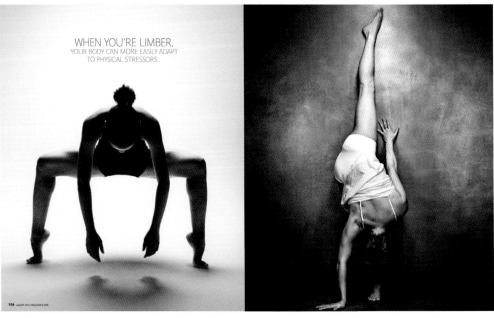

WHEN YOU'RE LIMBER,
YOUR BODY CAN MORE EASILY ADAPT
TO PHYSICAL STRESSORS.

AUGUST 9, 2010

Inside: Joe Klein on the challenge in Pakistan

TIME

What Happens if We Leave Afghanistan

BY ARYN BAKER

Aisha, 18, had her
nose and ears cut off
last year on orders
from the Taliban
because she fled
abusive in-laws

www.time.com

AISHA
TIME MAGAZINE
Magazine Editorial | Cover

Design Director
D. W. Pine
Director of Photography
Kira Pollack
Photographer
Jodi Bieber—INSTITUTE
for TIME
**International
Picture Editor**
Patrick Witty
Agency
Time Magazine
Client Jodi Bieber/TIME
Country United States

PORTRAIT OF PHILIP ROTH
THE WALL STREET JOURNAL
Newspaper Editorial
Miscellaneous

Creative Director
Tomaso Capuano
Art Director
Christian Drury
Designer Kelly Peck
Director of Photography
Jack Van Antwerp
Deputy Director of Photography
Lucy Gilmour
Photographer
Brigitte Lacombe
Photo Editor Carrie Levy
Agency The Wall
Street Journal
Client Review/The Wall
Street Journal
Country United States

This portrait was
assigned for the newly
launched Review section
of *The Wall Street Journal*.
In the rubric entitled
CREATING, reporters
interview individuals
about their creative pro-
cess. Black-and-white
portraits are assigned
to photographers to
interpret the same brief.
Photographer Brigitte
Lacombe took the por-
trait of writer Philip Roth.

THE POST-ADOLESCENT LIFE STAGE
THE NEW YORK
TIMES MAGAZINE
Magazine Editorial | Miscellaneous

Design Director
Arem Duplessis
Art Director Gail Bichler
Designer Gail Bichler
Director of Photography
Kathy Ryan
Photographer
Santiago Mostyn
Production Company
The New York
Times Company
Photo Editor
Luise Stauss
Agency The New York
Times Magazine
Client The New York
Times Magazine
Country United States

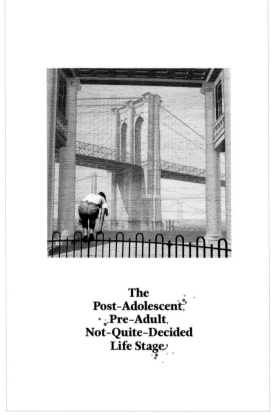

The
Post-Adolescent,
Pre-Adult,
Not-Quite-Decided
Life Stage

FORMER JAY-Z COHORT DAMON DASH'S IMPROBABLE BACKPACKER COMEBACK

JULY 21–27, 2010 ∎ VOL. LV NO. 29 ∎ AMERICA'S LARGEST WEEKLY NEWSPAPER

VILLAGEVOICE.COM ∎ FREE

the village VOICE

TOM ROBBINS WADES INTO THE MOSQUE FRENZY AT GROUND ZERO

YESTERDAY. TODAY. TILDA.

WITH A NEW MOVIE IN THEATERS, AND *ORLANDO* REAPPEARING, IT'S A SWINTON MOMENT

By Melissa Anderson *Photographed by* Sylvia Plachy

YESTERDAY. TODAY. TILDA.
THE VILLAGE VOICE
Newspaper Editorial | Newspaper Front Page

Art Director John Dixon
Designer Jesus Diaz
Photographer Sylvia Plachy
Editor Tony Ortega
Photo Editor John Dixon
Writer Melissa Anderson
Publisher Village Voice Media
Agency The Village Voice
Client The Village Voice
Country United States

It was a thrill to work with long time *Village Voice* contributing photographer Sylvia Plachy and welcome her back to our paper. Writer Melissa Anderson secured an interview with Tilda Swinton and director Sally Potter of the film *Orlando,* which was being re-released in theaters. A narrow window of time was allowed for photographing Tilda and Sally during their press junket. Sylvia and I booked a hotel room adjacent to the one where they were staying and "cased the joint." We scouted the room, calculated light-readings days ahead of time and set up hours before their arrival—all to capitalize on the short amount of camera-time we'd have with our subjects. Once Sylvia was locked and loaded on her targets, I promptly exited the set and allowed her to capture the magic. That's all it took, designing the cover layout afterward was a breeze—John Dixon, Art Director, *The Village Voice.*

WEAPONS
LEO BURNETT CHICAGO
AND ARC WORLDWIDE
CHICAGO
Poster or Billboard

Creative Director Dave
Loew, Jon Wyville
Art Director
Rainer Schmidt,
Chris von Ende
Copywriter Tohru Oyasu
Photographer James Day
Producer
Laurie Gustafson
Account Director
Antoniette Wico,
CJ Nielsen
Agency Leo Burnett
Chicago and Arc
Worldwide Chicago
Client Symtantec Norton
Country United States

The concept is that in
the hands of cybercrimi-
nals, computers are as
dangerous as weapons.
The crime may be digital,
but the damage inflicted
is real. We represented
this idea visually by
combining elements of
computers (keyboard
keys, power buttons, disc
drives) with traditional
weapons such as a
handgun, a switchblade
and a grenade. The post-
ers were used to create
internal communication
that acts as a global
rallying cry in the fight
against cybercrime.

IN THE HANDS OF A CYBERCRIMINAL, A COMPUTER IS A WEAPON.
EVERY CLICK MATTERS.

The New York Times Magazine

FEBRUARY 7, 2010

WINTER (FUN AND) GAMES!

A photo portfolio of Olympian heights, *by Ryan McGinley*

Also:

Lindsey Vonn on top (BILL PENNINGTON), Shani Davis on edge (MICHAEL SOKOLOVE), Canada as a brand (MICHAEL IGNATIEFF), figure skating as disaster porn (VIRGINIA HEFFERNAN) and more.

WINTER (FUN AND) GAMES!
THE NEW YORK TIMES MAGAZINE
Magazine Editorial | Miscellaneous

Design Director
Arem Duplessis
Art Director Gail Bichler
Designer Robert Vargas
Director of Photography
Kathy Ryan
Photographer
Ryan McGinley
Production Company
The New York
Times Company
Photo Editor
Clinton Cargill
Agency The New York
Times Magazine
Client The New York
Times Magazine
Country United States

AUGUST 2010: FOOD FEATURE
REAL SIMPLE MAGAZINE
Magazine Editorial | Food

Creative Director
Janet Froelich
Art Director
Cybele Grandjean
Designer
Cybele Grandjean
Photographer
Christopher Baker
Photo Editor
Casey Tierney
Deputy Photo Editor
Lauren Reichbach Epstein
Agency Real Simple
Magazine
Client Real Simple
Country United States

GOBBLER EXAM SPREAD
FIELD & STREAM MAGAZINE
Magazine Editorial
Miscellaneous

Creative Director
Sean Johnston
Designer Mike Ley
Illustrator Seb Lester
Photographer
Dan Saelinger
Photo Editor
Amy Berkley
Agency Field & Stream
Magazine
Client Field &
Stream Magazine
Country United States

This spread features a quiz testing the reader's knowledge of turkey hunting. The photographer worked with a live turkey in his studio to make the shot—without a doubt the most challenging aspect of this assignment. The chalk-board question mark illustration relates to the quiz element and also complements the profile of the turkey.

chocolate stout Bundt cake
This intensely flavorful Bundt is made more complex with the addition of a malty brew.

hazelnut ganache tart with sea salt
No matter how you slice it, this stunner offers a one-two punch of chocolate in each bite, thanks to a crunchy wafer-cookie crust and a silky-smooth filling.

DECEMBER 2010 | REALSIMPLE.COM **263**

Creative Director
Janet Froelich
Art Director
Cybele Grandjean
Designer
Cybele Grandjean
Photographer
Mitchell Feinberg
Photo Editor
Casey Tierney
Deputy Photo Editor
Lauren Reichbach Epstein
Agency
Real Simple Magazine
Client Real Simple
Country United States

ICING
MARTHA STEWART
LIVING OMNIMEDIA
Magazine Editorial | Food

Photographer Pal Allan
Director James Dunlinson
Agency Martha Stewart
Living Omnimedia
Client Martha
Stewart Living
Country United States

BASIC BUTTERCREAM
Ultrarich yet ultrasimple, buttercream is the go-to icing for birthday cakes and cupcakes.
Could this be frosting heaven? Just butter, confectioners' sugar, and vanilla, buttercream is easy to prepare and work with, making it an ideal choice for frosting novices. Use the tip of an offset spatula to create swoops and swirls. To minimize graininess, add the confectioners' sugar slowly.

GANACHE
This sleek, mahogany glaze must be poured, not spread.
If buttercream is the fun, fluffy flirt, ganache is the serious sophisticate. Bittersweet chocolate and cream make it smooth; corn syrup gives it gloss. Before you pour it, set the cake on a wire rack over a baking sheet. Match ganache with a Bundt or other single-layer cake.

MARTHASTEWART.COM | 149

MOLASSES
LEO BURNETT
SYDNEY
Magazine Advertisement

Creative Director
Andy DiLallo
Art Director Dan Oliva
Copywriter Rob Kleckner
Designer
Masataka Kawano
Photographer
Chris Budgeon
Agency Leo Burnett
Sydney
Client Diageo Australia
Country Australia

This campaign introduces the founders of Bundaberg Rum, a group of sugar millers from the 1880s. They had the ingenious idea to turn a molasses surplus into rum. Now they inspire other ingenious solutions to serious problems.

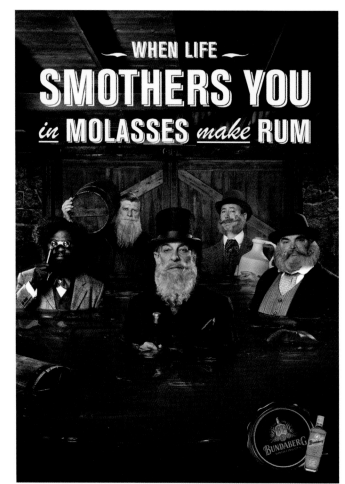

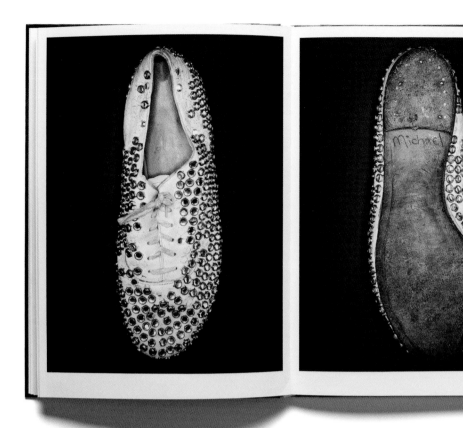

NEVERLAND LOST—A PORTRAIT OF MICHAEL JACKSON
HENRY LEUTWYLER
STUDIO
Book

Designer
Ruba Abu-Nimah,
Kevin Ley
Photographer
Henry Leutwyler
Image Post Production
Kulton Inc.
Publisher Gerhard Steidl
Agency Henry Leutwyler
Studio
Client Henry Leutwyler
Country United States

Prior to Michael Jackson's
death, Henry Leutwyler
photographed crates of
artifacts removed from
Jackson's Neverland
ranch in California. The
resulting series of photographs documents the
inner turmoil of the public
person who chose to
model his private life on
Peter Pan and the Lost
Boys—children who
never wanted to grow up.
Leutwyler's unemotional
portraits are almost too
intimate to behold, but
when one digs beneath
the surface, what emerges
is the profound truth of a
star's sequestered reality.
Leutwyler's photographs
unearth the "Lost Boy"
forced to leave Neverland,
and now these still lifes
are as close as anyone
will ever get to what
Jackson once had, and
ultimately left behind.

POWER GAMES: WOMEN WHO HIT VERY HARD
THE NEW YORK
TIMES MAGAZINE
Magazine Editorial | Miscellaneous

Design Director
Arem Duplessis
Art Director Gail Bichler
Designer Caleb Bennet
Director of Photography
Kathy Ryan
Photographer
Dewey Nicks
Production Company
The New York
Times Company
Photo Editor
Stacey Baker
Agency The New York
Times Magazine
Client The New York
Times Magazine
Country United States

RARIN' TO RIDE
CANADIAN GEOGRAPHIC
ENTERPRISES
Magazine Editorial | Miscellaneous

Creative Director
Suzanne Morin
Art Director
Suzanne Morin
Copywriter Peter Sibbald
Designer Suzanne Morin
Photographer
Peter Sibbald
Editor-in-Chief
Eric Harris
Editor Monique Roy-Sole
Photo Editor
Suzanne Morin
Publisher Canadian Geo-
graphic Enterprises
Agency Canadian
Geographic Enterprises
Client Canadian
Geographic Magazine
Country Canada

Rarin' to ride

*A chance stop at a rodeo in southern Ontario unleashes
photographer Peter Sibbald's inner cowboy, sending him on
a behind-the-chutes quest to understand the culture*

PHOTOGRAPHY AND STORY BY PETER SIBBALD

Jangling her bull-rope cowbell, junior bull rider Shelby Pattison (OPPOSITE), 14, of Erin,
Ont., jubilantly reacts to her first winning ride of the rodeo season in May at Lindsay,
Ont. Eric Isabelle (ABOVE) of Saint-Lin-Laurentides, Que., hangs on during his first buck
out of the chute on a bull named #23 Tramp Stamp at the Lindsay Rodeo.

CANADIAN GEOGRAPHIC 61

The Secret Lives of Girls

*Five actresses who broke
through in 2009 — in movies portraying
young women.*

PHOTOGRAPHS BY
HELLEN VAN MEENE

Gabourey Sidibe
PRECIOUS

Abbie Cornish
BRIGHT STAR

Emily Blunt
THE YOUNG VICTORIA

**THE SECRET LIVES
OF GIRLS**
THE NEW YORK
TIMES MAGAZINE
Magazine Editorial | Fashion

Design Director
Arem Duplessis
Art Director Gail Bichler
Designer Leo Jung,
Hilary Greenbaum
Director of Photography
Kathy Ryan
Photographer
Hellen Van Meene
Production Company
The New York Times
Company
Photo Editor
Joanna Milter
Agency The New York
Times Magazine
Client The New York
Times Magazine
Country United States

THE WELLNESS ISSUE
THE NEW YORK
TIMES MAGAZINE
Magazine Editorial | Cover

Design Director
Arem Duplessis
Art Director Gail Bichler
Designer Gail Bichler
Director of Photography
Kathy Ryan
Photographer
James Welling
Production Company
The New York Times
Company
Photo Editor
Joanna Milter
Agency The New York
Times Magazine
Client The New York
Times Magazine
Country United States

TRY-ONS
HANS SEEGER
Book

Designer Hans Seeger
Photographer
Clay Weiner
Stylist Jenna Wright
Agency Hans Seeger
Client Clay Weiner
Country United States

Try-Ons chronicles Clay Weiner's attempts to "Be Somebody" through living the lives of an eccentric array of real and imaginary characters. "Growing up, I was always told to be somebody. In an attempt to find myself, I tried 85 personas. I'm still confused."

HARVEST PIES
MARTHA STEWART
LIVING OMNIMEDIA
Magazine Editorial | Food

Photographer
Gentl & Hyers
Director
James Dunlinson
Agency Martha Stewart
Living Omnimedia
Client
Martha Stewart Living
Country United States

WASTES ENERGY/
SAVES ENERGY
LEO BURNETT SYDNEY
Magazine Advertisement

Creative Director
Andy DiLallo,
Jay Benjamin
Art Director
Gary Dawson
Copywriter
Gary Dawson
Photographer
Chris Budgeon
Agency
Leo Burnett Sydney
Client Energy Australia
Country Australia

LEICA
M9

LEICA M9, LEICA SUMMILUX-M 35 mm f/1.4 ASPH., ISO 160, f/5.6, 1/500 s

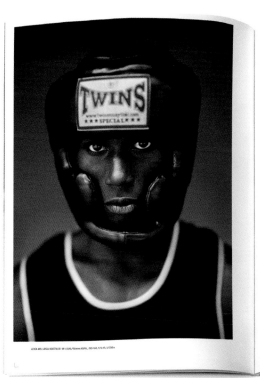

LEICA M9, LEICA NOCTILUX-M 1:0.95/50 mm ASPH., ISO 160, f/0.95, 1/250 s

LEICA NOCTILUX-M 50 mm f/0.95 ASPH.
King of the night.

In 2008 Leica proudly announced the fastest aspherical lens the world had ever seen: the remarkable Leica Noctilux-M 50 mm f/0.95 ASPH., a replacement for the legendary Leica Noctilux-M 50 mm f/1, which had been a highlight of the Leica M lens range since 1975. The combination of cutting-edge optical and mechanical technologies has made it possible to achieve a marked improvement in its performance compared to its illustrious predecessor. Although its dimensions are almost identical, a significantly higher speed has been successfully attained. At full aperture, its extremely shallow depth of field allows the photographer to create compelling portraits and scenic impressions characterized by an incomparably natural-looking play of sharpness and softness. Stop down a little and the lens delivers outstanding image quality comparable to that of the Leica Summilux-M 50 mm f/1.4 ASPH., the lens generally considered to be the reference standard for all other normal lenses. When used for available light photography, the Noctilux-M actually exceeds the resolving power of the human eye. The use of a floating element ensures that this lens provides top performance down to its closest focusing distance. Vignetting and distortion have also been noticeably improved compared to the 50 mm f/1.

(All views of lenses full-size unless otherwise indicated)

LEICA M LENSES | 91

LEICA M9 BROCHURE
G2 FRANKFURT/
G2 GERMANY
Corporate/Institutional

Creative Director
Felix Dürichen, Anita Stoll
Art Director
Sabine Brinkmann
Copywriter Anita Stoll,
Sabine Weber
Designer
Sabine Brinkmann
Photographer
Maik Scharfscheer
Project Manager
Maik Hofmann,
Silvana Meyer
Agency G2 Frankfurt/
G2 Germany
Client Leica Camera AG
Country Germany

Since the 1920s the M series has represented the soul of Leica, and every new M model sparks intense anticipation. With the M9, the stakes were even higher: it would either answer the Leica fan's prayers or confirm that Leica had truly missed the digital-photography boat. To demonstrate how the M9's performance sets new benchmarks without losing any of its ancestors authenticity, we reduced the design down to a stage for the (much more important) photographic story: a classic M-style assignment documenting a day in the life of an amateur boxer in Havana, where boxing remains pure, simple, non-commercial, even noble. The same values that Leica lives by.

**YOUR UNSTOPPABLE
HEART**
MEN'S HEALTH MAGAZINE
Magazine Editorial | Healthcare

Creative Director
Brandon Kavulla
Designer
Brandon Kavulla
Photographer
James Wojcik
Director Brenda Milis
Photo Editor
Jeanne Graves
Agency Men's Health
Magazine
Client Men's Health
Magazine
Country United States

MILITARY CUISINE OF AFGHANISTAN
VII NETWORKS
Newspaper Editorial | Food

Photographer
Ashley Gilbertson
Photo Editor
Jeffrey Scales (The New York Times)
Agency VII Network
Client The New York Times
Country United States

**MAYA TAKES TO
THE STREETS**
THE NEW YORK
TIMES MAGAZINE
Magazine Editorial | Fashion

Design Director
Arem Duplessis
Art Director Gail Bichler
Designer Gail Bichler
Director of Photography
Kathy Ryan
Photographer
Ryan McGinley
Production Company
The New York Times
Company
Photo Editor
Joanna Milter
Agency The New York
Times Magazine
Client The New York
Times Magazine
Country United States

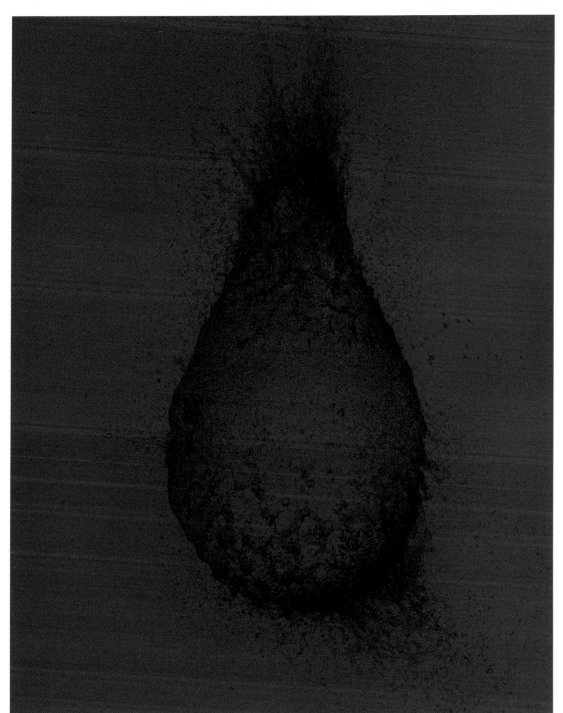

MY ABOVE-AVERAGE STROKE
MEN'S HEALTH MAGAZINE
Magazine Editorial | Healthcare

Creative Director
Brandon Kavulla
Designer
Brandon Kavulla
Photographer
Steve Pyke, Kenji Aoki
Photo Editor
Brenda Milis,
Jeanne Graves
Agency Men's Health
Magazine
Client Men's Health
Magazine
Country United States

Illustration: There were a number of strong entries in the Illustration category. I especially noticed some very good student work. Overall I was surprised that there weren't more entries, though. It seemed to me that I saw a lot of exceptional work over the past year, perhaps prize-winning, that simply hadn't been entered. I have always believed that the Art Directors show is the best place for illustrators to be seen, because the audience is not just one's peers, but also one's potential clients. After all, assignments come from art directors worldwide, on magazines and newspapers, in ad agencies, design studios and at corporations, and they are the ADC judges and readers. I'd also like to urge art directors to consider using more illustration again. Photography seems to be the default solution for advertising and publishing lately, and it's convenient enough, but great illustration can add unique character and impact to visual projects.

—Paul Davis, Illustrator,
Illustration Jury Member

SENSETIAN

BIG BUSINESS III

THE BEST GLOBAL BRAND DESIGN

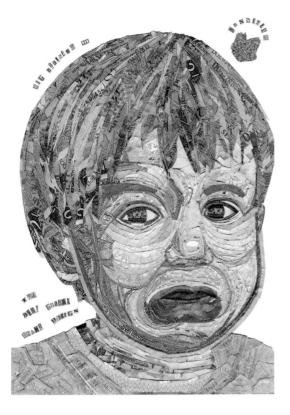
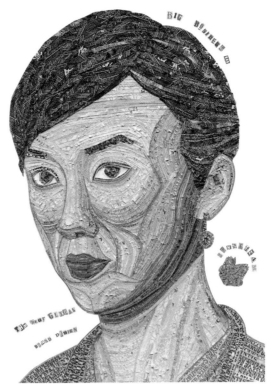

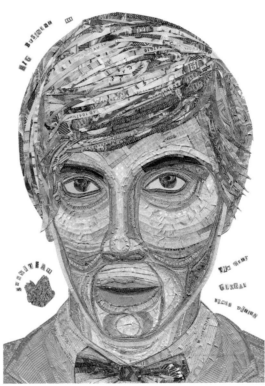

BIG BUSINESS 3
SENSETEAM
Poster or Billboard

Creative Director
Hei Yiyang
Art Director Hei Yiyang
Designer Hei Yiyang,
Wang Xiaomeng
Illustrator Hei Yiyang,
Wang Xiaomeng, Gao
Peng, Chen Silin, Zhao
Xinyu, Zhang Chi, Yan
Yizhen, Cai Zhenhao
Director Hei Yiyang
Publisher SenseTeam
Agency SenseTeam
Client SenseTeam
Country China

Big Business, published in
March 2010, was created
and edited by SenseTeam.
The poster is collaged
with money, combining
faces with ideas of wealth
and brands. It provides
people with a new vision
to understand brand and
identity and to rethink the
influence of money and
desire on human beings.
Big Business, introduces
the best global brand
design among top 500
companies in the world,
selecting in 222 global
brand design. Tragedy
and comedy perform life
through faces. When you
read and understand
happiness, it will show
on your face. Not only can
it make you smile, but it
can also make you cry.
It's like a mirror. You
smile and it replies with a
smile. You can see your
inner heart when you look
it in the eye. It belongs
only to those who can
face it calmly.

SNOWFLAKE MEN
TAKAHISA HASHIMOTO
Self-Promotion

Creative Director
Takahisa Hashimoto
Art Director
Takahisa Hashimoto
Illustrator
Takahisa Hashimoto
Photographer
Megumu Wada
Producer
Yasuharu Mitsumura
Agency Takahisa
Hashimoto
Client Takahisa
Hashimoto
Country Japan

A series of three pieces
of riders on the snow
illustrating their deep
passion and enthusiasm
for snowboarding, who
love to fall, stand up, fall
again and keep trying
until they make a great
trick—basically those
who absolutely love just
to be on the snow. The
"Snowflake Men" series
illustrate the pure simple
love of snowboarding.

**FAMOUS SPEECHES
COLLECTION**
MARCEL PARIS
Magazine Advertisement
Poster or Billboard

Creative Director
Anne de Maupeou,
Frederic Temin
Art Director Souen Le
Van, Romain Galli
Copywriter Souen Le
Van, Romain Galli
Illustrator Kim F. Lucas,
E. Forgot, AMI Collective
Production Company
Marcel Paris
Agency Marcel Paris
Client EDITIONS POINTS
Country France

Multiple Winner
Advertising Merit | Magazine
Consumer | Print Craft

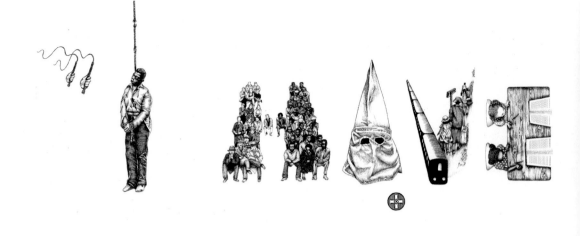

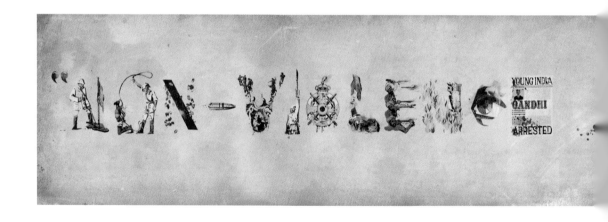

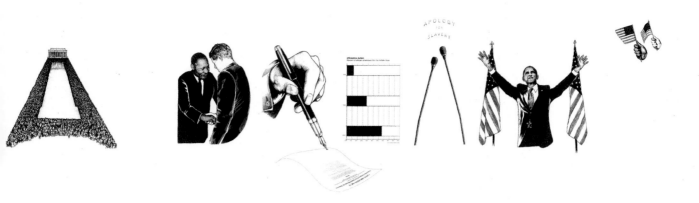

Words that changed the world. Famous speeches in pocket book collection. **P●INTS**

Words that changed the world. Famous speeches in pocket book collection. **P●INTS**

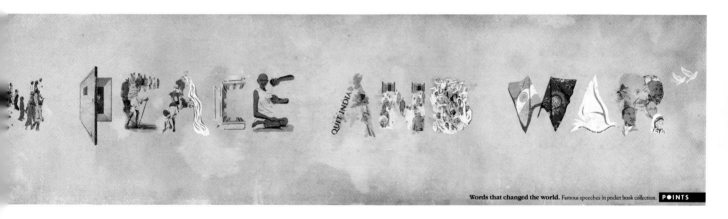

Words that changed the world. Famous speeches in pocket book collection. **P●INTS**

WWF CUTOUTS
BBH CHINA
Miscellaneous

Creative Director
Johnny Tan, Leo Zhang
Art Director Jeffrey Sun,
Jenny Jin, Leo Zhang
Copywriter Leo Zhang,
Jeffrey Sun
Designer Jeffrey Sun,
Jenny Jin, Rei An Huang
Illustrator Jeffrey Sun,
Jenny Jin, Rei An Huang
Account Jasmine Huang,
Joyce Hong, Natalie Ann
Agency BBH China
Client WWF China
Country China

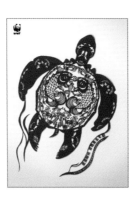

Objective: At the 2010
Shanghai World Expo,
WWF wanted to draw
visitors to the WWF
Pavilion and understand
the importance of saving
our endangered species.
Idea: Save one. Save
them all. Solution: Using
traditional paper cutting,
we showed how delicately
interrelated and intri-
cately codependent our
whole ecosystems are.
The actual species in a
habitat were connected
to one other to form a
striking image of the
endangered wildlife that
WWF protects in the area.
To draw more interest to
the campaign, the artist
mounted the work
himself at the WWF
Pavilion during the Expo.
Results: The poster series
was exhibited at the
WWF Pavilion in June
2011 and drew more than
210,000 visitors.

LAND ROVER PHONE
Y&R LIMA/RKCR Y&R
LONDON
Photo-Illustration

Creative Director Flavio
Pantigoso, Graham Lang,
Guillermo Vega
Art Director Christian
Sánchez, Mirko Cuculiza
Copywriter
Daniel de León
Illustrator Salamanca
Photographer
Salamanca
Retoucher Salamanca
Agency Y&R Lima/RKCR
Y&R London
Client Land Rover
Country Peru, United
Kingdom

We wanted the virtually
indestructible Land Rover
phone to play off the
legendary ruggedness,
strength and adventurous
spirit that the vehicles
themselves are known for.
By creating incredible
visual torture tests we
were able to reflect the
different consumer
groups that the phone
is aimed at. The result is
a simple yet intricate
demonstration of the
phone's toughness.

THE LAND ROVER S1 PHONE Incredibly tough

STREET DANCE FESTIVAL
PERFIL 252
Photo-Illustration

Creative Director
Waldemar França,
Marcia Lima
Art Director
Waldemar França
Designer
Waldemar França
Copywriter Waldemar
França, Marcia Lima
Illustrator
Waldemar França
Photographer
BC Imagens
Photo Editor
Waldemar França
Agency Perfil 252
Client Prefeitura de Belo
Horizonte
Country Brazil

The challenge was to
show the rich movements
of street dance in a static
medium such as a poster.
We chose to use the tech-
nique referred to as photo
illusion, overlaying several
photos with different
models and dance posi-
tions. This created other
outlines and colors in the
same image, giving move-
ment to the piece. Those
looking at the image can
observe details, random
abstract figures formed
when the photos were
overlaid with different
filters. That being done,
we highlighted some
colors and redrew some
details. Newspaper paper
and digital printing in a
rigid substrate printer
were chosen to give an
artistic handicraft edge to
the posters, as well as to
allow a smaller circula-
tion. Thirty posters in
each model were printed
and posted in participat-
ing schools.

Multiple Winner
Design Merit | Poster Design | Wild
Postings

WWW.PBH.GOV.BR   PREFEITURA
BELO HORIZONTE

AFRICAEMO SQUATTER
DENTSU INC.
Poster or Billboard

Art Director
Yoshinaka Ono
Designer Yoshinaka Ono
Illustrator Yoshinaka Ono
Agency Dentsu Inc.
Client Zankyo Record Inc.
Country Japan

It is a poster of alternative rock band Africaemo's debut album *Squatter*. The visual area is occupied by characters from hieroglyphs of ancient Africa, inspired by the band name Africaemo and the album title.

**EXHIBITION OF KIDA
YASUHIKO/100 VIEWS
OF MT. FUJI AND
FAMOUS MOUNTAINS**
FURAIBO INC.
Poster or Billboard

Creative Director
Yasuhiko Kida
Art Director
Yasuhiko Kida
Designer
Taro Matsuyoshi
Illustrator Yasuhiko Kida
Director Yasuhiko Kida
Publisher Shibunkaku
Museum
Agency Furaibo Inc.
Client Shibunkaku
Museum
Country Japan

This series was for my
exhibition "Exhibition of
Kida Yasuhiko: 100 Views
of Mt. Fuji and Famous
Mountains." Mt. Fuji,a
symbol for the Japanese
people, has been the
subject of many famous
paintings since ancient
times. Other famous
mountains in various
areas are often called
"Our Mt. Fuji"as a term
of endearment. Moun-
tains appear different in
different seasons and
from different viewpoints.
I want to produce works
that convey the unique
beauty of these different
moments in a way other
artists have not done. The
method I use is painting
on the back side of glass.
This technique requires
careful planning when
painting, but it brings out
vivid, brilliant colors. I
hope to keep improving
and experimenting with
these materials.

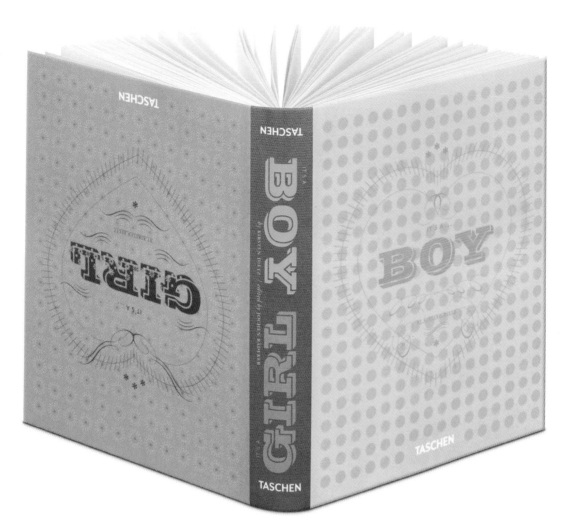

IT'S A BOY—IT'S A GIRL
STRICHPUNKT GMBH
Book

Creative Director
Kirsten Dietz
Designer Kirsten Dietz
Photographer
Kirsten Dietz
Editor Jochen Rädeker
Publisher TASCHEN
GmbH Verlag
Agency
Strichpunkt GmbH
Client Kirsten Dietz
Country Germany

The book is a collection of people-less portraits. It takes an innovative approach to the naming of a newborn child, presenting an arresting and entertaining guide to what the next generation of newborns might be called—and where their names might end up. The photographs each show a business that proudly displays the name of its owner. Taken together, they paint an affectionate and yet honest picture of such premises, while also revealing some of the highs and lows of international signage design. They take us on a journey, capturing a slice of contemporary life in the process. Their subjects are, after all, increasingly threatened by the growing anonymity and globalization of our cities.

GO RED! PRINTS
THE PARTNERS
Poster or Billboard

Creative Director
Jack Renwick
Design Director
Michael Paisley
Senior Designer
Sam Griffiths
Designer Sean Rees,
Tim Brown
Junior Designer
Henry Hadlow
Illustrator Various Artists
Artworker Alex John,
Bernadette Feely
Project Manager
Suzanne Neal
Agency The Partners
Client Richard House
Country United Kingdom

Richard House is London's first children's hospice and needs to raise £1.8 million each year, just to keep going. GO RED! is its largest annual fund-raiser. Borne of the children's game Consequences, the GO RED! identity unfolds in multiple images and words combined to create amusing and informative examples of how people might GO RED! What better way to get involved than to develop the spirit of the original identity and play a huge game of Consequences? We asked some of the top illustrators working today to draw a head, body or legs, so we could play the game in aid of Richard House. They donated their artwork and time for free. With 120 brilliant illustrators and 64,000 unique combinations, visitors to the website can create and order their own archival-quality giclée print. But get in there quick—there is only one of each combination. goingoinggone-red.org/

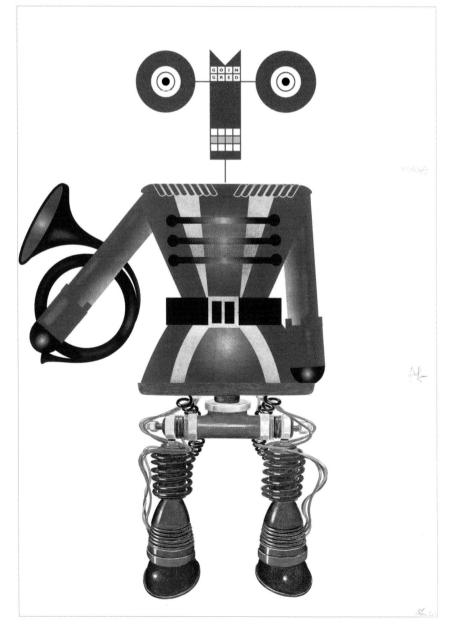

3 BODY SECTIONS
× **120** BRILLIANT ILLUSTRATORS
= **64,000** UNIQUE COMBINATIONS
£3.8M FOR RICHARD HOUSE
2 YEARS OF RUNNING COSTS COVERED
ONE SIMPLE IDEA FOR A GREAT CAUSE

JUDGES!!!
Don't forget to head to
goinggoinggone-red.org
to get your unique print
and help the children
at Richard House

THE TERRORIST MIND: AN UPDATE
METALMOTHER
Newspaper Editorial | Miscellaneous

Art Director Kelly Doe
Illustrator Matt Dorfman
Agency MetalMother
Client The New York Times—Week in Review
Country United States

Kelly Doe at *The New York Times* called me late on a Thursday with an assignment requesting six illustrations in less than 24 hours. They were to accompany a piece for the "Week in Review," which examined the nascent science of studying terrorism via direct interviews conducted with ex-radicals who have abandoned their causes. Wrestling a brutal cold at the time, I turned the assignment down. But Kelly persisted, and I pitched concepts that would require using only one illustration. Kelly again persisted and strongly encouraged me to work with multiples. I mainlined caffeine that evening and gave those pictures all the energy that I had.

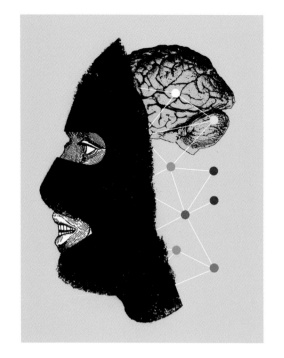

渡
watary

WATARY
DENTSU INC.
Poster or Billboard

Creative Director
Naoto Ohdate
Art Director
Yoshinaka Ono
Copywriter
Tomohiro Sawada
Designer Yoshinaka Ono
Illustrator Yoshinaka Ono
Agency Dentsu Inc.
Client Victor
Entertainment, Inc.
Country Japan

Watary is a Japanese pop
singer and a jazz pianist.
I designed the CD jacket
and the poster for his
first album. By drawing a
piano man in a Japanese-
style painting, I expressed
Watary's world of com-
bined Japanese pop and
jazz music.

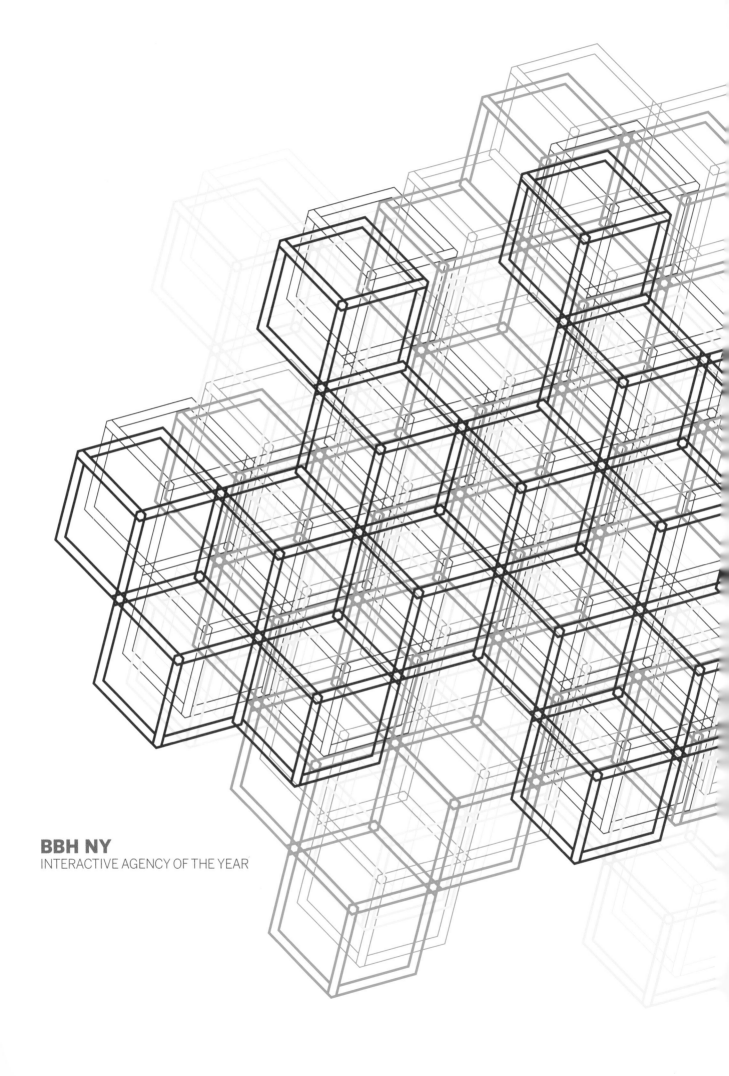

BBH NY
INTERACTIVE AGENCY OF THE YEAR

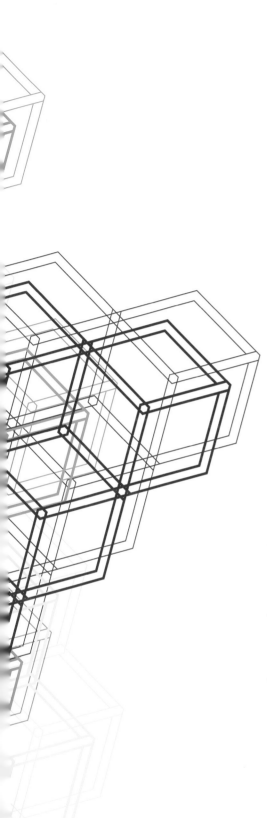

Interactive: What is digital or interactive advertising anyway? A banner, game, e-mail, website, microsite—wait, no, microsites are dead. Is it a mobile app, installation, or social media? Should it be social? What does it really mean to be social? Can it be a film or, god forbid, a commercial, a new product innovation, a file format, an invention or some strange hybrid of a bunch of these things? Can it be a music video or a strange game that takes place on the streets of Stockholm? Interactive is all of the above and more. Which is what makes it the most exciting category to judge. It also can make it a bit maddening at times. The beauty of it, though, is that you have no choice but to throw out your preconceived notions of what advertising is supposed to be and focus on the basics. We're in the communication business and we tell stories. It may be an application, OOH experience, website or video on YouTube. Regardless of the shape it comes in, the best entries tell you a story about the brand. However you encounter the idea, when it's good you know it. You feel it. It speaks to you. It has something to say and it's worth paying attention to. What began as banner ads and websites has become something far greater. The term digital applies to almost everything. It's changed the way we think. The work in this book can serve as a snapshot or a glimpse into the thinking that has been changing the way we communicate; a harbinger of what advertising will become in the future.

—Will McGinness, Executive Creative Director, Venables Bell & Partners, Interactive Chair

MAKE SURE
YOUR MAN SMELLS LIKE A MAN.

Old Spice

RESPONSE CAMPAIGN
WIEDEN+KENNEDY
Online Content | Branded
Short Films

**Executive Creative
Director** Mark Fitzloff,
Susan Hoffman
**Global Interactive
Creative Director**
Iain Tait
Creative Director
Jason Bagley,
Eric Baldwin
Art Director
Craig Allen, Eric
Kallman, Jason Bagley
Eric Baldwin
Copywriter
Craig Allen, Eric Kallman,
Jason Bagley, Eric Baldwin
Programmer
Trent Johnson,
John Cohoon
Editor Kamp Grizzly
Executive Producer
Emily Fincher
Interactive Producer
Ann-Marie Harbour
Production Company
Don't Act Big
**Digital Strategist/
Community Manager**
Dean McBeth
Digital Strategist
Josh Millrod
Interactive Studio Artist
Matthew Carroll
Agency Wieden+Kennedy
Client Old Spice
Country United States

"The Man Your Man Could
Smell Like" made a big
splash in early 2010. But
how could this character
engage with fans on a
more personal level? The
result was the "Response"
campaign, an experiment
in real-time branding in
which "The Man Your
Man Could Smell Like"
recorded 186 personalized
YouTube messages over
the course of two and a
half days. The work would
go to record more than 60
million views, making it one
of the fastest-growing and
most popular interactive
campaigns in history.

Multiple winner
Interactive Black Cube | Online
Content | Branded Short Films
Hybrid Cube | Online Content
Branded Short Films

SOUR/MIRROR

MASASHI + QANTA +
SAQOOSHA + HIROKI
Online Content | New Media
Innovation

Creative Director
Masashi Kawamura
Art Director
Masashi Kawamura
Copywriter
Masashi Kawamura
Director Masashi + Qanta
+ Saqoosha + Hiroki
Producer Qanta Shimizu,
Yasuhito Nakae,
Hisaya Kato
Production Company
Aoi Promotion, AID-DCC,
Katamari
Music SOUR
Programmer Qanta
Shimizu, Saqoosha,
Yuma Murakami
Agency Masashi + Qanta
+ Saqoosha + Hiroki
Client Zenith Co., Ltd.
Country United States,
Japan

This is an interactive music
video for the Japanese
band SOUR. The song
"Utsushi Kagami" (Mirror)
explores the notion that
everything and everyone
around you is a mirror
that reflects who you are.
The lyrics gave us the
idea of a journey to find
yourself through your
connections with people
online. By connecting to
Facebook, Twitter and
webcam, the video will be
customized every time,
based on the viewer's
personal data and social
networking status. In
order to engage fans and
allow them to participate
in early phases, we
successfully raised the
production budget through
Kickstarter, and also allow
Twitter followers of @SOUR
official to automatically
become a part of the
color pixels in the video.
The video itself was an
effort of user participation
on the social network.

Multiple winner
Hybrid Merit | Media Innovation
Non-Broadcast Media

Advertising Gold | Media Innovation
Non-Broadcast Media

PAY WITH A TWEET
R/GA
Website | E-Commerce Experience

Associate Creative Director Leif Abraham, Christian Behrendt
Agency R/GA
Client Innovative Thunder
Country United States

When we wrote our book Oh My God What Happened and What Should I Do? We had one problem: no one knew who we were or how to find the book. To promote the book, we decided to give it away for free as long as the person tweeted about it. And with this, the idea of "Pay with a Tweet" was born. It's simple-when you pay with a Tweet you tell your friends and followers about the product and this will lead to more people paying with a Tweet. In the first six months more than 400,000 people paid for something with a Tweet. And if you want to sell your goods in exchange for buzz, just go to www.PaywithaTweet.com and fill out the form. Boom.

Multiple Winner
Hybrid Cube | Website
E-Commerce Experience

Advertising Silver | Media Innovation
Non-Broadcast Media

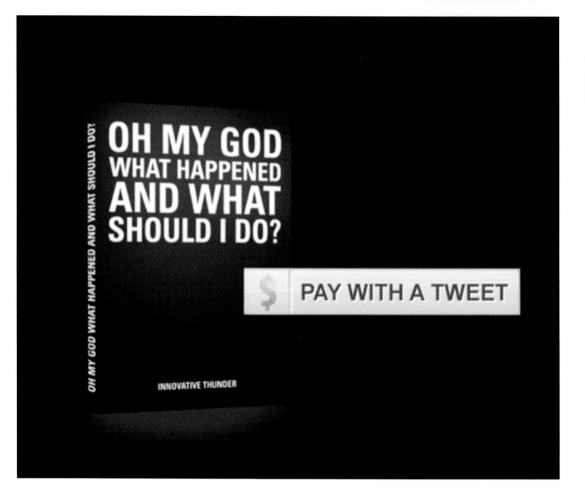

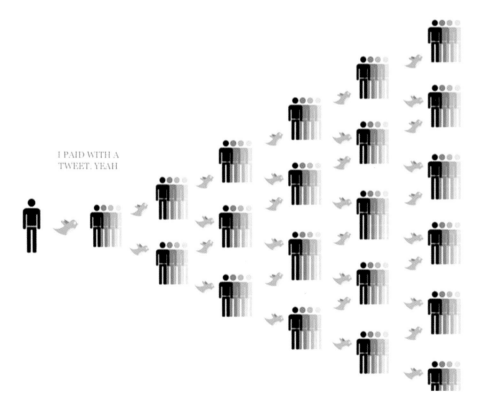

MINI GETAWAY STOCKHOLM
JUNG VON MATT
Mobile | Mobile Experience
Marketing

Creative Director
Johan Jäger
Art Director
Daniel Wahlgren
Copywriter
Magnus Andersson
Designer Daniel Forero
Final Art Jon Palmqvist
Production Company
Carat, Monterosa,
Suddenly, Duoblau
Account Director
Jan Casserlöv
Project Manager
Ida Modin
Planner Leon Phang
Client MINI/BMW
Agency Jung von Matt
Country Sweden

Background: MINI launched the new MINI Countryman with the global concept "Getaway." Challenge: Create MINI evangelists. Solution: For seven days, everybody with an iPhone was invited to hunt and catch a virtual MINI in Stockholm city and win a real MINI Countryman. You used an app where you could see the location of the virtual MINI, all other players and yourself. If you got closer than 50 meters away from the virtual MINI, you could "take" it with your iPhone. Then you had to get away, because anyone else within 50 meters could take the MINI from you. The person with the virtual MINI in their iPhone when the game finished won a real MINI Countryman.

SAVE AS WWF
JUNG VON MATT AG
Online Content | Online Guerrilla

Creative Director
Doerte Spengler-Ahrens,
Jan Rexhausen
Art Director Michael
Kittel, Alexander Norvilas
Copywriter Henning
Mueller-Dannhausen,
Lisa Glock
Designer Michael Kittel
Programmer Michael
Behrens, Sven Loskill,
Tom Schallberger,
Michael Seifert, Franziska
Loeffler, Simone Bitzer,
Susanne zu Eicken
Producer Florian Paul,
Lana Nugent
Other Gerrit Winterstein,
Klaas Nocken,
Rose Tribble
Agency Jung von Matt AG
Client WWF Deutschland
Country Germany

Millions of square meters
of rain forest are cleared
every year to make paper
on which pointless
documents are printed
out, all around the world.
We wanted to stop this
unnecessary printing
and start raising global
awareness of the destruc-
tion it causes. That's why
we invented the world's
first green file format: the
WWF, a file format that
simply cannot be printed
out, a simple idea to save
trees. Every individual,
every company and
every organization
can join in by simply
downloading, using and
sharing WWF files. Our
simple message: SAVE
AS WWF, SAVE A TREE.
Only a few days after
starting the campaign the
WWF was a number one
topic in the news, Tweets
and blogs all over the
world. After four weeks,
200,000 users from 183
countries had visited
the website and down-
loaded the software more
than 30,000 times.

How does the WWF work?

Simply download the free WWF software for PC and Mac at
www.saveaswwf.com. Once installed it enables you to convert
files with just one click to a WWF file.

Every last page of a WWF file acts as a response element.
It includes a campaign explanation and a link to the website.

LORD VADER + YODA RECORDING FOR TOMTOM GPS
POOL WORLDWIDE
Online Content | Viral Video

Creative Director
Pool Worldwide
Art Director
Pool Worldwide
Copywriter
Pool Worldwide
Designer Pool Worldwide
Director of Photography
Director Willem Gerritsen
Daan Nieuwenhuijs
Editor Brian Ent
(The Ambassadors)
Agency Producer
Matthijs Horsman
Producer
Michel de Goede
Production Company
Czar.nl
Account
Mayke van de Rijt
Agency Pool Worldwide
Client TomTom
Country Netherlands

The briefing was simple: let the world know that everybody's favorite *Star Wars* voices are available for TomTom devices. In two virals, we see Lord Vader and Master Yoda recording their voices for TomTom. Each, in their own way, makes the lives of the sound engineers a living hell. We tried to explain the product in the most logical, natural and entertaining way possible, by simply showing how it was made. Nothing is more compelling and funny than watching the Dark Lord and his green nemesis struggle to fit into our mortal world. Results: 5 million views combined for both virals 1500% ROI Number one and two on the Guardian Viral Video Chart And best of all... The Darth Vader viral and its sister viral, starring Master Yoda, will be included in the Official *Star Wars* Blu-Ray box set.

YES, I AM PRECIOUS
BREAKFAST
Beyond The Web

Creative Director
Andrew Zolty
Copywriter
Janeen McCrae
Producer Michael Lipton
Programmer
Mattias Gunneras
Agency BREAKFAST
Client Benefiting
LIVESTRONG
Country United States

Janeen McCrae planned to ride her bike, Precious, across the U.S. to raise money to benefit LIVESTRONG. Our challenge was to get the word out that this was all happening, and in turn get people to open their wallets. Our solution? Build Precious a brain that allowed him to share his thoughts, experiences, body temperature and much more as he made his way across the country. Fitted with a "brain" of wires, circuits and a whole lot of code, Precious used his new silicon senses to share what it feels like to have a sweaty chain while riding up the side of the Rockies. He even shared his subconscious dreams from time to time, which can get a little, well, bike-freaky. The site gave a real-time and historical view of everything Precious went through, while also displaying his comments, which kept his thousands of devoted followers entertained throughout the journey.

AUG 〈 SEP SEP 5 ◀ 12:38 PM ▶

YES I AM PRECIOUS

AND I AM CURRENTLY **2,207**.23 MILES ACROSS AMERICA
RAISING MONEY TO BENEFIT LIVESTRONG®

currently in:
CO-96, Arlington,
CO 81021

1	**5**	**73**	**186**
FLATS	RAINY DAYS	CHASED BY DOG	ROADKILLS

WHAT'S THIS ALL ABOUT?

It's pretty simple really. It's about taking a self-indulgent goal—riding across the USA—and using it as a two-wheeled vehicle for helping those fighting the biggest douchebag of all, cancer.

Join Precious (the bike) and Janeen (the rider) as they put aside their differences and attempt to raise a gob-load of money for LIVESTRONG as part of Team Fatty. Follow every sweatin' mile, every dog chase, every brain fart Precious has, and then show your support by donating to their LIVESTRONG Challenge page.

DONATE
THE RIDER'S BLOG
WHY LIVESTRONG
TEAM FATTY GEAR

JUST HAULED HER ASS OVER 104.0 MILES. DRAGGED THAT PARASITE ZIMMERMAN, TOO. IS THERE NOTHING I CANNOT DO?

7 months ago

FOLLOW ME ON TWITTER

60 90 120 F

1,500 3,000 4,500 0 6,000 DOLLARS RAISED

10 20 30 0 40 mph

6 JNDER THE STARS

19 HONKED AT

59 AVG MILES PER DAY

37 DAYS ON THE ROAD

DOES IT ALL WORK?

us's brain is an on-board device that captures all of his experiences, ned with a cloud-based system that analyzes those experiences. Put together and get a bike that's able to express itself in his own He shares his up-to-the-moment thoughts and has a subconscious allows him to dream about all he's been through. Take a peek into s brain functions below…

am Precious - A Bike with a Brain

CHROME FASTBALL
BBH NEW YORK/GOOGLE CREATIVE LAB
Games | Online Game

Executive Creative Director Pelle Sjoenell, Calle Sjoenell, Robert Wong (Google Creative Lab)
Art Director Erik Holmdahl
Copywriter Beth Ryan
Producer Jennifer Usdan McBride, Sandra Nam
Production Company B Reel
Agency BBH New York/ Google Creative Lab
Client Google
Country United States

To promote a browser to people immune to banners, we created Chrome FastBall, a race across the Internet. This first YouTube game of its kind showed how the Web is faster and easier with Google Chrome. More than 1 million unique visitors moved a ball through our series of linked YouTube videos. When the ball stopped they solved a challenge utilizing Google Maps, Search and Translate, Twitter and last. fm that tested their wits and reflexes and proved the browser's speed.

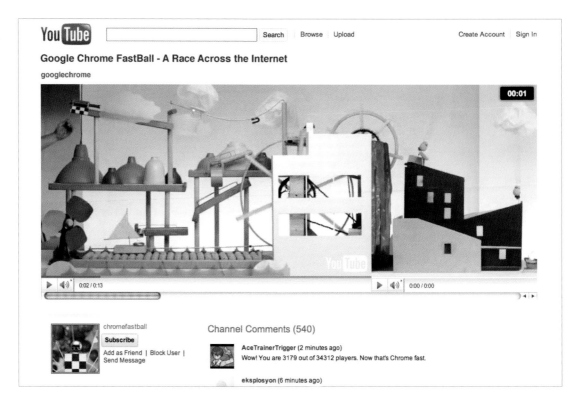

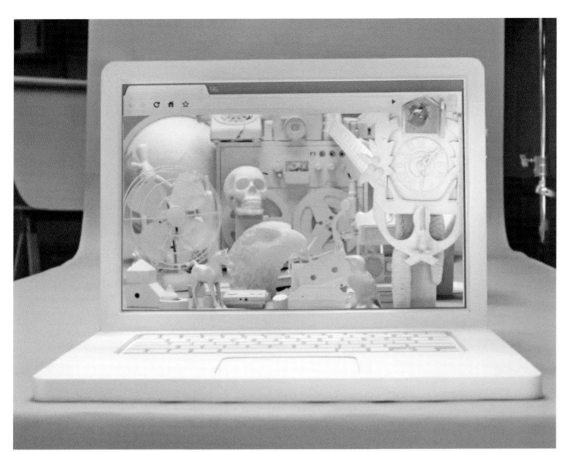

CHROME EXTENSIONS
BBH NEW YORK
Online Content | Branded
Short Films

**Executive Creative
Director** Pelle Sjoenell,
Calle Sjoenell
Art Director
Maja Fernqvist,
Joakim Saul
Copywriter
Maja Fernqvist,
Joakim Saul
Editor Charlie Johnston
Producer Melissa Bemis,
Sam Penfield
Production Company
1st Avenue Machine
Agency BBH New York
Client Google
Country United States

**FOURTEEN ACTORS
ACTING**
THE NEW YORK TIMES
MAGAZINE
Online Content | Branded
Short Films

Creative Director Solve
Sundsbo
Producer Kathy Ryan,
Joanna Milter, Miki Meek
Production Company
The New York Times Co.,
Spring Studios
Music Owen Pallett
Agency The New York
Times Magazine
Client The New York
Times Magazine
Country United States

DALÍ MUSEUM IPHONE APP

GOODBY, SILVERSTEIN & PARTNERS
Mobile | Mobile Phone Application

Creative Director
Jeff Goodby, Luca Buick
Art Director
Brian Gunderson
Copywriter Jody Horn
Designer
Brian Gunderson
Producer Carey Head,
Alex Burke
Production Company
Hipstamatic
Programmer
Ryan Dorshorst
**Director of Brand
Strategy** Gareth Kay
Agency Goodby,
Silverstein & Partners
Client Dalí Museum
Country United States

We were asked by The Dalí Museum to help build awareness for the opening of their fantastical new building. The mere mention of a Salavador Dalí–related project sent our thinking pie-in-the-surrealist-sky. The budget, however, was very realistic: zero dollars. We concepted a picture-editing app that created dreamy surrealist overlays to photos turning any iPhone snapshot into a Dalí-esque work of art. Rather than trying to create yet another app, we approached the style-makers at Hipstamatic, the most popular photo-editing app of the time, to see if they would work with us. They liked the idea so much that they waived their fee and pledged to donate all proceeds to the museum. The Hipstamatic community helped propel the app into a global spotlight while a high-profile photo contest judged by provocateur John Waters fueled sales. We're proud to have helped support the arts with an idea that not only didn't cost the museum a cent but in fact netted them tens of thousands of much-needed dollars.

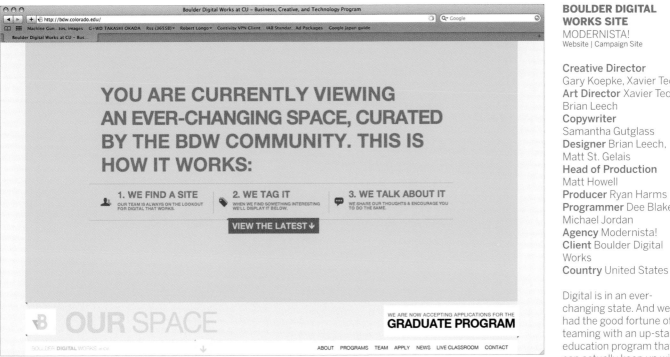

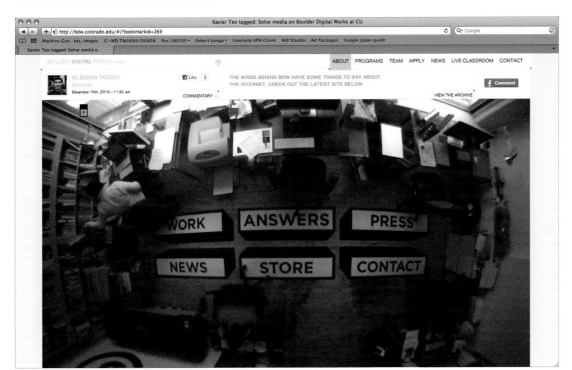

BOULDER DIGITAL WORKS SITE
MODERNISTA!
Website | Campaign Site

Creative Director
Gary Koepke, Xavier Teo
Art Director Xavier Teo,
Brian Leech
Copywriter
Samantha Gutglass
Designer Brian Leech,
Matt St. Gelais
Head of Production
Matt Howell
Producer Ryan Harms
Programmer Dee Blake,
Michael Jordan
Agency Modernista!
Client Boulder Digital
Works
Country United States

Digital is in an ever-changing state. And we had the good fortune of teaming with an up-start education program that can actually keep up with it. When we first started working with the folks at Boulder Digital Works, they hadn't graduated a single student, and weren't much more than some classroom space and an ambitious agenda to disrupt the current state of digital education. With a powerful core ideal, we decided to highlight their greatest promotional strength—the high-profile industry thought-leaders from the likes of Apple, Microsoft, Goodby, AKQA, Modernista! and others. Our final creation is what we call the "Inspiration Site."

NIKE FOOTBALL+TEAM EDITION FOR IPAD

AKQA
Mobile | I-Reader Application
or Book

Creative Director
Phil Haworth
Group Creative Director
Duan Evans
Art Director
Rodrigo Sobral
Copywriter Nat Cantor
Designer Andreas Levin
Project Manager
Joel Godfrey
Account Director
John Wilson
Client Partner
Geoff Northcott
Agency AKQA
Client Nike Football
Country United Kingdom

The Nike Football+ Team Edition iPad app is designed for football coaches at all levels. It gives them the tools to improve their squad's skills and performance using drill videos, challenges and insights from the world's top teams and their coaches. It enables coaches to build custom training programs for each of their players, focusing on areas of improvement identified by its rigorous tests. Coaches can test their players against the ultimate football benchmarks: the Cristiano Ronaldo Speed Challenge; the Fernando Torres Accuracy Challenge and the Cesc Fabregas Control Challenge; and for fitness, the globally recognized SPARQ test. Each player's results are recorded alongside the custom training regimen prescribed for them. Intuitive, innovative and video-rich, the Nike Football+ Team Edition revolutionizes football training in every way - and is accessible on any training ground with the iPad.

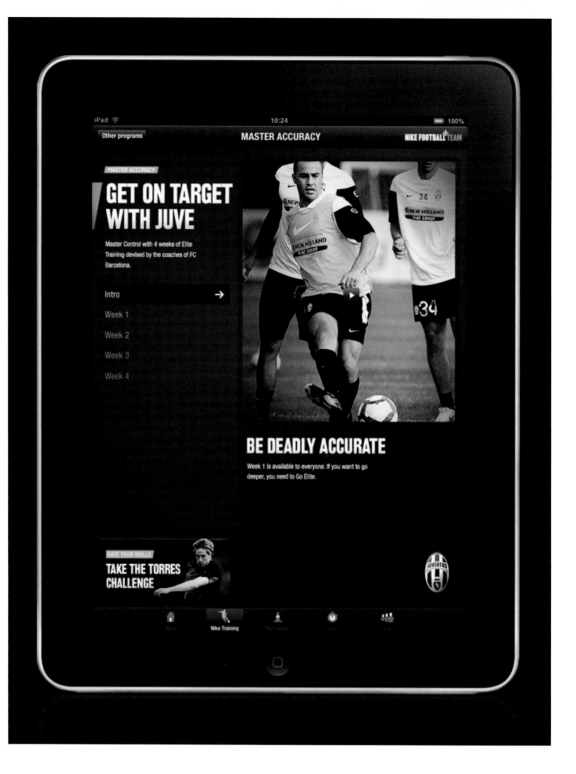

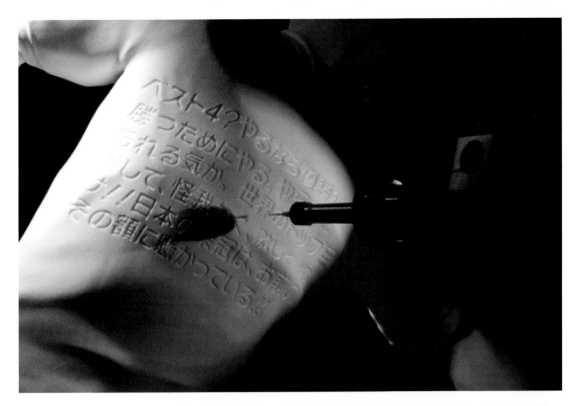

WTF NIKE TULIO
WIEDEN+KENNEDY
TOKYO
Beyond The Web

Creative Director
Frank Hahn, Naoki Ito
Art Director Naoki Ga
Copywriter
Hiroshi Kuyama
Interactive Copywriter
Takayuki Rokutan
Designer Masanori
Sakamoto (Deltro)
Producer Seiichi Saito
(Rhizomatiks),
Toru Terashima
(Root Communications)
Production Company
Rhizomatiks, Root
Communications, Deltro
Project Manager
Jun Yanazaki
(Rhizomatiks)
Account Director
Ted Yukawa
Account Supervisor
Shig Seng
Art Buyer Akio Iida
Programmer Seiichi Saito
(Rhizomatiks), Ken Horii
(Deltro), Kawasaki Heavy
Industries
Web Director
Hiromi Yoshikawa
(Root Communications)
Space Design
Time Tron, Limb Co.
Agency Wieden+Kennedy
Tokyo
Client Nike Japan
Country Japan

GLASTOTAG
POKE
Website

Creative Director
Nik Roope, Ben Tomlinson,
Jason Fox,
Emma Cakehead
Art Director Jason Fox
Copywriter Liam Nicholls
Designer Katie Marcus,
Matt Booth
Producer Ollie Wright,
Lauren Matthews
Production Company
Poke
Programmer Tom Quick,
Jamie Ingram
Agency Poke
Client Orange UK
Country United Kingdom

We wanted to drive
awareness of the Orange
partnership with Glaston-
bury and celebrate the
festival's 40th anniver-
sary, so we took a huge
photo to capture the
event. "GlastoTag" was
created by stitching
together 36 photos taken
in quick succession using
two Hasselblad cameras,
a skilled photographer
and 180-degree panning
action covering the entire
Pyramid Stage field and
everyone in it. The picture
was presented online and
viewers invited to zoom
in and out to find and tag
themselves in the crowd
using Facebook Con-
nect. The final image was
used as display assets
in retail channels, print
and traditional PR. We
smashed all the targets
with 1.3 million visits to
the site, 7,000 tags, more
than 6,000 Facebook
likes and more than 2 million page impressions of
blogs and news coverage.
Contagious declared it an
example of the "golden
age of the industry." It
was also the Guinness
World Records' most
tagged photo.

PHILIPS WAKE UP THE TOWN
TRIBAL DDB AMSTERDAM
Online Content | Branded Short Films

Creative Director
Neil Dawson, Chris Baylis,
Paul Fraser, Mariota Essery
Art Director
Mariota Essery
Copywriter Paul Fraser
Designer Simon Cook,
Leigh Hibell,
Joris Blomjous, Stella Yu
Head of Art
Mike Hambleton
Director of Photography
Denzil Armour-Brown
Director Doug Pray
Producer Jeroen Jedeloo,
Jolly Banjeree
Production Company
Stamp Films (Scott O
Donnell), Group 94
Account Sandra Krstic,
Nick Bassermann
UXD David Vogel
Technical Lead
Jan-Willem Penterman
Strategic Planner
Joey Duis
Music Garron Chang
Colorist Michael Gossen
Agency Tribal DDB
Amsterdam
Client Philips
Country Netherlands

A HUNTER SHOOTS
A BEAR
BUZZMAN
Online Content | Viral Video

Creative Director
Georges Mohammed-
Cherif
Art Director
Louis Audard
Copywriter
Tristan Daltroff
Producer
Mélanie Rohat Meheust
TV Producer E. Jonquille
Production Company
Elegangz
Managing Director
T. Granger
Account Executive
A. Ferrari
Agency Buzzman
Client Tipp-Ex/Bic
Country France

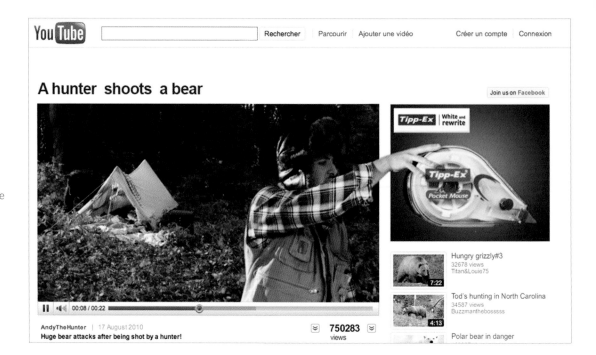

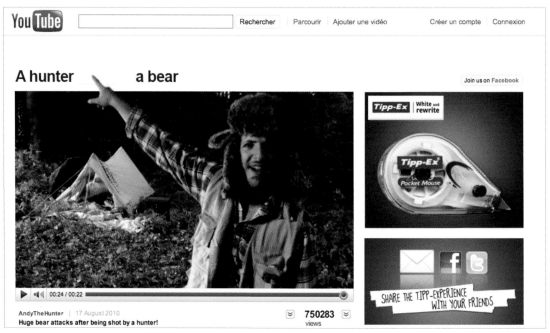

AIRWALK
Y&R NEW YORK
Online Content | Augmented Reality

Executive Creative Director Ian Reichenthal, Scott Vitrone
Executive Director, Content Production Lora Schulson, Nathy Aviram
Creative Director Graeme Hall, Menno Kluin, Steve Whittier
Art Director Alexander Nowak
Copywriter Feliks Richter
Producer Jo Kelly, Devon Dentler
Production Company Goldrun
Agency Y&R New York
Client Airwalk
Country United States

When Airwalk decided to do a limited-edition relaunch of their classic sneaker, the Airwalk Jim, we came up with an entirely new way to do it. We made the world's first ever "invisible pop-up stores" coupling together cell phones, GPS technology, and Augmented Reality, customers could only buy the Jim if they downloaded the app, went to a predetermined location, held up their phones, and took a photo of the AR Jim floating there. That allowed them to purchase the sneaker there and then. An exclusive product sold to an exclusive audience with an entirely new retail experience.

DONATE WORDS
RC COMUNICAÇÃO
Website

Creative Director
Guilherme Araújo
Art Director Eduardo
Araújo, Rafael Gil
Copywriter Guilherme
Araújo, Tiago Pereira,
Gustavo Costa,
Mateus Martins
Designer Herbert Rafael
Production Company
3bits
**Planning and
Management** Raquel
Ratton, Pedro Souza,
Denise Panisset
Agency RC Comunicação
Client Mario Penna
Institute
Country Brazil

Challenge: Motivate
patients at Mário Penna
Institute to fight cancer
with more positivity and
willpower—healing oncol-
ogy patients is directly
connected to their
emotional state. Idea:
Call people up to donate
something that money
can't buy. We created a
platform in which any person in the world can send
a message of willpower to
patients at Mário Penna,
through a website or Twitter account. Messages are
shown on TVs at the hos-
pital. Result: More than
600,000 messages from
249 countries and 249
Brazilian cities in the first
month, 1,800,000 visits
to the site in eight months
as well as exhibition on
the greatest Brazilian
TV broadcasts and the
participation of thou-
sands of people in Brazil
and worldwide, including
celebrities and the vice
president of Brazil.

DOT CONS
CP+B
Online Content | Branded
Short Films

Chief Creative Director
Rob Reilly, Andrew Keller,
Jeff Benjamin
Creative Director Tim
Roper, Dave Steinke
**Associate Creative
Director** Caprice Yu,
Tim Geoghegan
Art Director Slava
Morshch, DJ Pierce
Copywriter Ian Falcon,
Justin Ebert
Editor Evan Nix
Executive Producer
Chris Kyriakos
Producer Colin Narver
Production Company
Smuggler
Agency CP+B
Client Microsoft
Country United States

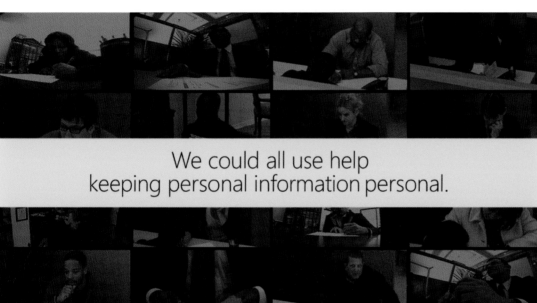

Internet Explorer's
competitors were fighting
over who was the fastest,
while IE was bleeding
share. So, IE8 decided to
tout a benefit they could
own: online security.
Filled with new innovative
safeguards, IE8 offered
users far more protec-
tion from online attacks
than all their competitors.
But the question still
remained— how does IE8
prove that people actually
need a safer browser? To
prove just how vulner-
able peoples' personal
information can be while
online, notorious Web
scams were re-created
live, in one of the most
street-smart cities in the
world: New York. Over the
course of a week, a phony
bank and two other faux
storefronts mimicking
actual Web scams were
erected and opened.
Each lured unsuspecting
"customers" into giving
up ridiculously personal
information. Actors and
extras were cast and
professional-looking sig-
nage was created for each
business. Every encounter
and personal exchange
was documented, using
an elaborate array of hidden cameras.

M&M'S FIND RED
PROXIMITY CANADA
Games | Online Game

Creative Director
John Gagné
Art Director
Jeffrey Da Silva,
Ari Elkouby
Copywriter
Rene Rouleau, Jon Ruby,
Ryan Lawrence
Designer Jeffrey Da Silva
Editor Topix
Producer Joanne Sincich
Production Company
Soft Citizen
Programmer
Iftikhar Ahmed,
Darrin Patey, Edwin
Locke, Patrick Jordan
Other Priyanka Gowami,
Shari Balga, Jesse
Abrams, Chris Perron
Agency Proximity
Canada
Client Mars Canada
Country Canada

OS RINGTONICOS
ALMAPBBDO
Mobile | Mobile Website

Creative Director
Sergio Mugnaini
Art Director
Guiga Giacomo
Copywriter Ricardo Wolff
Designer Lucas Amaral
Programmer Yves Apsy,
Daniel Carvalho
Mobile Technology
Pontomobi
Agency AlmapBBDO
Client Casa do Zezinho
Country Brazil

**PEPSI
REFRESH PROJECT**
HUGE
Social Networks | Social Network
Platform

**Partner, Director of User
Experience** Gene Liebel
Creative Director
Joe Stewart,
Felipe Memoria
Art Director Liang Zhang,
Ryan Frank
Copywriter
Ross Morrison
Designer Badrul Rupak
Producer Kate Watts,
Ana Breton
Programmer Rafael
Mumme, Lukas Mairl
Technology Director
Philip Cotty
Agency HUGE
Client PepsiCo
Country United States

**HALO REACH:
REMEMBER REACH**
AKQA
Website

Chief Creative Officer
Rei Inamoto
Creative Officer Pierre
Lipton, Stephen Clements
Art Director Ian Aldous
Copywriter Justin Pedone
Designer Jeremiah
Wassom, Kyle Yugawa
Producer
Andrea Bustabade
Agency AKQA
Client Xbox
Country United States

Our challenge was to
excite core fans while
capturing the imagina-
tions of new gamer
recruits worldwide. We
created a live collabora-
tive monument of light
honoring the fallen
heroes of *Halo Reach*.
Visitors to Remember-
Reach.com selected
coordinates and watched
as a giant robot illumi-
nated those points of
light in real time, revealing
the full 3-D monument.
In 20 days, more than a
million people visited the
site and shared it across
social networks. The cam-
paign was also featured in
national publications like
Wired magazine, popular
blogs like Gizmodo and
even on NBC television
news. *Halo Reach* posted
record sales, generating
over $200 million in the
first 24 hours.

Advertising: I read in our archives that at the close of the ADC's first-ever award show, in the spring of 1921, the chair of the jury declared, "It will not be possible to present in any other year a show of so high a standard." Clearly, our first chairperson underestimated the remarkable work that has been honored by this club by many future generations. Ninety years later, as Advertising Chair, I took my cue from his remark as I challenged this year's jury to forget the past. The past was something invented by others. We would focus our attention on sparking the future. To select work that we believe would inspire a course for the next generation, many look to the ADC show as a reference point. An ambition. A standard to surpass. As many of you know, the ADC uses its profits from this very show to sponsor programs for students and juniors. We believe that investing in the future of our industry is the most sustainable way to keep it healthy and relevant. I am happy to report that every judge took the mission to heart. As a group they were unbiased and committed. And they rewarded few. In fact, less than 1% won, among an unprecedented number of entries. The result is a show that is one of our finest. The work is as surprising as it is inspiring. With few exceptions, it steps boldly outside conventional advertising boundaries. The only common territory in this eclectic body of work is that all the winners have at the core— besides all the great ideas—a passion for executing those ideas in a convincing and compelling way. As advertising chairman, on behalf of an outstanding ADC 90th jury, and with middle finger proudly raised to the past skeptics of 1921—I congratulate this year's winners.

—Paul Lavoie, Chairman, Co-Founder, TAXI, Advertising Chair

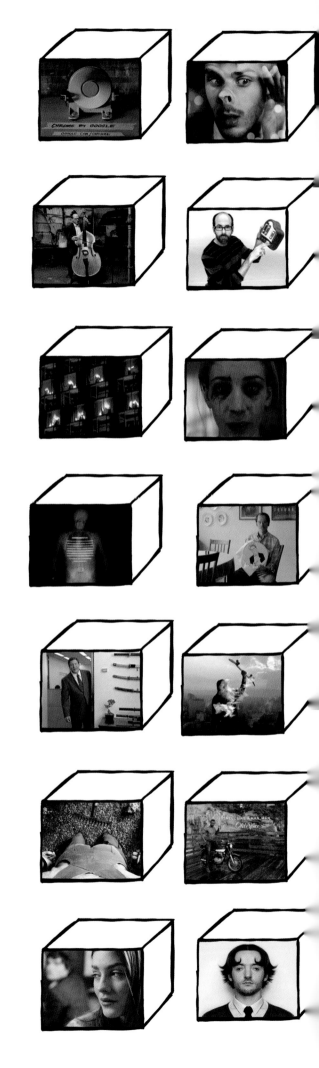

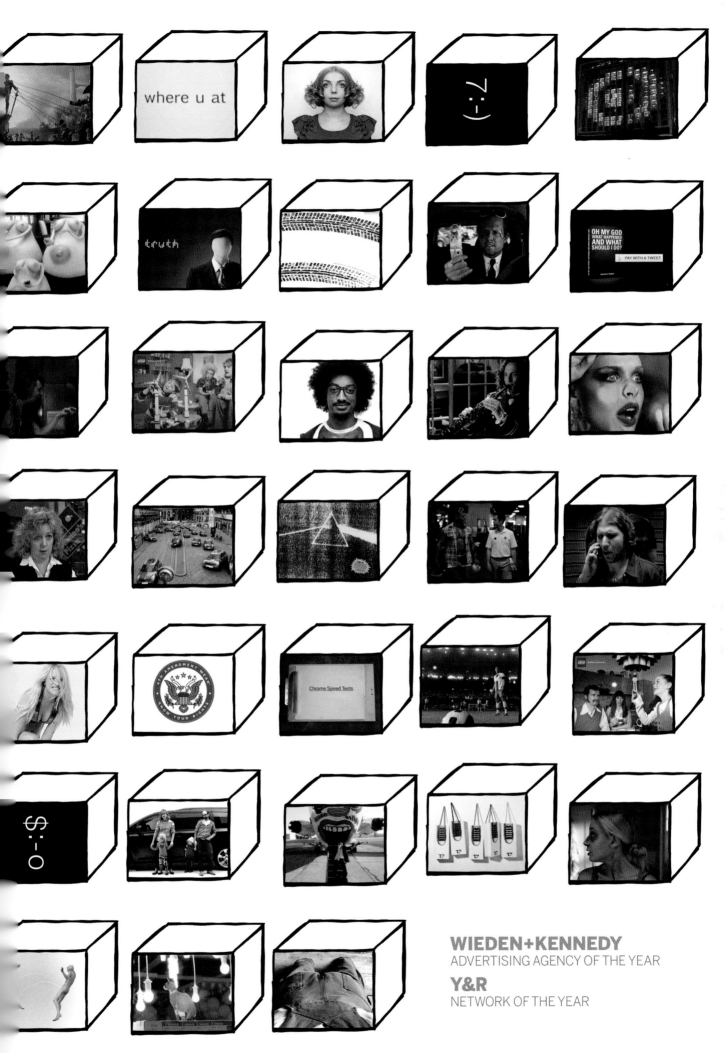

WIEDEN+KENNEDY
ADVERTISING AGENCY OF THE YEAR

Y&R
NETWORK OF THE YEAR

4TH AMENDMENT WEAR

4TH AMENDMENT
WEAR—METALLIC
WEAR— INK PRINTED
UNDERCLOTHES
Collateral | Promotional

Creative Director
Matthew Ryan,
Tim Geoghegan
Art Director
Matthew Ryan
Copywriter
Tim Geoghegan
Designer Matthew Ryan
Illustrator Matthew Ryan
Photo Editor
Matthew Ryan
Agency 4th
Amendment Wear
Client 4th
Amendment Wear
Country United States

Now there's a way to
protest those intrusive
TSA X-ray body scanners
without saying a word—
underclothes printed
with the Fourth Amend-
ment in metallic ink.
Let them know they're
spying on the privates
of a private citizen. The
Fourth Amendment to the
Constitution of the
United States, meant
to prevent unwarranted
search and seizure, is
readable on TSA body
scanners. 4th Amend-
ment Wear is specifically
designed to broadcast
messages to TSA X-ray
officers just when they are
peeking at your privates.
We invented a proprietary
metallic ink that displays
any designed image or
message on the TSA scan-
ner screens, thus creating
the only clothing that
would display the Fourth
Amendment when passed
through airport security
scans. The clothes are
designed as a silent
protest against the new
reality of being searched
to the point where we're
basically naked.

Multiple Winner
Design Silver | Corporate/
Promo | Promotional Apparel

Hybrid Cube | Collateral
Promotional

Designism Cube | Collateral
Promotional

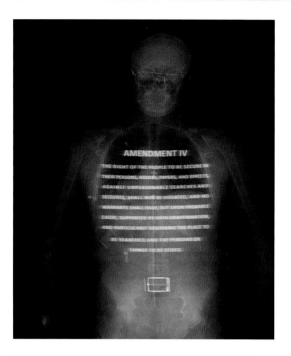

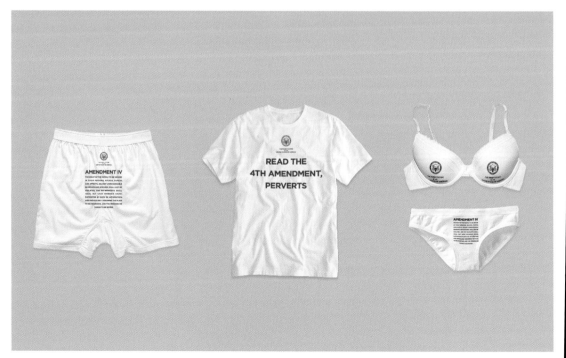

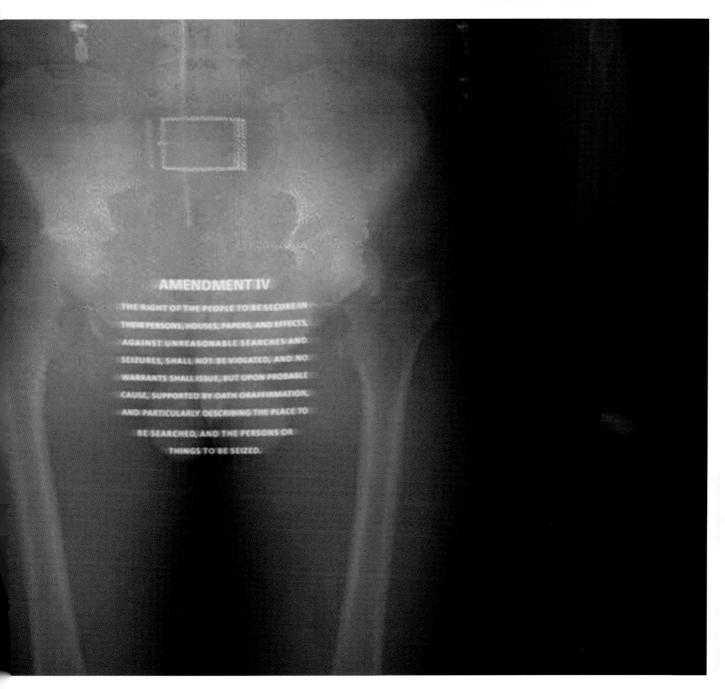

AMENDMENT IV

THE RIGHT OF THE PEOPLE TO BE SECURE IN THEIR PERSONS, HOUSES, PAPERS, AND EFFECTS, AGAINST UNREASONABLE SEARCHES AND SEIZURES, SHALL NOT BE VIOLATED, AND NO WARRANTS SHALL ISSUE, BUT UPON PROBABLE CAUSE, SUPPORTED BY OATH OR AFFIRMATION, AND PARTICULARLY DESCRIBING THE PLACE TO BE SEARCHED, AND THE PERSONS OR THINGS TO BE SEIZED.

ANTI-ROCK STAR
Y&R NEW YORK
Broadcast Craft | Direction

**Executive Creative
Director** Guillermo Vega,
Ian Reichenthal,
Scott Vitrone
**Executive Director,
Content Production** Lora
Schulson, Nathy Aviram
Art Director Guillermo
Vega, Menno Kluin
Copywriter Scott Vitrone,
Ian Reichenthal,
Icaro Doria
Director Bryan Buckley
Editor Carlos Arias
(Final Cut)
Producer Jo Kelly
Production Company
Hungry Man
Agency Y&R New York
Client VH1
Country United States

The wonderful world of
VH1 is music and culture
in a blender.

Multiple Winner
Advertising Silver | Broadcast
Media | Television Commercial

CHROME SPEED TESTS
BBH NEW YORK/GOOGLE CREATIVE LAB
Broadcast Craft | Cinematography

Executive Creative Director Pelle Sjoenell, Calle Sjoenell, Robert Wong (Google Labs)
Art Director Steve Peck
Copywriter Jared Elms
Director Aaron Duffy (1st Avenue Machine)
Editor Charlie Johnston (Lost Planet)
Producer Orlee Tatarka, Sam Penfield
Production Company 1st Avenue Machine
Agency BBH New York/ Google Creative Lab
Client Google
Country United States

What does "fast" mean online? Since there is no benchmark for speed on the Internet, we created one and dubbed it Chrome Fast. To demonstrate how fast Chrome Fast really is, we created the *Chrome Speed Tests* films, comparing the rendering speed of Google's Chrome browser against extremely fast things in real life—a potato gun, sound waves, lightning. We filmed everything in slow motion with no CG effects, capturing them as live science experiments. The result was an engaging way to visualize speed and prove that Google Chrome is indeed a very fast web browser.

Multiple Winner
Interactive Gold | Online Content | Viral Video

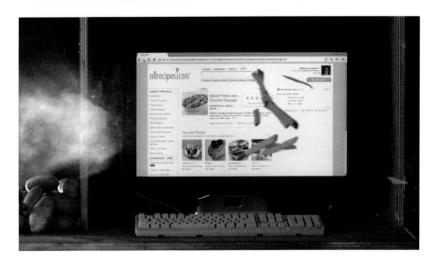

DORTMUND CONCERT MILK
JUNG VON MATT AG
Integrated

Executive Creative Director Sascha Hanke
Creative Director Tobias Grimm, Jens Pfau, Jo Marie Farwick
Art Director Damjan Pita
Copywriter Henning Robert, Jan-Hendrik Scholz
Designer Nicolas Schmidt-Fitzner, Christoph Maeder, Sven Gabriel
Director Silvio Helbig
Editor Tobias Suhm, Niels Muenter
Producer Meike van Meegen, Johannes Bittel, Claudia Westermann
Production Company Markenfilm GmbH & Co. KG, Infected Postproduction GmbH, VCC Agency for Postproduction
PR Agency Mhoch4 GmbH & Co.KG
Agency Jung Von Matt AG
Client Dortmund Concert Hall
Country Germany

Set deep in the heart of Germany, Ruhr region, where hardly anyone is interested in classical music, the Dortmund Concert Hall has to offer something pretty unusual to attract new visitors. So we invented a completely new medium, to make our classical music tasty to people: milk. It has been scientifically proven that classical music has a positive effect on cows milk yield. So we played music to them from selected artists of the new season. As a result, the cows produced the very first music worldwide for the taste buds. This special milk was then bottled directly on the farm. There were nine different tastes, depending on the artist the cows listened to. This way even people who otherwise hardly encounter classical music got a taste of the Dortmund Concert Hall, making it the most successful season in their history. Dortmund Concert Hall, Experience music like never before.

Multiple Winner
Hybrid Merit | Integrated

IT RARELY STOPS

Y&R CHICAGO
Broadcast Media | Non-Broadcast
Commercial
Broadcast Craft | Special Effects

Creative Director
Ken Erke
Art Director Ken Erke,
Brian Smego
Copywriter Ken Erke
Designer Adam St. John
Director Dave Meyers
Editor Chris Davis
Producer Brian Smego
Production Company
@radical.media
Visual Effects MPC
Agency Y&R Chicago
Client National Domestic
Violence Hotline
Country United States

Each year, women experi-
ence about 4.8 million
intimate-partner-related
physical assaults. Most
often these assaults are
not isolated but instead
continue. Our goal was to
relate to the overwhelming
desperation of such a
terrible situation, communicate just how lonely the
experience of domestic
violence is and offer real
hope and a solution.

Multiple Winner
Advertising Merit | Broadcast
Craft | Direction

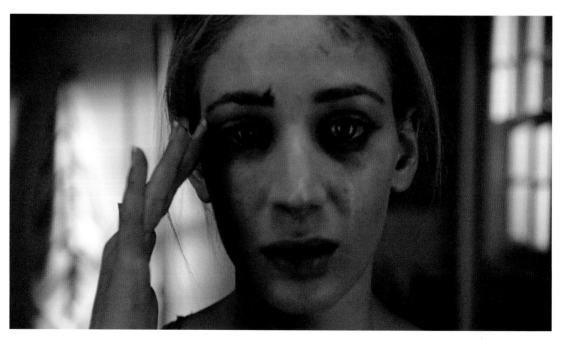

LOGITECH—LOGITECH REVUE—WITH GOOGLE TV—IVAN COBENK
GOODBY, SILVERSTEIN & PARTNERS
Broadcast Media | Television Commercial

Creative Director
Margaret Johnson,
David Kolbusz
Art Director
Croix Gagnon
Copywriter Nat Lawlor
Director
Ringan Ledwidge
Editor Rich Orrick
Producer Jan O'Malley
Production Company
Smuggler
Agency Goodby,
Silverstein & Partners
Client Logitech
Country United States

Multiple Winner
Advertising Bronze | Broadcast
Craft | Copywriting
Advertising Merit | Broadcast
Craft | Art Direction

TARGET KALEIDOSCOPIC FASHION SPECTACULAR

MOTHER NEW YORK
Media Innovation | Ambient/ Environmental

Creative Director Mother
Director Legs
Producer Mother
Music Sam Spiegel
Choreography
Ryan Heffington
Stylist Mel Ottenberg
Lighting Design
Bionic League
Agency Mother New York
Client Target
Country United States

Last spring, Target asked for a fashion show that would showcase their new fall line and create buzz during New York Fashion Week. But as a department store known for affordable style, stacking up against the world's couture fashion labels was no easy task. To be noticed in an already oversaturated and cynical market, Target needed to produce something spectacular. It took 66 dancers, 25 models, an original score, 44,640 LED bulbs, a month of rehearsals, one cordoned-off city block, and 155 rooms in New York's Standard Hotel. Named the Target Kaleidoscopic Fashion Spectacular, the event reinvented the fashion show by using all 18 stories of the hotel's windows to showcase the brand and its fall fashion line while providing a 20-minute light, sound and dance spectacle for thousands of spectators on the streets below and millions of viewers online.

Multiple Winner
Advertising Bronze | Media Innovation | Non-Broadcast Media

WRITE THE FUTURE

WIEDEN+KENNEDY AMSTERDAM
Broadcast Craft | Art Direction
Broadcast Media | Television
Commercial

Executive Creative Director Jeff Kling
Creative Director Mark Bernath, Eric Quennoy
Art Director Freddie Powell, Stuart Harkness
Copywriter Stuart Harkness, Freddie Powell
Director Alejandro Gonzalez Inarritu
Editor Work Post London, Rich Orrick, Ben Jordan, Stephen Mirrione
Producer Elissa Singstock, Olivier Klonhammer
Production Company Independent Films/ Anonymous Content
Head of Broadcast Erik Verheijen
Account Team Gene Willis, Jordi Pont, David Anson, Marco Palermo
Planner Dan Hill, Graeme Douglas
Nike Clients Enrico Balleri, Colin Leary, Todd Pendleton
Visual Effects The Mill, London and New York
Music Hocus Pocus by Focus
Music Remix Massive Music Amsterdam
Sound Design Grand Central London, Raja Sehgal, Phaze UK
Mix Company Grand Central Studios London, Raja Sehgal
Agency Wieden+Kennedy Amsterdam
Client Nike
Country Netherlands

How could Nike dominate the world's biggest football tournament without being a sponsor? Every four years, the keys to football heaven are dangled in front of the international elite. One goal, one pass, one game-saving tackle can be the difference between fame and forgotten. What happens on the pitch in that split second has a ripple effect that goes beyond the match and the tournament. "Write the Future" was a messaging platform that allowed Nike to show how football creates this ripple effect. It gave a glimpse

WRITE YOUR FUTURE

Experience life at the top of the game and see how you can handle the pressure from signing a contract to making the big plays. The spotlight's on you. Time to shine.

into the future to see what the players were really playing for, in their own lives and the lives of those who follow them. Our goal was to weave the brand into the conversations around this major tournament in a way that celebrated the participating teams and athletes and engaged football fans around the world.

Multiple Winner
Advertising Black Cube | Broadcast Media | Television Commercial
Advertising Silver | Integrated

DELIVER HOPE
AGENCYTWOFIFTEEN
Broadcast Craft | Art Direction

Executive Creative
Director Scott Duchon,
John Patroulis
Art Director Ben Wolan
Copywriter Joe Rose
Director Noam Murrow
Editor Angus Wall
Producer Joyce Chen
Production Company
Biscuit Filmworks
Agency agencytwofifteen
Client Microsoft/Xbox
Country United States

SMELL LIKE A MAN, MAN.
Old Spice

QUESTIONS
WIEDEN+KENNEDY
Broadcast Craft | Direction

Executive Creative Director Mark Fitzloff, Susan Hoffman
Creative Director Jason Bagley, Eric Baldwin
Art Director Craig Allen, Eric Kallman
Copywriter Eric Kallman, Craig Allen
Designer Andy Reznik
Director Tom Kuntz
Editor Carlos Arias(Rock Paper Scissors)
Agency Executive Producer Ben Grylewicz, Lindsay Reed
Agency Producer Ben Grylewicz
Producer David Zander, Jeff Scruton
Production Company MJZ
Music and Sound Stimmüng
Agency Wieden+Kennedy
Client Old Spice
Country United States

Anything is possible when you smell like an Old Spice man, and our hero, Isaiah Mustafa, is back to illustrate just a few of the amazing things that an Old Spice man can do. The latest effort is a fully integrated campaign with TV, print and digital executions, targeted at both men and women, once again touting the manly scents of Old Spice body wash.

"YOUR PLANET" CAMPAIGN

MULLEN
Broadcast Media | Television
Commercial

Chief Creative Officer
Mark Wenneker
Creative Director
Brian Tierney,
Stephen Mietelski
Art Director Chris Toland
Copywriter Brian Tierney
Director Dave Laden
Editor Lawrence Young,
Bikini Edit
Producer Zeke Bowman,
Mary Donington
Production Company
Hungry Man
Visual Effects Brickyard
Audio Post Mike Secher,
Soundtrack
Agency Mullen
Client Planet Fitness
Country United States

Planet Fitness is different
from most gyms in that
it actually discourages
roided-out muscle heads
from joining. They want
their gyms to be clean,
comfortable places where
ordinary people can get
a workout without being
intimidated by weights
being slammed down and
loud grunting. They actu-
ally have an alarm that
they sound when these
offenses occur, called the
lunk alarm. The challenge
was to show that Planet
Fitness is not the right
place for these guys.
Planet Fitness is not their
planet; it's yours.

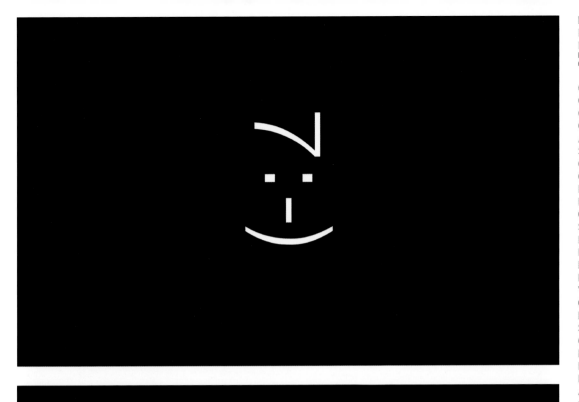

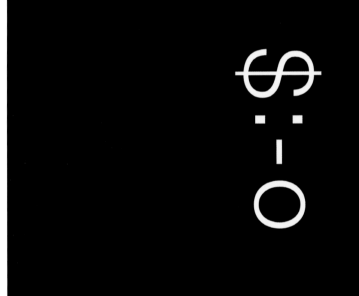

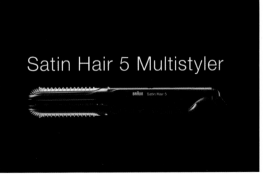

Any mood. Any style.

Satin Hair 5 Multistyler

HAIRMOTICONS
BBDO GERMANY GMBH,
DÜSSELDORF
Broadcast Media | Television
Commercial

Chief Creative Officer
Christian Mommertz
Creative Director
Christian Mommertz
Art Director
Stephan Eichler
Copywriter
Christopher Fink
Designer Philipp Alings
Director
Christian Mommertz,
Steffen Gentis
Editor Florian Alt,
Markus Jaeschke
Producer Steffen Gentis
Production Company
VCC GmbH
CGI Das Werk
Head of TV
Steffen Gentis
Composer
Leroy Anderson
Music Publisher EMI
Music Publishing
Agency BBDO Germany
GmbH, Düsseldorf
Client Braun GmbH
Country Germany

Emoticons like : -) and
: - (are well established
in modern communica-
tion. However, these
faces had one thing in
common: they were
bald. But in "real" life our
moods and own styles
are often expressed with
a personal hairstyle. So
we summarized both for
Braun: emoticons, that
carry a suitable hair-style
to express our personal
mood and style. This
way we engage women
in a modern conversa-
tion about style. Inviting
them to "play" with us
and explore all the sides
of their femininity—par-
ticularly women who are
quite expressive in all
aspects of their life. The
"terms of entry" are
quite easy: just use one
of our hair emoticons in
your communication or
get inspired to create one
of your own. The ads are
just an inspiration to
get creative—because
there are so many styles
for any mood.

DOG RADIO
GRABARZ & PARTNER
Radio | Radio Commercial

**Executive Creative
Director** Ralf Heuel
Creative Director
Tom Hauser, Ralf Heuel
Art Director Jan Woelfel
Copywriter
André Hennen
Director
Torsten Hennings,
Ralf Heuel
Production Company
Studio Funk, Hamburg
Sound Engineer
Torsten Hennings
Agency
Grabarz & Partner
Client
Galaxxy Pet Food GmbH
Country Germany

The challenge was pretty easy: advertise the high quality of Naturia dog food and increase sales. The hard part: a highly competitive market and a tiny budget. Our solution was the highest radio frequency: 15 KHz. Luckily, it's exactly the frequency that dog whistles have. People can't hear this frequency or can only barely hear it, but dogs hear it very sharply. We recreated a 15 KHz tone and played it every time Naturia was mentioned in the ad. For dog owners, it appeared as if their dogs really did react to the Naturia name in the ad. That worked out very well: 12,768 cans of naturia dog food were sold in the month of the ad was aired; 28% more than in the previous month!

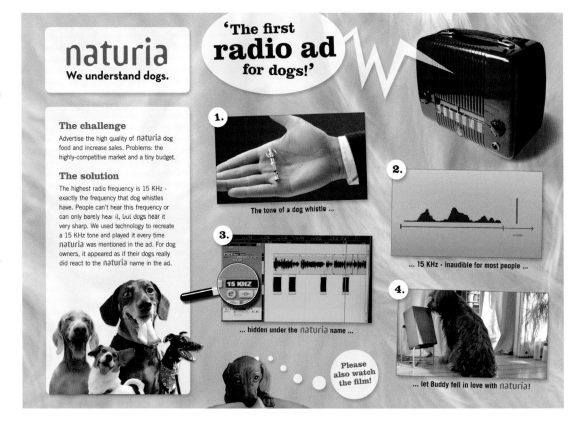

PEOPLE WHO
BOUGHT THIS ITEM
ALSO BOUGHT

ALTITUDE
SICKNESS
PILLS

AUTUMN/WINTER 2010
HARVEY NICHOLS

**ACCESSORIES
REQUIRED**
Y&R DUBAI
Magazine Consumer | Print
Advertisement

Creative Director Shahir
Zag, Komal Bedi Sohal
Art Director Komal Bedi
Sohal, Shahir Zag
Copywriter Shahir Zag,
Komal Bedi Sohal
Designer Shahir Zag
Photographer
James Day
Account Director
Nadine Ghossoub
Agency Y&R Dubai
Client Harvey Nichols
Country
United Arab Emirates

SWORD COLLECTOR

Y&R NEW YORK
Broadcast Media | Television
Commercial

**Executive Creative
Director** Ian Reichenthal,
Scott Vitrone
**Executive Director,
Content Production** Lora
Schulson, Nathy Aviram
Creative Director
Guillermo Vega, Graham
Lang, Dan Morales,
Icaro Doria
Art Director Dan Treichel
Copywriter
Brandon Henderson
Director Jim Jenkins
Editor Jason MacDonald,
(Number Six Edit)
Producer Lora Schulson,
Nathy Aviram
Production Company
O Positive
Agency Y&R New York
Client Land Rover
Country United States

Land Rover drivers
experience a feeling of
safety that drivers of
other vehicles don't.
This is why we created
the "You'll Feel Safe Inside"
campaign. It humorously
demonstrates the sense
of confidence that a Land
Rover driver feels when
they are inside one of the
toughest, safest, most versatile vehicles ever made.

Multiple Winner
Advertising Merit | Broadcast Craft
Copywriting

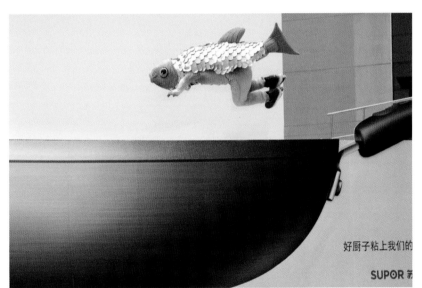

SUPOR NON-STICK PANS
LEO BURNETT SHANGHAI
Media Innovation | Ambient/Environmental

Creative Director
Amanda Yang, Gordon
Hughes, Forest Young
Art Director Amanda
Yang, Gordon Hughes
Forest Young, Lin Wei-Jun,
Sean Qu
Copywriter
Amanda Yang,
Donna Dong
Designer Sean Qu,
Lin Wei-Jun,
Handsome Wong
Illustrator Dicky Lui
Photographer Eric Dang,
Nicholas Siau
Agency Leo Burnett
Shanghai
Client Supor
Country China

Break through the clutter
of an already very
crowded marketplace to
build awareness for
Supor's premium range
of non-stick pans. A
spectacular event using
a giant wok and in-line
skaters dressed as prawns,
pork, eggs, carrots and
fish was set up outside
shopping malls in
Shanghai, China. The food
skaters flew up and down
a ramp constructed
inside the wok to
demonstrate the nonstick
surface. A rise in sales
of 20% in the selected
Shanghai malls has led
to plans being made
to take the event into
second and third-tier
cities
across China.

MAYHEM
LEO BURNETT CHICAGO
Broadcast Media | Television
Commercial

Executive Creative Director Jeanie Caggiano, Charley Wickman
Creative Director Britt Nolan, Jo Shoesmith
Associate Creative Director Matt Miller
Art Director Greg Nobles, Chris Rodriquez
Copywriter Matt Miller, Josh Mizrachi
Director Phil Morrison
Editor Haines Hall, Matthew Wood
Producer Veronica Puc, Bryan Litman
Production Company EPOCH Films
Agency Leo Burnett Chicago
Client Allstate Insurance
Country United States

Meet Mayhem. The personification of trouble. He's every reason to have the right insurance. Sometimes he's a texting teenager. Sometimes he's an act of nature. But he's always proof that, when it comes to insurance, nobody protects you better than Allstate.

PIANO
MOTHER
LONDON LIMITED
Broadcast Media | Television
Commercial

Creative Director
Ed Warren, Al MacCuish,
Robert Saville, Mark
Waites, Stephen Butler
Art Director
Daniel Mencak,
Erik Nordenankar, David
Colman, Nick Hallbery
Copywriter Al MacCuish,
Daniel Mencak,
Erik Nordenankar, David
Colman, Nick Hallbery
Director Si & Ad
Editor Jonnie Scarlett
Producer Clare Wallis
Production Company
Academy Films
Agency Mother London
Limited
Client Match.com
Country United Kingdom

Matchmaking, online
dating, filling out forms
to match you up with
someone compatible.
Not only is it considered
to be something for the
people left over, it also
becomes a bit technical
and functional. It's not
about that. Match.com
is really about Love.

Karen Kaiser
Marketing Director

Brandon Solano
Head Chef

PIZZA TURNAROUND
CP+B
Integrated

Chief Creative Officer
Rob Reilly, Andrew Keller,
Jeff Benjamin
Creative Director
Tony Calcao, Mark Moll
**Associate Creative
Director** Craig Miller,
Matt Denyer
Art Director Andrew
Lincoln, Brian Lambert
Copywriter Matt Talbot,
Roberto Lastra
Interactive Designer
Shannon Brown
Director
Henry Alex Rubin
Editor Fred Fouquet
Producer Julie Vosburgh,
Christina Carter
Production Company
Smuggler
Agency CP+B
Client Domino's
Country United States

Domino's came to us with
a new pizza that scored
better in taste tests than
any they'd ever made.
But 50 years of pushing
speed and efficiency had
eroded the brand's repu-
tation for taste. We had
a great new product our
battered brand couldn't
credibly announce. Our
solution: Come clean.
Admit we'd made bad
pizza in the past, prove
we'd listened to people's
complaints and give
them a reason to believe
in us again. The resulting
campaign yielded the
largest quarterly same
store sales increase in
fast-food history.

RIDE
PUBLICIS MOJO, SYDNEY
Broadcast Craft | Cinematography

Creative Director
Micah Walker
Art Director Andrew
Ostrom, Ruth Bellotti
Copywriter
Ian Williamson
Director Garth Davis
Editor Jack Hutchings
Producer Karen Sproul
Production Company
Exit Films
Cinematographer
Greig Fraser
Agency Producer
Philippa Smart
Head of TV Corey Esse
Postproduction Editor
Colin Renshaw
Sound Mix Jason Murphy
Music Supervisor
Karl Richter
**Agency Account
Director**
Simon Ludowyke
Agency Publicis Mojo,
Sydney
Client The Coca-Cola
Company
Country Australia

Made in collaboration
with skate legend Steve
Berra, this film forms
part of our approach
for Coke's energy drink,
Burn, involving preexist-
ing communities where
energy plays a legitimate
role in fueling creative
expression. Using real fire
and actual skaters from
a street skateboarding
collective in Mexico City,
it follows the skaters on
their journey from dawn
till dusk as they cross
the city, catching fire as
they pick up speed and
perform tricks and stunts.
The film sets out to
capture both the sense of
community and individu-
alism synonymous with
the pursuit.

SYMMETRY
TBWA PARIS
Magazine Consumer | Print
Advertisement

Creative Director
Eric Holden, Remi Noel,
Alasdhair
Macgregor-Hastie
Art Director Ingrid Varetz
Copywriter Glen Troadec
Photographer
Cindy Gravelat
Other Ewan Veitch
Agency TBWA Paris
Client Nissan
Country France

NISSAN launched in 2010 its new Cube car in Europe, the very first car conceived as much as a design product as a car. A print campaign was created to promote the iconic design of the car to a design audience. The sources of inspiration for the design included a bulldog with sunglasses for the front bonnet. This gives credibility to the Cube as the perfect car for people with an appeal for design, who like to challenge their mind with interesting and unexpected visuals. A series of three print visuals demonstrate how symmetry is boring and fails to dramatize one of the most iconic design aspects of the car, the asymmetry of its back. The aim of the campaign is to start people thinking about the uniqueness of the Cube, which flies in the face of standard car design.

**HIDDEN CAMERA INTERVIEW
DUSTIN H.
APRIL 16, 10:18 AM**

**STOP ME/OKAY/
OFFER**
ARNOLD WORLDWIDE
Broadcast Media | Television
Commercial

Creative Director
Pete Favat, Roger
Baldacci, John Kearse,
Meg Siegal
Art Director
Eric Stephenson,
Rob Kottkamp
Copywriter
Gregg Nelson,
Will Chambliss
Director
Henry-Alex Rubin
Director of Photography
Matthew Woolfe,
Jonathan Furmanski
Editor Lawrence Young,
Aaron Langley
Producer Carron Pedonti,
Drew Santarsiero
Production Company
Smuggler
Agency Arnold Worldwide
Client Truth
Country United States

Why would we hire a fake recruiter, set up a fake recruiting office and use hidden cameras to secretly film 60 candidates going through fake job interviews? Well, to answer one very real question: Do you have what it takes to be a tobacco exec? In the past, truth has exposed the public to Big Tobacco and its questionable practices. This time we wanted to know if, even in the worst economy in 79 years, could regular people do what tobacco execs do. Could you be the executive, making decisions about a product that kills millions a year? Because if we can get kids thinking about that, maybe it will make them think twice about the whole issue of tobacco, and whether to start smoking or not.

REAR ASSIST
GRABARZ & PARTNER
Newspaper, Trade | Print
Advertisement

**Executive Creative
Director** Ralf Heuel
Creative Director
Timm Weber, Goesta
Diehl, Oliver Heidorn
Art Director
Thomas Schmiegel
Copywriter
Kerstin Correll
Photographer Tom
Mennemann c/o Christa
Klubert
Agency Grabarz &
Partner
Client Volkswagen AG
Country Germany

As a contractor, your
everyday work presents
you with any number
of tasks and challenges
that demand your
full concentration. So
wouldn't it be great to
have someone at your
side who looks out
for potential risks and
dangers? Such as the
rearview camera "Rear
Assist." Our campaign
convinces tradesmen
and company owners of
the advantages and
benefits of the practical
"Rear Assist" camera
now installed in many
commercial vehicles
made by Volkswagen.

Multiple Winner
Advertising Silver | Magazine, Trade
Print Advertisement

The "Rear Assist" rear-view camera.
Now also available in the Crafter.

Commercial
Vehicles

12 SECOND STRIP
PUBLICIS LONDON
Integrated

Creative Director
Tom Ewart, Adam Kean
Art Director
Johnny Leathers
Copywriter Gavin Kellett
Designer Spin
Photographer Perou
Director Perou
Producer Gabi Besevic
Agency Producer
Colin Hickson,
Verity Saunders
Agency Publicis London
Client Renault UK Ltd
Country
United Kingdom

Renault's Wind Roadster
is a new car in a new seg-
ment for them—the small
convertible category.
We needed fun-loving
show-offs to take a good
look at it. Its most notable
feature is the roof,
which retracts in just 12
seconds, but we wanted
consumers to be aware
of its other features, so
Web visits would be vital.
Whether or not viewers
joined in, we needed a
device whose attitude
spoke of the car's spirit
as well as led them to
its product benefits. We
launched 12secondstrip.
co.uk—a race to win the
car by removing clothing
in the time it takes the
Wind's roof to retract.
Digital posters appeared
and contestants filmed
themselves stripping
from winter woollies to
summer skimpies in front
of them, then uploaded
their entry via YouTube
or their mobile. They also
stripped at home using
their webcams. The most
fun video won the car.

BUILDERS OF TOMORROW
SERVICEPLAN
Magazine Consumer | Print
Advertisement

**Executive Creative
Director**
Matthias Harbeck
Chief Creative Officer
Alex Schill
Creative Director
Oliver Palmer
Art Director Sandra
Loibl, Julia Koch,
Franz Röppischer
Copywriter Frank Seiler
Photographer
Susanne Dittrich, c/o
KristinaKorb.com
Director
Susanne Dittrich, c/o
KristinaKorb.com
Production Company
Alexa Günther,
Sebastian Eberhard
(Embassy of Dreams
Filmproduktion GmbH)
Agency serviceplan
Client LEGO GmbH
Country Germany

The builders of tomorrow
are the LEGO builders
of today. And yesterday!
LEGO is and has always
been the toy of the smart
and creative ones—those
who have always been
one step ahead.

ANDES TELETRANSPORTER

DEL CAMPO NAZCA
SAATCHI & SAATCHI
Media Innovation | Ambient/
Environmental

**Executive Creative
Director** Maxi Itzkoff,
Mariano Serkin
Creative Director
Javier Campopiano
Art Director
Carlos Muller
Copywriter
Patricio del Sante
Designer
Bruno Tortolano,
Juan Pedro Porcaro
Director of Photography
Leandro Filloy
Director Nico & Martin
Editor Cinecolor
Producer Caro Cordini
Agency Producer
Adrian Aspani, Camilo
Rojas, Patricio Martínez
Production Company
Primo Buenos Aires
Account Team
María Lorena Pascual,
Jaime Vidal
Agency Del Campo
Nazca Saatchi & Saatchi
Client Inbev
Country Argentina

The context: Andes is
the number 1 beer in
Mendoza, Argentina
The situation: Men love
to go to the bar to drink
beer and have fun with
friends. The problem: The
girlfriends hate it when
their boyfriends go to the
bar. The solution: Andes
Teletransporter, sound-
proof booth with a sound
panel that re-creates
lots of different environment sounds to get men
out of the bar without
actually leaving home.
Results: More happy men.
Less broken-up couples.

SFX: *Tools clanging throughout.*

VO: *Bill's digging a bottomless pit. It's a job that takes an infinite amount of dedication, but infinity is exactly what Bill has, because Bill has Craftsman hand tools. With Craftsman's lifetime warranty, Bill's tools can last forever, so he can build something that takes forever. And for Bill, that something is a bottomless pit. It has a beginning, kind of a middle, but surely, will not have an end. When concerned loved ones ask Bill how his hole is going, Bill says he's just beginning, because when you're digging a pit with no ending, you're always just beginning. Only quitters will say you can't dig a bottomless pit forever into infinity. And Bill's no quitter.*

TAG: *Craftsman. Trust in your hands.*

BOTTOMLESS PIT
Y&R NEW YORK
Radio | Radio Commercial

Executive Creative Director Ian Reichenthal, Scott Vitrone, Ken Erke
Executive Director, Content Production Nathy Aviram, Lora Schulson
Creative Director Jon Eckman
Copywriter David Canning
Producer Jona Goodman
Agency Y&R New York
Client Craftmans Tools
Country United States

The objective was to encourage people to buy Craftsman hand tools by reminding them that they come with a lifetime warranty and are guaranteed for life. In a crowded hand-tools category, a certain amount of durability is expected, so we needed to up the ante on the types of projects Craftsman hand tools can handle. If Craftsman hand tools are guaranteed for life, even virtually impossible projects—that conceivably take forever—are always within your grasp. Because with Craftsman's lifetime warranty, time is always on your side.

CATS
MOTHER LONDON
LIMITED
Broadcast Craft | Direction

Creative Director
Feh Tarty, Robert Saville,
Mark Waites,
Stephen Butler
Art Director
Freddy Mandy,
Tim McNaughton
Copywriter Freddy
Mandy, Tim McNaughton
Director Adam Berg
Editor Paul Hardcastle
Producer Ben Croker
Production Company
Stink
Agency
Mother London Limited
Client IKEA
Country United Kingdom

Cats are the undisputed champions of comfort. Whether it's your bed, your sofa, or your lap, once they are happy, they settle in. So, to launch IKEA's 2011 catalog and its new brand positioning, "Happy Inside," we decided to conduct an experiment, and put IKEA products to the test. We released 100 felines into IKEA's Wembley store, for real, to see where they went and what furniture made them happy inside. The experiment was manifest in multiple ways, from a behind-the-scenes film to an online competition. "Wembley Cats" was a commercial that brought "Happy Inside" to life featuring the music of Mara Carlyle.

FLOW

BSUR AMSTERDAM
Broadcast Craft | Special Effects

Creative Director Jason Schragger, Paulo Martins
Art Director Rolando Cordova, Rob Phillips
Copywriter Gian Carlo Lanfranco, Ben Tucker
Director Brian Beletic
Producer Corey Bartha
Production Company Smuggler
Account Director Mia Drexl-Schegg
Account Executive Thijs van Dam
Agency BSUR Amsterdam
Client BMW-MINI
Country Netherlands

The global launch of the MINI Countryman the first four-door, four-seat and four-wheel drive MINI. We wanted to demonstrate its versatility creating a film where we show every way you can get from A to B. And getting to B is where the true adventure lies in this film. The MINI splits from one to two to five to 100 and eventually it reaches its destination on the back of a ferry with a lot of small stories along the way. We show its flexibility while staying true to the MINI soul and values: agility and the classical MINI go-kart feeling.

GET TESTED PROJECT
SHALMOR AVNON
AMICHAY/Y&R INTERAC-
TIVE TEL AVIV
Media Innovation | Radio

**Executive Creative
Director** Tzur Golan
Chief Creative Officer
Gideon Amichay
**Executive Client
Director** Adam Polachek
Creative Director
Amit Gal
Art Director
Shirley Bahar
Copywriter Orit Bar-Niv
Production Company
Shapa
Account Supervisor
Shiran Chen Gross
Account Manager
Inbal Stern
**Head of Strategic
Planning** Yoni Lahav
Planning Director
Hila Tamir
Planner Niva Ziv
Agency Shalmor Avnon
Amichay/Y&R Interactive
Tel Aviv
Client Aids Task Force
Country Israel

To mark World AIDS Day
and raise awareness,
all radio stations in the
country launched the
"Get Tested" Project
for the Israel AIDS Task
Force. Live HIV tests were
taken by the country's
leading radio anchors
in the country to promote
the message: Take an
HIV test and know your
status. Get Tested.
Results were given within
half an hour—all of which
were broadcast live as
well (everyone tested
negative). During the
promotion, the public was
invited to the stations
to take their own tests.
Apart from the Live
testing during the entire
day radio stations
broadcasted items,
interviews and spots
underscoring the impor-
tance of HIV testing.

KLEENEX FEELINGS CAMPAIGN
JWT London
Magazine Consumer | Print
Advertisement

Creative Director
Dominick Lynch-
Robinson
Art Director
Christiano Neves
Copywriter
Christiano Neves
Illustrator
Gail Armstrong
Photographer
Jonny Thompson
Director Russell Ramsey
Producer Kevin Noble
Agency JWT London
Client Kimberly-Clark
Country United Kingdom

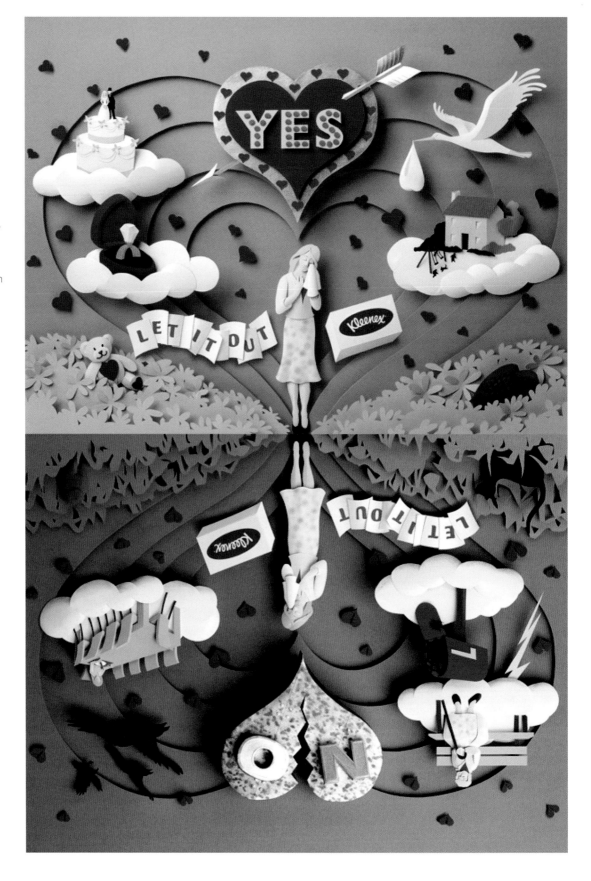

U BY KOTEX
JWT NEW YORK
Broadcast Media | Television
Commercial

Executive Creative Director Sarah Barclay
Creative Director Samira Ansari, Georgina Hofmann, Lisa Topol, Tia Lustig
Art Director Yangjie Wee, Raquel Gimenez
Copywriter Leanne Amann, Bee Reynolds, Kelly Diaz
Director Tim Godsall
Editor Erik Laroi, Mackenzie Cutler, Angela Buck, Gavin Cutler
Director of Production Joe Calabrese, Matthew Anderson, Clair Grupp
Senior Executive Producer Shawn Lacy
Executive Producer Holly Vega
Senior Producer Angela Buck
Production Company Biscuit Filmworks
Postproduction Company 3, Method, Melissa Miller, Angela Lupo
Visual Effects Tom McCullough
Account Supervisor Merrie Harris
Account Manager Gabe Goldberg, Kaitlyn Nolan
Sound Design Andrew Green, JWTwo
Music Amber Music
Agency JWT New York
Client Kimberly-Clark
Country United States

Why is vagina a four-letter word? Why is a female body part unmentionable? When it came to talking about periods or period-related issues, we were stuck in the 1950s. It was time to stop talking in old-school codes and metaphors and be truthful.

**PARALLEL
CONSEQUENCES
CAMPAIGN**
LEO BURNETT HONG
KONG
Magazine Consumer | Print Craft

Creative Director Connie
Lo, Brian Ma, Alfred Wong
Art Director Brian Ma,
Nicky Sun, Kenny Ip
Copywriter Alfred Wong,
Joey Chung, Wen Louie
Designer Nicky Sun
Illustrator
Matt Johnstone
Agency Leo Burnett
Hong Kong
Client Greenpeace
Country China

Cars are a major source
of climate-warming
greenhouse gases. As
the earth gets hotter,
extreme weather events
will become common
and threaten lives around
the world. Every year,
Greenpeace promotes
Car Free Day, trying to
change people's driving
behavior by getting
them to stop driving for
a day. To help people
realize that driving and
climate change go hand
in hand, we used a visual
consisting of parallel tire
tracks. In one, we show
a story of the fun and
merriment driving brings
you. In the other, we show
the death and destruction
caused by the resulting
climate change. These
parallel stories illustrate
the message that "You're
not just driving your car,
you're driving environ-
mental devastation."

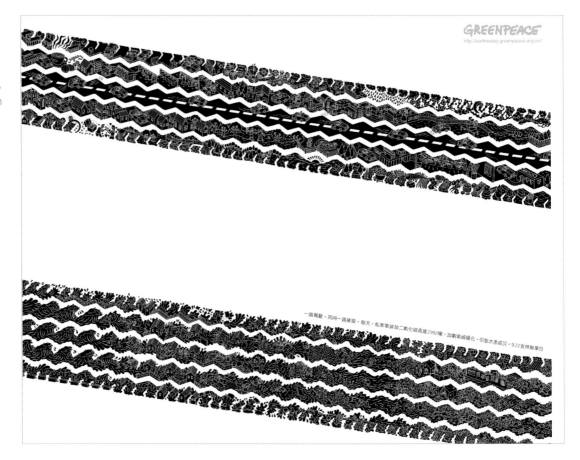

REVOLUTION
AGENCYTWOFIFTEEN
Broadcast Craft | Art Direction

**Executive Creative
Director** Scott Duchon,
John Patroulis
Art Director
Steve Couture, Jeremy
Diessner, Aramis Israel
Copywriter Michael Illick
Director Laurent Ledru
Editor Brett Nicoletti
Producer Alex Spahr
Production Company
Psyop LA
Agency agencytwofifteen
Client Microsoft/Xbox
Country United States

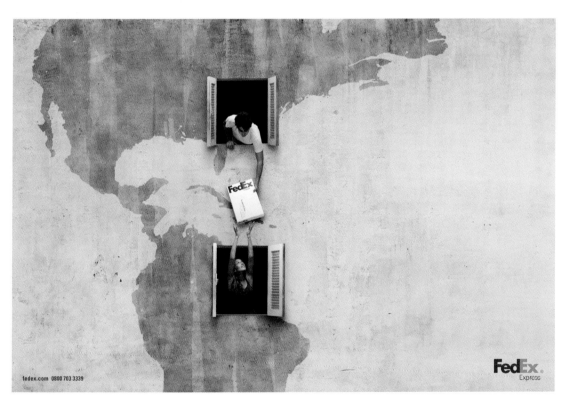

NEIGHBORS/AMERICA
DDB BRASIL
Poster or Billboard | Promotional

Creative Director Sergio
Valente, Renata Florio,
Rodrigo Almeida,
Moacyr Netto
Art Director Max Geraldo
Copywriter Aricio Fortes
Photographer
Manolo Moran
Agency DDB Brasil
Client Fedex/Courier
Services
Country Brazil

**NEVER ENDING
PROJECT**
Y&R NEW YORK
Radio | Radio Commercial

**Executive Creative
Director** Ian Reichenthal,
Scott Vitrone, Ken Erke
**Executive Director,
Content Production**
Nathy Aviram,
Lora Schulson
Creative Director
Jon Eckman
Copywriter
David Canning
Producer Jona Goodman
Agency Y&R New York
Client Craftmans Tools
Country United States

The objective was to
encourage people to buy
Craftsman hand tools by
reminding them that they
come with a lifetime war-
ranty and are guaranteed
for life. In a crowded
hand-tools category, a
certain amount of dura-
bility is expected, so we
needed to up the ante
on the types of projects
Craftsman hand tools
can handle. If Craftsman
hand tools are guaran-
teed for life, even virtually
impossible projects—that
conceivably take forever—
are always within your
grasp. Because with
Craftsman's lifetime
warranty, time is always
on your side.

SFX: *Man breathing heavily and tools clanging throughout.*

VO: *Gary's building a ladder to heaven. It's hard work and it takes a long time, but Gary has Craftsman hand Tools. With Craftsman's lifetime warranty, Gary's tools can last forever. So he can build something that takes forever. Like a ladder to heaven. Step by step, nail-by-nail, eon after eon, Gary puts his tools to the test. And while some might see it as an eternal wake up at dawn horror fest of frustration and infinite sadness, Gary just knows he'll be working the weekend. When Gary's glorious ladder is complete, which will be forever from now, he will notice he read the Ladder to Heaven instruction manual incorrectly, and will have to start all over again. But that's okay; Craftsman hand tools will let Gary start all over again. Forever.*

TAG: *Craftsman. Trust in your hands.*

SFX: *Tools clanging throughout.*

VO: *Tim is building a diorama of the universe. To scale. The job is hard, but Tim's will is strong, because Tim has Craftsman hand tools. With their lifetime warranty, his tools can last forever. So Tim can build something that takes forever. Hence the universe diorama thing, which is nowhere near completion, or ever will be. But as Tim says, it's getting there. Of course it is, Tim. Keep bolting on sections to your seven rings of Saturn; they're only seventy four million miles long each. After that, it's just a simple matter of chipping away at the rest of space, which you'll soon discover is constantly expanding, in every direction, forever. Good thing your Craftsman hand tools will let you keep working, forever.*

TAG: *Craftsman. Trust in your hands.*

THE LAST TEXT
BBDO NEW YORK
Broadcast Media | Non-Broadcast
Commercial

**Executive Creative
Director** Greg Hahn
Chief Creative Officer
David Lubars, Bill Bruce
Art Director
Brandon Mugar
Copywriter Adam Reeves
Director of Photography
Matthew Woolf
Director
Henry-Alex Rubin
Editor Geoff Richmond
Executive Producer
Bob Emerson
Production Company
Smuggler
Account Team
Gayle Weiss, Brandon
Fowler, Kristen Roche
Music Producer
Melissa Chester
Music Rumor Mill (Music
House)
Agency BBDO New York
Client AT&T
Country United States

WikiLeaks updated its current location to
Switzerland, Tuvalu and 712 other locations.
Julian Assange likes this.

SHORT. DIFFERENT.
PRINTED.

SPRINT—VALUE
GOODBY, SILVERSTEIN &
PARTNERS
Broadcast Media | Television
Commercial

Creative Director
Jamie Barrett,
Christian Haas
Art Director Kevin Koller,
Kristin Graham
Copywriter Rus Chao,
Mitchel Gage
Director David Shane
Editor Geoff Hounsell,
Patrick Griffin
Producer Ed Galvez,
Yogi Graham
Production Company
O Positive
Agency Goodby,
Silverstein & Partners
Client Sprint
Country United States

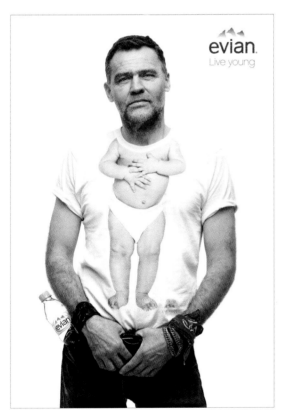

BABY INSIDE
BETC EURO RSCG
Poster or Billboard | Outdoor

Creative Director
Rémi Babinet
Art Director
Agnès Cavard
Copywriter
Valérie Chidlovsky
Photographer
Nathaniel Goldberg
Agency Betc Euro RSCG
Client Evian
Country France

In 2009, Evian chose a single global communications platform based on a high value-added benefit: youth. The "Rollerbabies" campaign with youth at the heart of its communications platform reinstated the baby as spokesman of the brand and the reason for its health value. The campaign generated unprecedented interest on the Web with more than 150 million views and nearly 50,000 posts on blogs. In 2010, Evian continued to build territory through a poster campaign that communicates youth as a universal and inspirational attitude that can be adopted by everyone. A "Live Young" attitude is embodied through a gallery of portraits of men and women, from varied ages and ethnic backgrounds, printed on a Tshirt with a baby's body. Refreshing, accessible and trendy, simple and minimalistic, this campaign describes youth in a universal language that is easily understood whatever one's age, gender or nationality.

GOERTZ 17
SHOELACE BOX
KEMPERTRAUTMANN
GMBH/LOVED GMBH
Collateral | Promotional

Creative Director
Heiko Freyland,
Tim Belser
Copywriter
Heiko Freyland
Designer Tim Belser,
Christiane Eckhardt
Photographer
Peter Ruessmann
Producer
Alexander Kate
Production Company
Cross Marketing GmbH
Agency
Kempertrautmann
GmbH/Loved GmbH
Client Goertz 17 GmbH
Country Germany

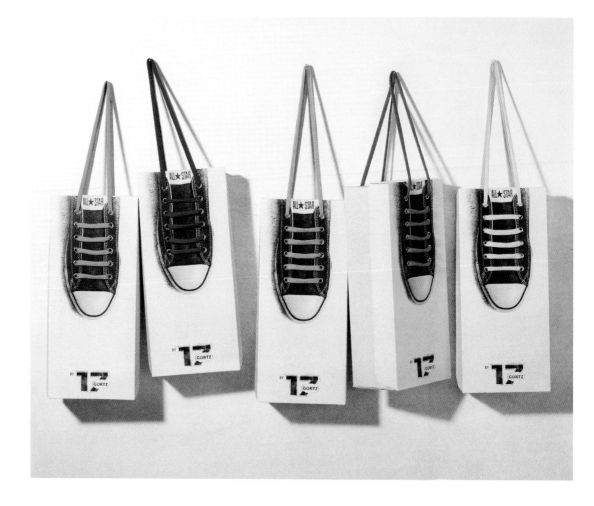

IF YOU LIKE
Y&R NEW YORK
Broadcast Media | Television
Commercial

**Executive Creative
Director** Guillermo Vega,
Ian Reichenthal,
Scott Vitrone
**Executive Director, Con-
tent Production**
Lora Schulson,
Nathy Aviram
Art Director
Guillermo Vega,
Menno Kluin
Copywriter Icaro Doria,
Scott Vitrone,
Ian Reichenthal
Director Bryan Buckley
Editor Carlos Arias
(Final Cut)
Producer Jonna Kelly
Production Company
Hungry Man
Agency Y&R New York
Client VH1
Country United States

The wonderful world
of VH1 is music and
culture in a blender. The
more extreme the artist
becomes, the more popu-
lar they get.

**ACCESSORIES/
MENSWEAR/
WOMENSWEAR**
DDB UK
Newspaper Consumer | Print
Advertisement

Creative Director
Jeremy Craigen
Art Director
Pablo Arellano,
Miguel Gonzalez
Copywriter
Pablo Arellano,
Miguel Gonzalez
Designer Pete Mould,
Oliver Watts
Illustrator Marc Philbert
Photographer
Marc Philbert
Head of Art
Grant Parker
Art Buyer Helen Parker
Retouching
Steve Sanderson,
Greg Chapman,
Andrew Walsh
Artworker
Trevor Slabber,
Gutenberg Networks
Agency DDB UK
Client Harvey Nichols
Country United Kingdom

Communicate that the
most fashionable sale
is now on. Most of our
customers are fashion
lovers but don't neces-
sarily belong to the
fashion elite. They go to
Harvey Nichols to keep
up-to-date with the latest
trends. But because of
the prices of top designer
brands, they don't buy
a single garment. The
sale offers the chance to
briefly leave the sidelines
and enter that luxury
world. Stop window-
shopping. With prices up
to 70% off, customers
have the opportunity to
afford those garments
they've been dreaming of
for months.

Narrator: *The image was still vivid-d-d in his mind. As clearly as if it was happening all over again. Gleaming light fell through tall, multicoloure-d-d-d win-d-d-dows. The chil-d-d-d looke-d-d-d up ... with a look of trepi-d-d-dation an-d-d-d curiosity. Then the man slowly bowe-d-d-d his hea-d-d-d and sai-d-d-d: In the name of the Father, an-d-d-d the Son, an-d-d-d the Holy Ghost I christen you: D-D-Dirk D-D-Dennis D-D-Daniel.*

VO: *Re-experience important moments over and over again as if they were happening now: With the Finepix Real 3D W3 by Fujifilm. Photography in 3D-D-D.*

RELEASE THE HOUNDS
VENABLES BELL & PARTNERS
Broadcast Media | Television Commercial

Creative Director
Paul Venables,
Will McGinness,
Erich Pfeifer
Art Director
Erich Pfeifer
Copywriter
Crockett Jeffers
Designer David Skinner
Director of Photography
John Lindley
Director Bryan Buckley
Editor Rick Russell
Producer Mino Jarjoura
Agency Producer
Emily Moore
Production Company
Hungry Man, Inc.
Visual Effects/ Postproducer
Ari Davis
Visual Effects/ Postproduction
The Mill LA
Lead Flame Phil Crowe
Matte Painter
Shannan Burkley
Colorist
Stefan Sonnenfeld (Co3)
Agency Venables Bell & Partners
Client Audi of America
Country United States

One challenging aspect of the production was trying to getting an actor to rappel down the side of a castle on a rope made of ascots tied together before the sun came up. Once that was in the can, we knew we had the film to tell the story of two men attempting to escape Old Luxury. We understood this task would not be easy, and were it not for our very bold client, our director Bryan Buckley, The Mill, a genius production designer named Skinner and of course, Prison Sax himself, Kenny G, those two inmates would probably still be inside that prison eating Cornish game hens and telling old whaling stories.

SANDWICH
ABBOTT MEAD VICKERS
BBDO
Media Innovation
Non-Broadcast

Agency Abbott Mead
Vickers BBDO
Client Pepsico Walkers
Country
United Kingdom

SAW 3-D MOVIE
PROMOTION
SAATCHI & SAATCHI
DÜSSELDORF
Collateral | Promotional

**Executive Creative
Director** Stephan Zilges
Creative Director
Marco Obermann
Art Director
Jean-Pierre Gregor,
Thomas Demeter
Copywriter
Till Koester,
Philipp Hentges
Producer
Alexandra Beck,
Reiner Hunfeld
Agency
Saatchi & Saatchi
Düsseldorf
Client UFA-Palast Movie
Theatres
Country Germany

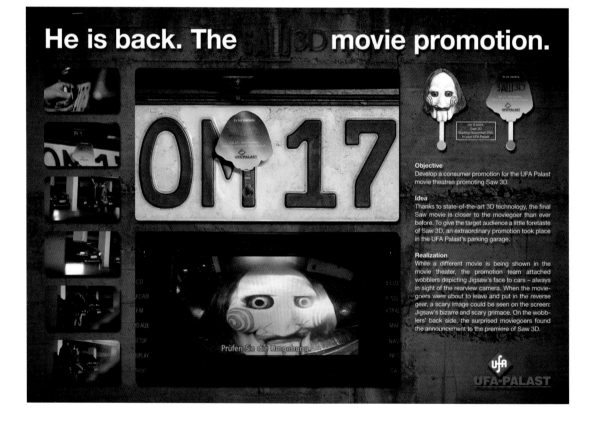

THE COPIED CITY
SCHOLZ & FRIENDS
Media Innovation | Ambient/
Environmental

**Executive Creative
Director** Martin Pross,
Matthias Spaetgens
Creative Director
Robert Krause,
David Fischer,
Philipp Woehler
Art Director
Anke Vera Zink,
Lisa Baur, Carlo Joest
Copywriter Tobias
Deitert, Folke Renken
Designer Dominik Tetzlaff
Agency Producer
Benito Schumacher
Account Manager
Anna Fishman
Agency Scholz & Friends
Client Copy & More
Country Germany

TIME UP, LIVE
OVER–GREY SEAL
SCHOLZ & FRIENDS
Poster or Billboard | Outdoor

**Executive Creative
Director** Martin Pross,
Matthias Spaetgens
Creative Director
Florian Schwalme,
Mathias Rebmann
Art Director
Ksenia Slavcheva,
René Gebhardt,
Bjoern Kernspeckt,
Sebastian Frese
Illustrator
Peppermill Berlin
Account Manager
Christine Scharney,
Susanne Kieck
Agency Scholz & Friends
Client BUND e.V.
Country Germany

TRAMP A BENZ
JUNG VON MATT AG
Integrated

Creative Director
Armin Jochum,
Goetz Ulmer,
Thimoteus Wagner
Art Director
Tilman Gossner
Copywriter
Torben Otten,
Georg Baur
Designer
Daniel Gumbert
Photographer
Stefan Gbureck
Director
Viviane Blumenschein
Producer
Jannik Endemann
Agency
Jung von Matt AG
Client Daimler AG
Country Germany

CAT SITTER
Y&R NEW YORK
Broadcast Media | Television
Commercial

**Executive Creative
Director** Ian Reichenthal,
Scott Vitrone
**Executive Director,
Content Production**
Lora Schulson,
Nathy Aviram
Creative Director
Guillermo Vega, Graham
Lang, Dan Morales,
Icaro Doria
Art Director Dan Treichel
Copywriter
Brandon Henderson
Director Jim Jenkins
Editor Jason MacDonald
(Number Six Edit)
Producer Lora Schulson,
Nathy Aviram
Production Company
O Positive
Agency Y&R New York
Client Land Rover
Country United States

Land Rover drivers expe-
rience a feeling of safety
that drivers of other
vehicles don't. Which
is why we created the
"You'll Feel Safe Inside"
campaign. It humorously
demonstrates the sense
of confidence that a Land
Rover driver feels inside
one of the toughest,
safest, most versatile
vehicles ever made.

GREAT PHOTOS
DDB BRASIL
Magazine Trade | Print
Advertisement

Creative Director
Sergio Valente,
Renata Florio,
Rodrigo Almeida,
Moacyr Netto
Art Director
Rodrigo Bombana
Copywriter
Edson Oda
Photographer
Latin Stock
Agency DDB Brasil
Client Latin Stock
Country Brazil

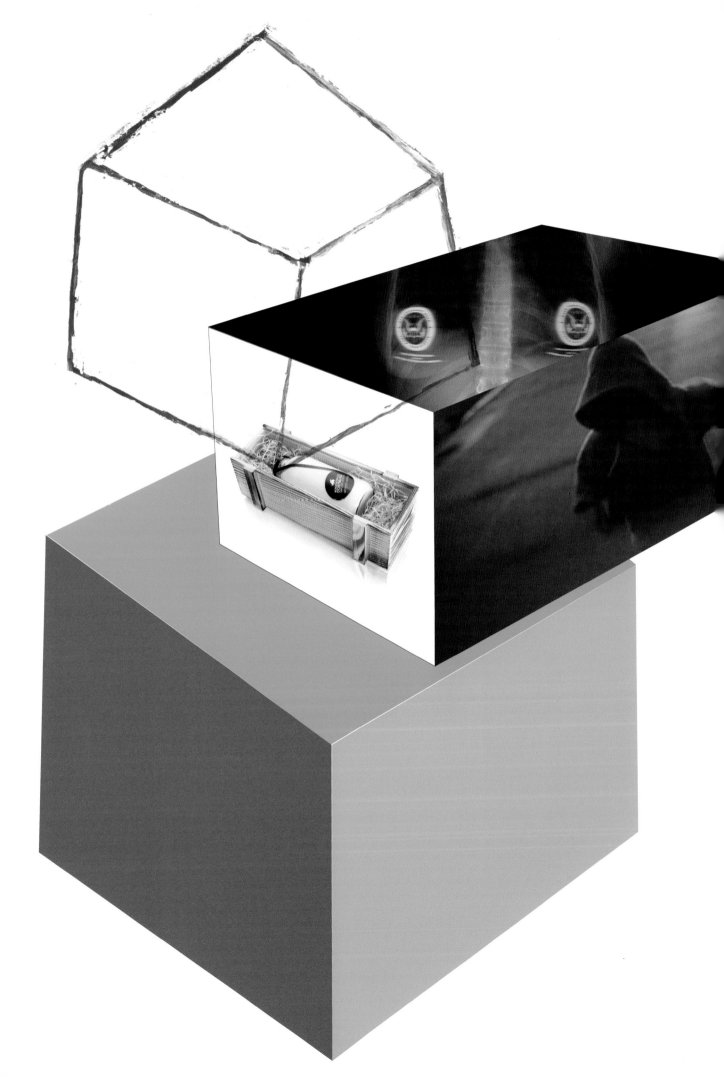

Hybrid: Great work often defies categories. Should it win for TV? Or digital? Is it integrated? Innovative? Or is it a hybrid? Often the answer was... all of the above. Or at least many of the above. So, the hardest thing about judging this year's show was deciding what buckets the work belonged in. That isn't a bad thing. We've all been talking about the changes in our industry for a while and this is proof that those changes aren't just happening, they've already happened. And that good ideas really can come from anywhere. In fact, some of the best work in the show wasn't created by an advertising agency or by advertising people. The industry continues to evolve. The challenge for the Art Directors Club will be to keep up and evolve with it.

—Wayne Best, Founder, Cog NYC, Hybrid Chair

4TH AMENDMENT WEAR—METALLIC WEAR—INK PRINTED UNDERCLOTHES

4TH AMENDMENT WEAR
Collateral | Promotional

Founder Matthew Ryan
Creative Director
Matthew Ryan,
Tim Geoghegan
Art Director
Matthew Ryan
Copywriter
Tim Geoghegan
Designer Matthew Ryan
Illustrator
Matthew Ryan
Photo Editor
Matthew Ryan
Agency
4th Amendment Wear
Client
4th Amendment Wear
Country United States

Now there's a way to protest those intrusive TSA X-ray body scanners without speaking a word. Underclothes printed with the 4th Amendment in Metallic Ink. Let them know they're spying on the privates of a private citizen. The Fourth Amendment to the Constitution of the United States, meant to prevent unwarranted search and seizure, is readable on TSA body scanners. 4th Amendment Wear is specifically designed to broadcast messages to TSA X-ray officers just when they are peeking at your privates. We invented a proprietary metallic ink that displays any designed image or message on the TSA scanner screens, thus creating the only clothing that will display the Fourth Amendment when passed through airport security scans. The clothes are designed as a silent protest against the new reality—being searched to the point where we're basically naked.

Multiple Winner
Designism Cube | Collateral Promotional

Advertising Gold | Collateral Promotional

Design Silver | Corporate/ Promo | Promotional Apparel

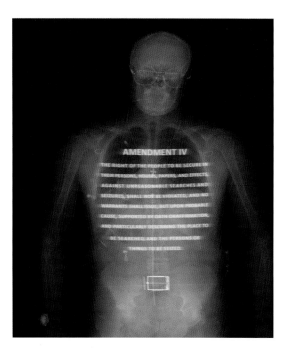

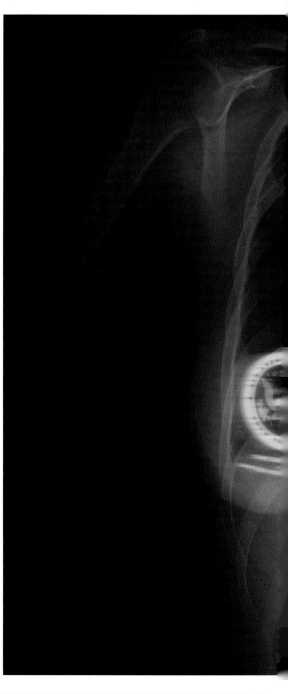

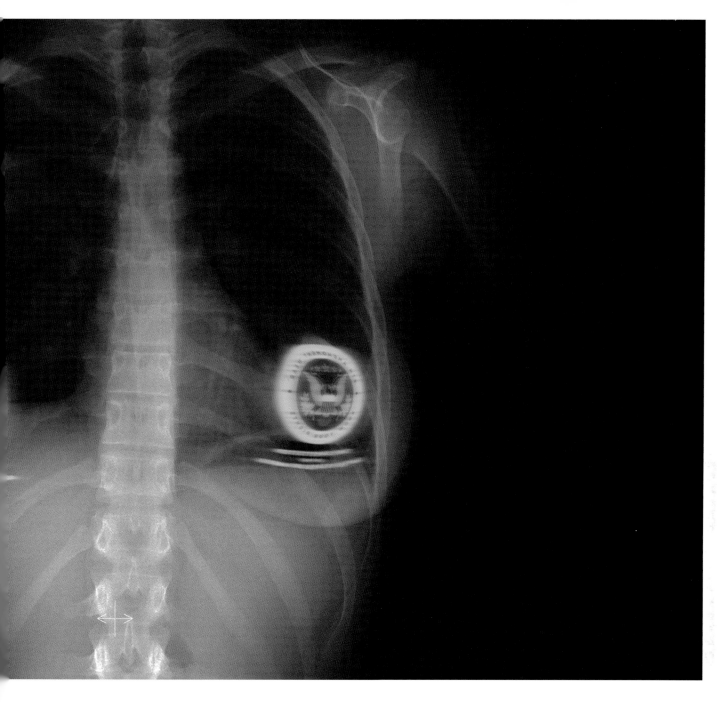

PAY WITH A TWEET
R/GA
Website | E-Commerce Experience

Associate Creative Director Leif Abraham, Christian Behrendt
Agency R/GA
Client Innovative Thunder
Country United States

When we wrote our book Oh My God What Happened and What Should I Do? We had one problem: no one knew who we were or how to find the book. To promote the book, we decided to give it away for free as long as the person tweeted about it. And with this, the idea of "Pay with a Tweet" was born. It's simple-when you pay with a Tweet you tell your friends and followers about the product and this will lead to more people paying with a Tweet. In the first six months more than 400,000 people paid for something with a Tweet. And if you want to sell your goods in exchange for buzz, just go to www.PaywithaTweet.com and fill out the form. Boom.

Multiple Winner
Advertising Silver | Media Innovation
Non-Broadcast Media

Interactive Silver | Website
E-Commerce Experience

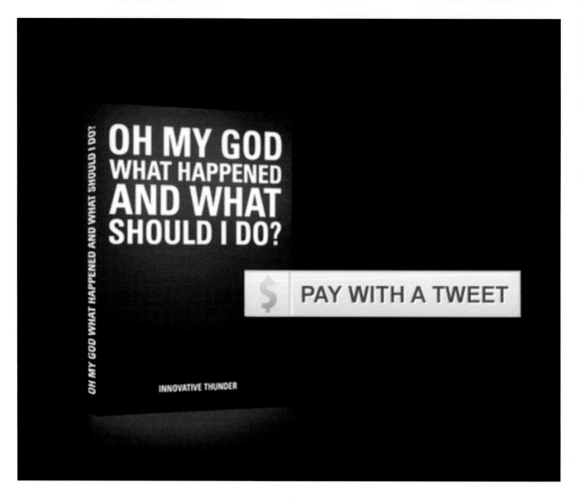

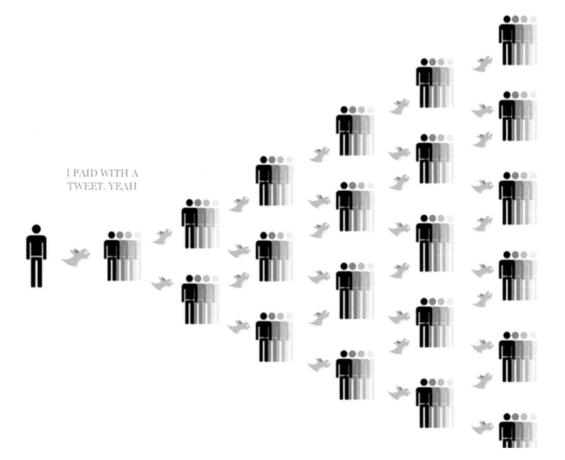

SMELL LIKE A MAN, MAN.
Old Spice+com

RESPONSE CAMPAIGN
WIEDEN+KENNEDY
Online Content | Branded
Short Films

Executive Creative Director Mark Fitzloff, Susan Hoffman
Global Interactive Creative Director Iain Tait
Creative Director Jason Bagley, Eric Baldwin
Art Director Craig Allen, Eric Kallman, Jason Bagley Eric Baldwin
Copywriter Craig Allen, Eric Kallman, Jason Bagley, Eric Baldwin
Programmer Trent Johnson, John Cohoon
Editor Kamp Grizzly
Executive Producer Emily Fincher
Interactive Producer Ann-Marie Harbour
Production Company Don't Act Big
Digital Strategist/ Community Manager Dean McBeth
Digital Strategist Josh Millrod
Interactive Studio Artist Matthew Carroll
Agency Wieden+Kennedy
Client Old Spice
Country United States

"The Man Your Man Could Smell Like" made a big splash in early 2010. But how could this character engage with fans on a more personal level? The result was the "Response" campaign, an experiment in real-time branding in which "The Man Your Man Could Smell Like" recorded 186 personalized YouTube messages over the course of 2 1/2 days. The work would go to record more than 60 millions views, making it one of the fastest growing and most popular interactive campaigns in history.

Multiple Winner
Interactive Black Cube | Online Content | Branded Short Films
Interactive Gold | Online Content Branded Short Films

http://www.thewildernessdowntown.com/container.html

THE WILDERNESS DOWNTOWN
@RADICAL.MEDIA LLC/
MILK+KOBLIN/GOOGLE
CREATIVE LAB
Motion | Music Video

Creative Director
Chris Milk, Aaron Koblin
Art Director
Ben Tricklebank
Copywriter Chris Milk
Director Chris Milk
Editor Livio Sanchez
Producer Jennifer Heath,
Nicole Muniz
Production Company
@radical.media LLC,
B-Reel
Account Director
Thomas Gayno
Agency @radical.media
LLC/Milk+Koblin/Google
Creative Lab
Client Arcade Fire
Country United States

The Wilderness Down-
town is an interactive film
using HTML5 program-
ming and Google Maps
and Streetview to create
startling individualized
videos to the Arcade Fire
song "We Used to Wait."
The complete work can
be viewed at www.TheWil-
dernessDowntown.com.

Multiple Winner
Design Gold | Motion | Music Video

DORTMUND CONCERT MILK
JUNG VON MATT AG
Integrated

Executive Creative Director Sascha Hanke
Creative Director Tobias Grimm, Jens Pfau, Jo Marie Farwick
Art Director Damjan Pita
Copywriter Henning Robert, Jan-Hendrik Scholz
Designer Nicolas Schmidt-Fitzner, Christoph Maeder, Sven Gabriel
Director Silvio Helbig
Editor Tobias Suhm, Niels Muenter
Producer Meike van Meegen, Johannes Bittel, Claudia Westermann
Production Company Markenfilm GmbH & Co. KG, Infected Postproduction GmbH, VCC Agency for Postproduction
PR Agency Mhoch4 GmbH & Co.KG
Agency Jung von Matt AG
Client Dortmund Concert Hall
Country Germany

Set deep in the heart of Germany, Ruhr region, where hardly anyone is interested in classical music, the Dortmund Concert Hall has to offer something pretty unusual to attract new visitors. So we invented a completely new medium, to make our classical music tasty to people: milk. It has been scientifically proven that classical music has a positive effect on cows milk yield. So we played music to them from selected artists of the new season. As a result, the cows produced the very first music world-wide for the taste buds. This special milk was then bottled directly on the farm. There were nine different tastes, depending on the artist the cows listened to. This way even people who otherwise hardly encounter classical music got a taste of the Dortmund Concert Hall, making it the most successful season in their history. Dortmund Concert Hall, Experience music like never before.

Multiple Winner
Advertising Gold | Integrated

SOUR/MIRROR
MASASHI + QANTA +
SAQOOSHA + HIROKI
Media Innovation | Non-Broadcast
Media

Creative Director
Masashi Kawamura
Art Director
Masashi Kawamura
Copywriter
Masashi Kawamura
Director Masashi + Qanta
+ Saqoosha + Hiroki
Producer Qanta Shimizu,
Yasuhito Nakae,
Hisaya Kato
Production Company
Aoi Promotion, AID-DCC,
Katamari
Music SOUR
Programmer Qanta
Shimizu, Saqoosha,
Yuma Murakami
Agency Masashi + Qanta
+ Saqoosha + Hiroki
Client Zenith Co., Ltd.
Country United States,
Japan

This is an interactive
music video for the Japa-
nese band SOUR. The
song "Utsushi Kagami"
(Mirror) explores the
notion that everything
and everyone around you
is a mirror that reflects
who you are. The lyrics
gave us the idea of a
journey to find yourself
through your connections
with people online. By
connecting to Facebook,
Twitter and webcam, the
video will be customized
every time, based on the
viewer's personal data
and social networking
status. In order to engage
fans and allow them
to participate in early
phases, we successfully
raised the production
budget through Kick-
starter, and also allow
Twitter followers of @
SOUR official to auto-
matically become a part
of the color pixels
in the video. The video
itself was an effort of
user participation on the
social network.

Multiple Winner
Advertising Gold | Media Innovation
Non-Broadcast Media

Interactive Gold | Online Content
New Media Innovation

SCHOOL OF VISUAL ARTS
SCHOOL OF THE YEAR

Student: Each year, that table of entries ripe for review always reminds me what an optimistic lot we are. The next table (or the next or the next) might offer that piece, that campaign, that extraordinary approach that reinvents it all. And so it is when searching through work from those still happy to list learning as a daily activity, those bright students intent on reimagining what the answer is; some breathtakingly unabashed use of craft because they're still in love with possibility. Even some risk, taken in the name of "because we can!" Nice ideas, you millennials, you innocent inventors, you forward thinkers. Continue to scare us. Keep proving that you can kick some ass and impress the world. Make us believe in what can be.

—Deb Morrison, Chambers Distinguished Professor of Advertising, University of Oregon, Advertising Jury Member

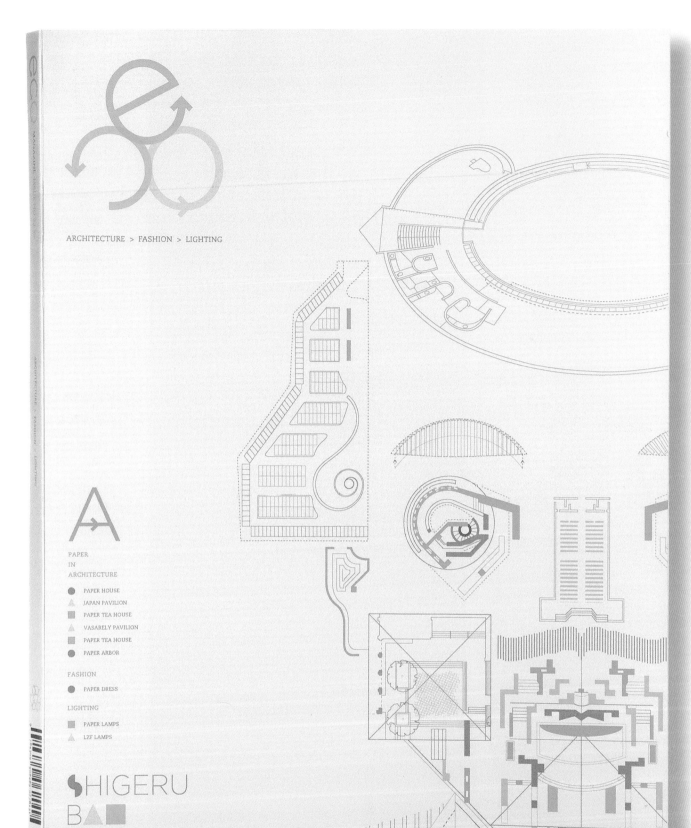

eco

ARCHITECTURE > FASHION > LIGHTING

A

PAPER
IN
ARCHITECTURE

● PAPER HOUSE
▲ JAPAN PAVILION
■ PAPER TEA HOUSE
▲ VASARELY PAVILION
■ PAPER TEA HOUSE
● PAPER ARBOR

FASHION

● PAPER DRESS

LIGHTING

■ PAPER LAMPS
▲ LZF LAMPS

SHIGERU
BAN

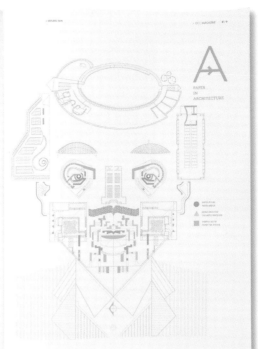

"Paper
is made
out of trees,"
Shigeru Ban says.
"Humans create
architecture
out of trees, so it must
be possible to create
architecture
out of paper."

THE ECO MAGAZINE
SCHOOL OF VISUAL ARTS
Editorial Design | Magazine Full Issue

Designer Jiwon Kim
Illustrator Jiwon Kim
Instructor Julia Hoffmann
School School of
Visual Arts
Country United States

The Eco Magazine is
designed to introduce
designers who worked
on environmental
designs. Contents include
architecture, fashion and
lighting design, all con-
structed using papers.
As papers are products
of trees, the magazine
layouts are designed
based on a tree form.
The underlying concept
is inspired by Shigeru
Ban, who is well known
for paper architectural
design. Shigeru Ban's
portrait is based on
blueprints he created
to create his architec-
tural design. Within the
Paper in Fashion section,
needles and threads
are also included, with
which readers also can
participate in creat-
ing their own patterns
and images. The Paper
in Lighting section is
designed to enable read-
ers to see writings and
images through vellum-
like paper.

MY FAVOURITE ANIMAL
KOOKMIN UNIVERSITY
Motion | Animation

Creative Director
Songeun Lara Lee
Interviewer Carl Rutter
School Kookmin
University
Country Republic
of Korea

This animation series
started as a personal
project for a little girl
named Nadia who loves
horses. She described
her favorite animal and I
then drew it according to
what she said, so that the
creature "grows itself" in
a completely unexpected
way. It is an experiment
based on the concept of
what things might look
like, when basic informa-
tion is described, if there
were absolutely no pre-
conceptions on the part
of the receiver. So a sweet
kitty might resemble an
alien monster. I expanded
the project, interviewing
several more children,
since I found there is an
interesting gap between
imagination and solid
concepts. An important
part of the process was
definitely the interviews.
While the concept was
clear and defined, it
depended on the sponta-
neity and naturalness of
the children. To achieve
this, the children were
interviewed by people
they knew and trusted in
an environment where
they felt comfortable.

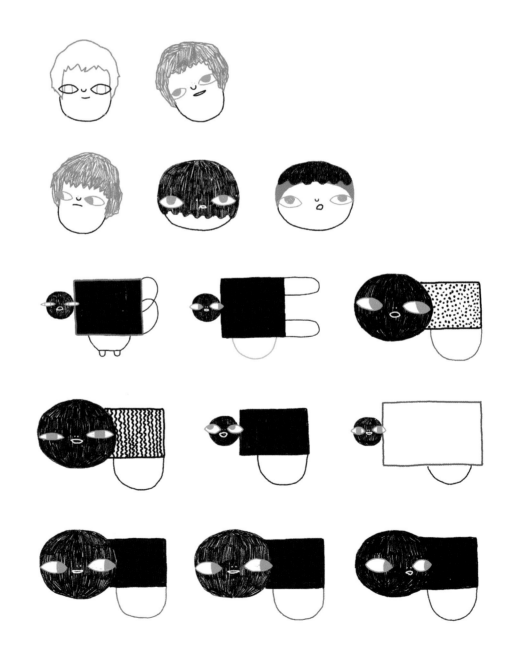

A DAVID CRONENBERG FILM

**THE FLY—TITLE
SEQUENCE**
ART CENTER COLLEGE
OF DESIGN
Motion | Cinematography

Creative Director
Doug Chang
**Assistant Production
Designer** Nicolette Wood
Director Doug Chang
Editor Doug Chang
Instructor Kaan Atilla
School Art Center College
of Design
Country United States

David Cronenberg's 1986
film *The Fly* is my all-time
favorite, childhood thriller.
I wanted to create a
contemporary opening
title sequence in hopes
it would be used if the
film were ever remade
again. My goal was to
capture the essence of
a mutating fly without
using any actual insects.
To achieve this, I gathered
seeds and plants with
textural qualities that
mimic the characteristics
of flies and experimented
with their reactions to
transformative materials
that change states such
as gels, creams, vinegar,
baking soda and even
melted cheese. Shooting
in macro helped me focus
on the subtle movements
and shifts in nature that
help create an atmo-
spheric expression of
the science of the movie.
Finally, I designed the
titles using the typeface,
Klavika, for its legibil-
ity in small sizes while
counterbalancing against
dynamic imagery. Special
thanks to Kaan Atilla and
Nicolette Wood.

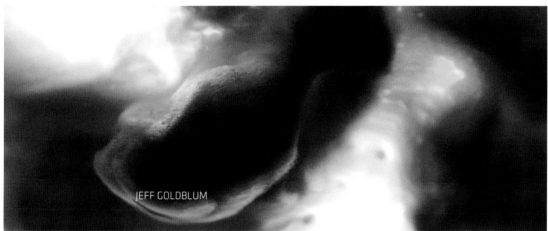

JEFF GOLDBLUM

MUSIC BY
HOWARD SHORE

THE FLY

ART CENTER VIEWBOOK
ART CENTER
COLLEGE OF DESIGN
Book Design | University Press Book

Creative Director
Winnie Li, Simon Johnston
Designer
Eliana Dominguez,
Seth Ferris
Photographer
Steven A. Heller,
Vahé Alaverdian
Director Jered Gold,
Ellie Eisner
Editor Vanessa Silberman
Writer Lara Warren,
Mike Winder
Production Manager
Audrey Krauss
Publisher Department of
Marketing and
Communications
School Art Center
College of Design
Client Art Center College
of Design
Country United States

The Viewbook is Art
Center's primary print
piece used for student
recruitment. We wanted
to create a unique user
experience distinct from
our website. Other objec-
tives included: making
the case for Los Angeles
as an art/design and
education destination;
highlighting the rigorous
nature of study at Art
Center; and showing the
passion and diversity of
our students and alumni
through their voices,
images and work. The
book speaks to prospec-
tive students through a
blend of the institutional
voice and student quotes.
We varied materials,
with coated stock used
for four-color images and
the more formal sections,
and uncoated colored
stocks with one-color
printing to present stu-
dent voices and informal
details about the Los
Angeles region. Exposed
binding and die-cut cover
typography make the
workings of the book, and
by extension the college,
visible. QR codes are
used throughout as a
bridge between print and
digital technologies.

Graphic Design

At Art Center, Graphic Design students learn to infuse words and
images with life and meaning, whether they are creating motion
graphics on the latest digital equipment, or setting type by hand in
Art Center's letterpress shop.

Our program begins with an accelerated education in the formal
principles of design, aesthetics and craftsmanship, after which
students may specialize in a single area of graphic design or continue
to explore the full scope of communication design. This approach is
consistently validated by the awards our students win in many of the
nation's top competitions.

Traditional manual skills, such as hand lettering and drawing, and
sophisticated graphics software are part of the spectrum of tools
available to today's graphic designers. We challenge students to
develop their design solutions while experimenting with a wide range
of media, including product packaging, book and magazine layouts,
interactive communication, 3D graphics, virtual environments and the
creation of graphic identities and branded experiences.

Through Transdisciplinary Studios, often sponsored by corporate
clients, and Designmatters projects on behalf of humanitarian organizations, our students apply their skills to commercial and nonprofit
causes while collaborating with students from other majors. For
example, our students recently designed new ways to engage the
Millennial generation for NASA, through movies, print campaigns,
environmental "interventions" and interactive solutions.

Our Graphic Design education is rounded off with courses on
design history and pop culture, the language of the moving image
and design research.

By learning to create solutions that are innovative, coherent,
artistic and engaging, we prepare students to become leaders in
communication design—whether they plan to join an established
firm or launch a studio of their own.

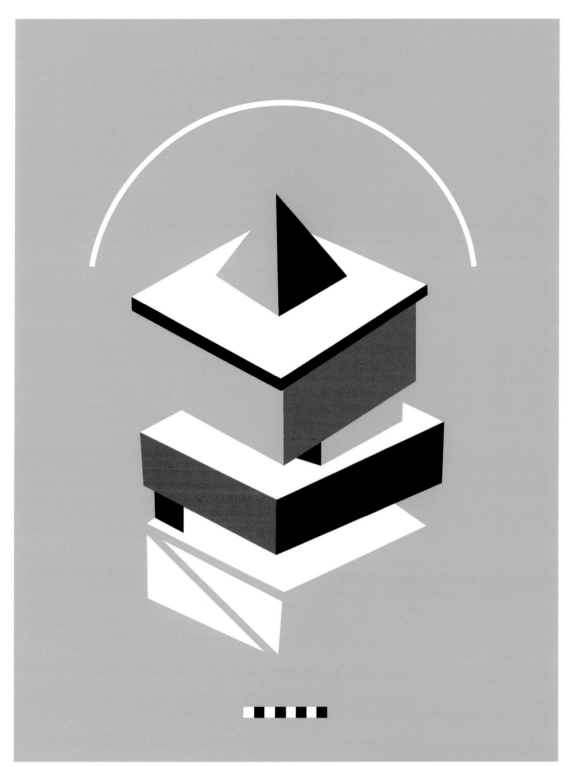

**IN PERSPECTIVE :
TYPOGRAPHY AND
THE THIRD DIMENSION**
KOOKMIN UNIVERSITY
Poster Design | Poster Typography

Creative Director
Songeun Lara Lee
School Kookmin
University
Country Republic of
Korea

This is a typographic experiment which looks at Hangul, the Korean script, from a new perspective. The word spelled out here is "sul-lae-jap-gi," which translates as "playing tag," and it was randomly chosen. Korean is syllable based; here, each syllable is represented as three-dimensional objects or "structures" built in a void. The shapes may look different from different angles, while they can be easily recognized in cross-section or front view. The poster is just one of the outcomes of the research, which resulted in the use of several different media, including pencil drawing, screen printing, and computer graphics. The project may be continued with different words and different scripts.

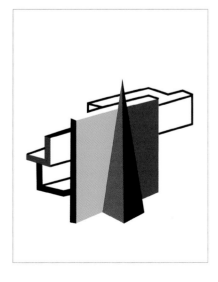

SVA YEARBOOK 2010
SCHOOL OF VISUAL ARTS
Book Design | Image Driven Book

Creative Director
Genevieve Williams
School School of
Visual Arts
Client School of
Visual Arts
Country United States

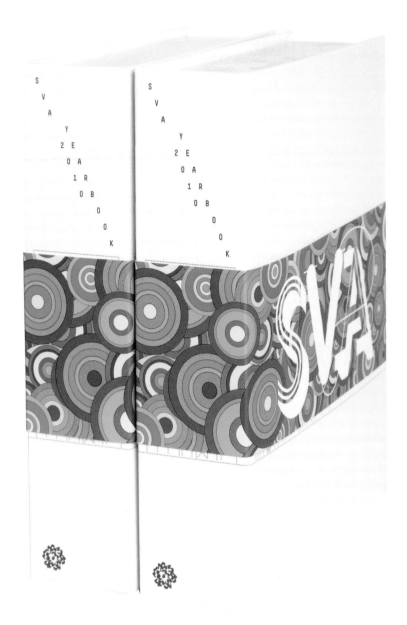

TYPESCAPE
GOLDEN TREE
Book Design | Typography

Creative Director
Namoo Kim
Designer Namoo Kim
Agency Golden Tree
Client GT Press
Country Republic of
Korea

Formal and contextual
experiments of types
based on time and space.

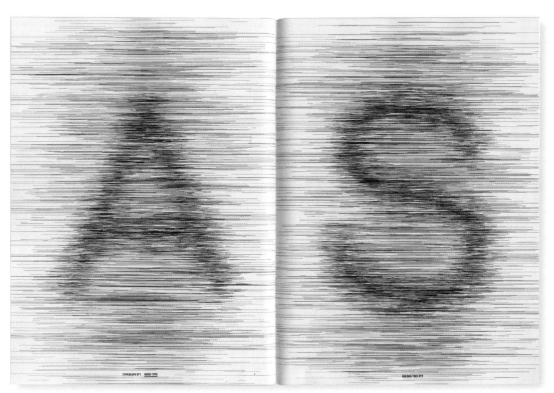

WASHINGTON SQUARE PARK

SCHOOL OF VISUAL ARTS
Branding | Typography Systems

Designer Jiwon Kim
Instructor Paula Scher,
Lisa Kitschenberg
School School of
Visual Arts
Country United States

Motivated by the shapes of the arch and water fountain in Washington Square Park, the Infinity logo is designed with circular and linear shapes in conjunction with three pro-environmental colors used in the typography. People can also participate in creating their own patterns by using the shapes of circle and line on the website or via brochure. The patterns can be applied to roadsides, the park entrance, and the floor of the fountain to vary what people can expect and what event follows the next.

WASHINGTON
SQUARE
PARK

WWF STICKERS
SCHOOL OF VISUAL ARTS
Corporate/Promo | Miscellaneous

Creative Director
Frank Anselmo
Art Director Michael Oh
Copywriter Michael Oh
School School of
Visual Arts
Client WWF
Country United States

THESE STICKERS CONSIST OF ANIMALS MOST COMMONLY SKINNED ALIVE FOR FUR PRODUCTS. WHEN PEELED, A DEMONSTRATION OF THIS ATROCIOUS ACT IS REVEALED.

Millions of animals lose their fur, before losing their lives.   WWF.ORG

HETEROSIS
YORK UNIVERSITY
Motion | Typography

Creative Director
Brian Banton
Designer Brian Banton
Director Brian Banton
Producer Brian Banton
Music Wataridori 2 by
Cornelius
Instructor
David Scadding,
Jan Hadlaw, Paul Sych
School York University
Country Canada

The term *heterosis* refers to the increased size and fecundity of plants that result when different varieties of a species are cross-bred. Recently, the term has been used to describe the benefits of both racial and cultural hybridity in contemporary society. Each character in this kinetic typeface was designed by "blending" two (essentially one-dimensional) vector lines across a spatial plane in order to produce a three-dimensional letter. The result is a set of characters that holds more possibilities than the standard two-dimensional alphabets to which we are accustomed. The letters were constructed from transparent acrylic and transparent elastic. Each character was photographed 60 times at intervals of 6 degrees of rotation in order to produce the motion loop. The typeface serves as a visual metaphor for how hybridity can open up new dimensions and new perspectives.

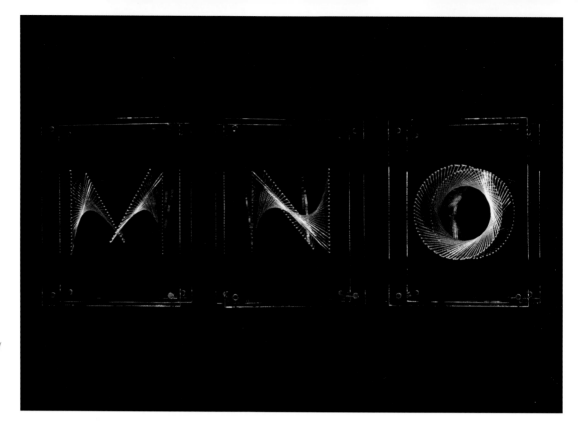

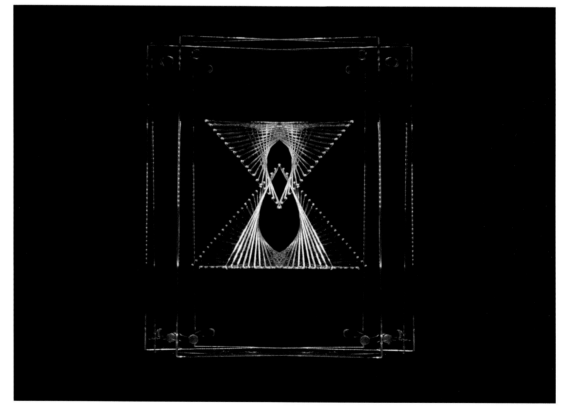

BOOM HA
MUSIC VIDEO
SCHOOL OF VISUAL ARTS
Motion | Music Video

Creative Director
Matt Luckhurst
Art Director
Matt Luckhurst
Designer Matt Luckhurst
Director Matt Luckhurst
Editor Matt Luckhurst
Composer Mike Grimes,
Pete Emes, Mandeep Ubhi
School School of
Visual Arts
Client Smalltown Romeo
Country United States

"Boom Ha" was a song created by Smalltown Romeo and Shad. The video is both satirical and manic, to reflect the need to moves one's mid-section that the beat and accompanying lyrical wit induce. It was illustrated by hand, then scanned and moved around on the computer.

A FEW WARM STONES/ ONDOL

KOOKMIN UNIVERSITY
Book Design | Limited Edition,
Private Press or Special Format Book

Creative Director
Dajeong Kim, Jihae Kim,
Haewon Ahn
Art Director Eunjung Lee,
Jisung Park, Joonki Min
Copywriter Jiyeon Lim,
Suyeon Kim
Designer Yujin Kim,
Jiyoung Lee, Deborah Kim
Illustrator Lara Lee,
Sunmi Yi, Jiwon Huh
Photographer Jaya Kim,
Jiyoung Lee
Director Sukju Lee,
Sangwon Bae,
Geehyun Joo
Editor Yunim Kim,
Chris Ro, Namoo Kim
Producer Jae Hyouk
Sung, Jin Yeol Jung
Photo Editor Ryung Hwa
Rhee, Hyesoo Kim,
Wonju Lee
Publisher Better Days
Institute
School Kookmin
University
Client Better Days
Institute
Country Republic
of Korea

"Ondol/A Few Warm
Stones" is a collaborative
student research project
aspiring to document,
discuss and archive some
of the rich but relatively
unknown world of Korean
graphic design, graphic
design history and typog-
raphy. With a selection
of projects that vary from
academic research to
interviews to just pure fun
and experimentation in
Hangul, this book is the
first of what we hope to
continue as a long-term
series. One of the few
bilingual publications in
this particular subject
area, this project also
aspires to share some
of the stories that are
shaping Korean graphic
design. *Ondol* translated
literally, refers to a set
of warm or hot stones
and to the heating
system warming many
homes here in Korea. It is
the hope of this project
that these metaphori-
cal stones can maintain
warmth for many
generations to come.

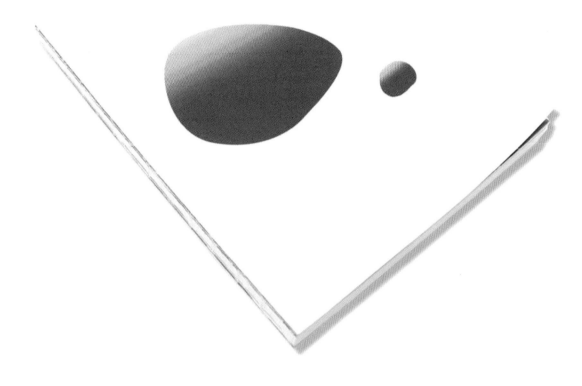

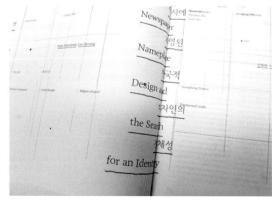

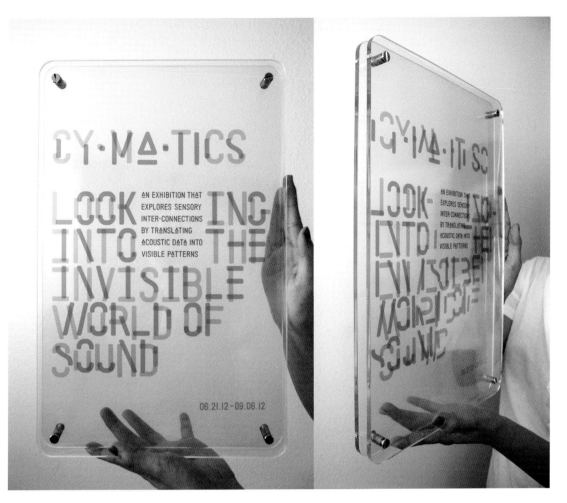

CYMATICS EXHIBITION
ART CENTER COLLEGE
OF DESIGN
Branding | Typography Systems

Art Director Ji Yong
(Raisa) Park
Designer
Ji Yong (Raisa) Park
Multimedia Developer
Ji Yong (Raisa) Park
**Web and Interface De-
signer** JiYong (Raisa) Park
Instructor Brad Bartlett
School Art Center College
of Design
Client Art Center College
of Design
Country United States

Cymatics Exhibition is
a forum to promote
the emerging art of
"sound visualization. The
mechanics of the exhibi-
tion allow each letter
form to be flexible in
its diverse manifestations
of motion in response to
an everyday sensory ele-
ment—sound. Exploring
sensory-interconnections
by translating acoustic
data into visible patterns,
Cymatics Exhibition
transforms the space
into an interactive
exposition, enabling us
to interact with the
invisible. The interactive
dialogue between the
anticipated visitors and
the designed promo-
tions—poster, plaques
and the interactive web-
site—allow us to foretaste
an exciting new art form
at Cymatics Exhibition.

BITTE LAßT DIE BLUMEN LEBEN (PLEASE LET THE FLOWERS LIVE)
UNIVERSITY OF APPLIED SCIENCES DARMSTADT
Book Design | University Press Book

Designer Marijana Babic, Alexander Brade, Rade Matic, Florian Renschke, Michaela Dechert, Linnea Erlich, Patrick Gasselsdorfer, Christoph Kronenberg, Pawel Napiorkowski, Oliver Schendzielorz, Andreas Strack
Tutor Matthias Görlich
Professor Frank Philippin
School University of Applied Sciences Darmstadt
Client University of Applied Science Darmstadt/Faculty of Design
Country Germany

What is good, what is bad, and what is ugly within design? These questions were the starting point of a three-day workshop at the Faculty of Design in Darmstadt. We separated students into three groups ("good, bad and ugly") with each one gathering representative design statements and design rules in the university library. The three groups then presented the collected materials to one an other. This process immediately sparked a discussion, as we found that putting the statements and rules into the given categories was extremely difficult, some even said ethically wrong. Who were we to judge? And who were those designers who in turn, judge and define rules for others? So we decided to display the collected statements, together with various images of flowers, in a single publication without any comment at all. The result is an eclectic compilation that questions rules, doctrines and design education in general.

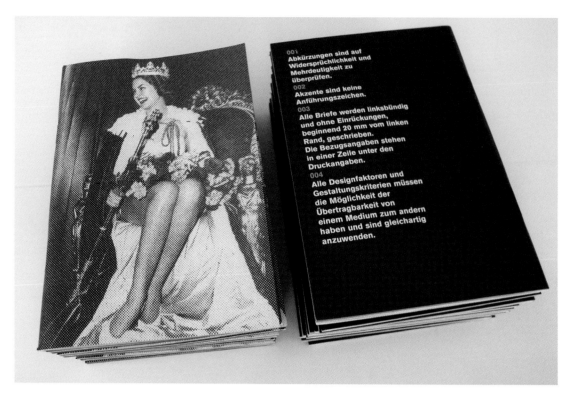

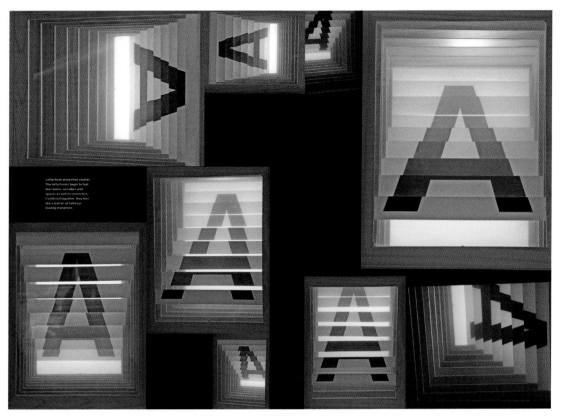

Copywriter Ann Benoit
Designer Ann Benoit
Photographer Ann Benoit
Thesis Advisor
Martin Venezky
School California College of the Arts
Country United States

This book documents my yearlong thesis process, and is heavily rooted in formal study. My work investigates ways of pushing the depth of the page in book design in direct response to the paradigm shift from physical to digital books. In the near future, fewer physical books will be published and the role of the designer will include the development of new strategies to enhance the book—both physical and digital. Viewing the page as a stage that extends past the normal boundaries of the x and y axes is one way of enhancing the reader's interaction with page, text and meaning. Considering a z axis creates new possibilities for text, image and narrative. My processes are deeply rooted in a combination of physical and digital making and the conversation created from this intersection.

82/83

**NEWPAPER
NEWSPAPER**
SCHOOL OF VISUAL ARTS
Editorial Design | Newspaper
Full Issue

Creative Director
Justina Zun-Zun Chang
Art Director
Justina Zun-Zun Chang
Designer Min Jin Shin,
Aaron Perez,
Devin Washburn
Photographer
Justina Zun-Zun Chang,
Charley Fang
Director Paul Sahre
Editor Paul Sahre,
Shawn Hasto
School School of
Visual Arts
Country United States

Newpaper Newspaper was
an in-class assignment I
did with classmates for
Paul Sahre, our instruc-
tor. Since traditional
prints are now facing the
problem of being replaced
by digital media and tools,
Paul asked us to explore
potential possibilities
for the future prints by
redesigning a newspaper.
Based on ideas of creat-
ing new communication
ways with traditional
media, we went for a more
experimental approach.
After the class, I decided
to expand the project into
a real publication with a
formal team. The study
then became *Newpaper
Newspaper*, a conceptual
newspaper about the
possibilities and new values of the new generation
of print.

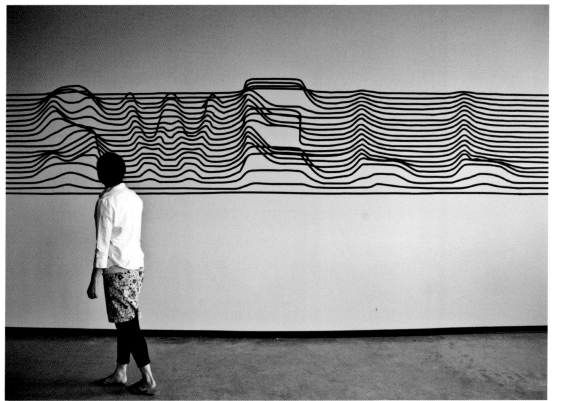

SWELL: A TYPEFACE
YALE UNIVERSITY
Environmental | Gallery/Museum
Exhibit or Installation

Creative Director
YuJune Park
Art Director YuJune Park
Designer YuJune Park
School Yale University
Country United States

This project is twofold: 1) A complete digital open typeface and 2) An installation of the typeface in black tape. My work often sets out to explore the boundary between presence and absence. In this project the letterforms appear concrete from a distance but, upon closer inspection, fragment into abstract lines. In this typeface, the "height" of the letterforms is determined by how often the letter is used in English. It highlights the architecture of words and maps the rhythmic ebb and flow of language. The tape installation is also an exploration between the representations of the digital and analog. The letterforms possess visual qualities reminiscent of the screen and advanced digital modeling programs. The digital is mapped onto the physical by rendering the forms in an everyday material—black tape.

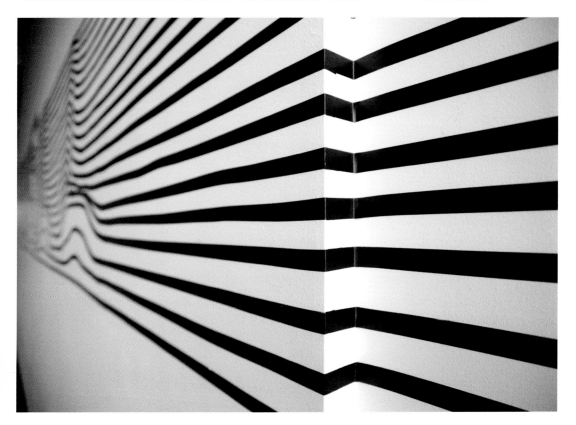

GRAMERCY FLOWER SHOP
SCHOOL OF VISUAL ARTS
Branding | Branding Campaign

Designer Jiwon Kim
Instructor Paula Scher,
Lisa Kitschenberg
School School of
Visual Arts
Country United States

Gramercy Flower Shop's logo is designed with organic shape based on tree and leaf. Distinguishing itself from other shops, windows are decorated with images of their own products and services in a tree form. To inform Gramercy Flower Shop's service to the public, different hues are used to catch one's eyes in different applications.

FLICKER
SAVANNAH COLLEGE OF
ART AND DESIGN
Motion | Direction

Creative Director
Landon Donoho
Art Director
Rebecca Ulmo
Copywriter
Landon Donoho
Designer Renn Brown,
Daniel Reed, Logan Roos
Director Landon Donoho
Editor Katia Simone
Producer Landon
Donoho, Rachel Cansler
School Savannah College
of Art and Design
Country United States

I wanted to create a short
film that built another
world, but focused on a
single character. The idea
was to explore the ideas
of light, hope, darkness
and despair all in a simple
short that would leave the
audience with something
to think about. A lot of
really talented friends
and other students
came together to help
make this happen. Over
two months we rented
a warehouse, built an
underground home out of
wood, chicken wire, two
tons of sod and 2,000
zip ties. Then we rented
a green screen room and
built a practical hill inside
of it with a trapdoor. We
shot in three days, and
then spent plenty of time
in postproduction on
sound, pacing, and VFX.
Thanks for watching.

GRAMPA KEVORKIAN
SAVANNAH COLLEGE OF
ART AND DESIGN
Motion | Animation

Director Claire Almon
School Savannah College
of Art and Design
Country United States

Grampa Kevorkian is
important to me because
it is more than just a
film; it is a personal
keepsake for my family
and me. My objective in
making this animation
was to create imagery
that reflects unfiltered
memories in order to
communicate emotion to
the audience. Instead of
using an anecdotal, linear
narrative to re-create
specific experiences we
shared, I wanted to cut
straight to the heart of
our relationship. This was
achieved by developing a
visual style, and carefully
sequenced imagery that
would best lend itself
to the experience of
remembering. Layering
the imagery with record-
ings of his grandchildren
describing their own
memories, I believe I was
able to share the story of
a special relationship that
audiences of all ages can
relate to.

**THE ILLUSIONIST
TITLE SEQUENCE**
SCHOOL OF VISUAL ARTS
Motion | Title Design

Art Director
Eunji Kim
Professor
Gerald Mark Soto
School
School of Visual Arts
Country United States

The title sequence for
The Illusionist is based
on the movie's storyline
of how chanced occur-
rences are, in fact,
planned beforehand.

ONCE UPON A TIME
THE TYPOGRAPHER
RHODE ISLAND
SCHOOL OF DESIGN
Book Design | Limited Edition,
Private Press or Special Format Book

Creative Director
Kwangyong Lee
Art Director
Kwangyong Lee
Copywriter Jacob Grimm
Director Kwangyong Lee
Producer Krzysztof Lenk
Production Company
That's Design Studio
School Rhode Island
School of Design
Country United States

The production of this
book and poster began
from exploration of effec-
tive typography studying
method for students
who wish to become
designers. First, 50
posters—inspired by the
bread crumbs and pebble
markings from the story
of "Hansel and Gretel"
were developed by taking
photographs in various
sites—streets, forests and
buildings. Each poster
delineates the harmony
of nature, scribbles, and
objects, and is created to
provide historical high
lightings and guidelines in
typography for students.
The book was created
based on research that
aims to deliver infor-
mation effortlessly by
allowing natural interac-
tion of readers with the
book and not forcing a
study. To pursue this, the
book tells 12 familiar children's stories and gives
information introducing
a range of fonts, size and
line spacing.

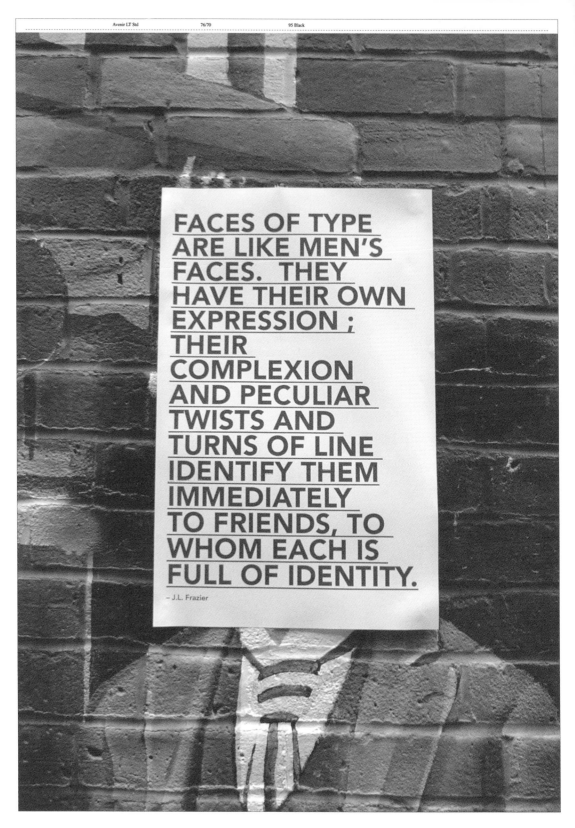

**SAFE AGUA CHILE -
THE BOOK**
ART CENTER COLLEGE
OF DESIGN
Book Design | University Press Book

Art Director Lisa Wagner
Designer Giancarlo Llacar
Creative Team Pei-Jeane
Chen, Evangeline Joo,
Karen Ko, Giancarlo
Llacar, Ping Zhu,
Eric Mathias
Publisher Designmatters
at Art Center
School Art Center College
of Design
Country United States

Safe Agua profiles the
unique social impact
design methodologies
and project solutions
behind the collaboration
between Designmatters
at Art Center College of
Design and Chilean-based
NGO, Un Techo para mi
Pais—an educational
partnership dedicated
to bringing water access
solutions to Chile's
poorest communities. For
more information: www.
designmattersatartcen-
ter.org.

Multiple Winner
Student Design Merit | Motion
Animation

CLEAR WATER COMES FROM NATURE   The Beginning

Cactus Leaves / Once upon a time, Father Felipe Berrios was traveling in
a remote region of Chile. He visited a village where the natives had hardly
any clean water for their daily activities. He was standing by a nearby
river, and noticed that the water was very dirty. As he watched, a native
woman came down to the river to collect water in a bucket. When Father
Felipe saw what she was doing, he warned her that the water was dirty
and that she shouldn't use it for her daily chores. / Calmly, the woman sat
down on the ground with the bucket full of dirty water that she had just
collected. She took a leaf from a cactus that was growing nearby and cut
it open sideways. She turned it inside out, so that she could put her hand
inside, as if the leaf were a glove. / She then dipped her hand, with the
cactus "glove" on, into the water and started to stir in a circular motion.
Suddenly, thanks to the effect of the cactus leaf, all the dirt from the
water started to come together, forming a small ball. Little by little, as
the dirt ball grew larger, the water became completely transparent and
clean. The dirt ball dropped to the bottom of the bucket and the woman
reached down and took it out. She proudly showed the newly clear water
to Father Felipe, and happily carried her full bucket back to the village.

By **Felipe Berrios**, Founder of *Un Techo para Chile*,
as told to **Liliana Becera**, Faculty, Product Design,
Art Center College of Design

ELEPHANTIS
SAVANNAH COLLEGE OF
ART AND DESIGN
Motion | Animation

Director Janie Stamm
School Savannah College
of Art and Design
Country United States

"Elephantis" was truly a
labor of love. The short
was originally created for
an experimental anima-
tion class, but with the
encouragement of friends
and peers, I decided to
continue work on the
project. While in produc-
tion I began to notice
that people would go out
of their way to avoid the
large elephant puppet. I
realized that my film was
exploring the phrase "the
elephant in the room"
and began to take the
elephant into areas that
an elephant would not
normally be found. Even
though I encountered a
few problems—including
strong winds and being
kicked out of a mall—this
film is everything I hoped
it would be, and I could not
be happier with the result.

BUILDING BLOCKS
SAVANNAH COLLEGE OF
ART AND DESIGN
Motion | Animation

Art Director Diem Hoang
Photographer
Alex Nelson
Director Vanessa Chan
School Savannah School
of Art and Design
Country United States

I came up with the idea
for "Building Blocks"
after I watched a great
TED video about hyper-
bolic geometry, using
crochet to physically visualize this form of math.
I wanted a story that
investigated this concept
of employing techniques
not normally thought of
to solve problems. One
of the biggest challenges
was the actual animation
and making sure that the
intentions of the charac-
ters came through since
there was no dialogue.
Thoroughly storyboard-
ing and planning out all
the movement really
helped me work through
the animation process.

**THE IMAGINARIUM OF
DOCTOR PARNASSUS
TITLE SEQUENCE**
SCHOOL OF VISUAL ARTS
Motion | Title Design

Designer Eunji Kim
Instructor Ori Kleiner
School School of
Visual Arts
Country United States

This title sequence
is based on the movie
*The Imaginarium of
Doctor Parnassus* and is
inspired by its beautiful
whimsical graphic.

BEAT STREET
RINGLING COLLEGE
OF ART AND DESIGN
Package Design | Miscellaneous

Designer Jeremy Rojas
Instructor Polly Johnson
School Ringling College of
Art and Design
Country United States

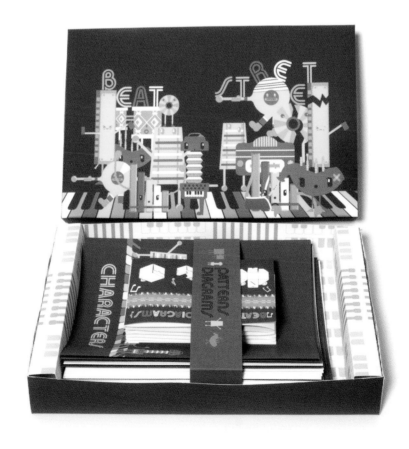

SAFE AGUA CHILE— THE BOOK & MOVIE
ART CENTER COLLEGE OF DESIGN
Motion | Animation

Creative Director
Ming Tai
Art Director James Kim,
Gurkan Erdemli
Designer James Kim,
Ian Abando, Elsa Chang
Director Gurkan Erdemli,
James Kim
Editor James Kim,
Gurkan Erdemli
2-D Animator Nadia Tzuo,
James Kim, Jason Yeh,
Gurkan Erdemli
3-D Animator Micael
Klok, Gurkan Erdemli
Production Company
Designmatters at Art
Center College of Design
Composer Jason Yeh,
James Kim,
Gurkan Erdemli
Narrator Martin Cox
School Art Center
College of Design
Country United States

Safe Agua: The Harry Gota Story is the motion-graphic companion piece for the Safe Agua project, a collaboration between Designmatters at Art Center College of Design and Chilean NGO Un Techo para mi Pais— the educational partnership dedicated to bringing water access solutions to Chile's poorest communities. Following the Safe Agua studio, this motion team set out to develop a short and compelling narrative that would effectively showcase the Safe Agua products, and demonstrate how each is used. By using the main character, Harry Gota, as the driving force of the story, the piece brings humor and lightheartedness to a tale that underscores the real challenges of water access in the *campamentos* of Chile.

Multiple Winner
Student Design Merit | Book
Design | University Press Book

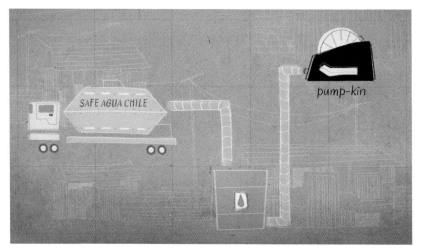

**STARTING IS
EVERYTHING**
SCHOOL OF VISUAL ARTS
Motion | Typography

Creative Director
Camille McMorrow
Instructor
Stefan Sagmeister
School
School of Visual Arts
Country United States

Stefan Sagmeister asked his class at SVA to write something we've learned in our lives in a brief sentence, and then design it. My sentence, "Starting is everything," is an expression of faith in the design process. I have tended to obsess over finding the perfect idea before beginning hands-on, but experience has taught me to just start making things. When I dive into the first steps of a project, momentum takes over, I'm happier, and surprises are revealed. I chose to create the sentence in a big domino run, and then knock it down for the video camera. The challenge I encountered was what you'd expect—dominos are very sensitive to premature collapse. It took two tries of 36 hours each to do the shoot, during which I pondered "Starting is important, but it's nothing without perseverance."

MISS EGGPLANT'S AMERICAN BOYS, BUYING LENIN, ALL ABOUT THE PUBLIC BATH
SCHOOL OF VISUAL ARTS
Cartoon/Comic Book

Art Director Marshall Arisman, Carl Titolo
Illustrator Jungyeon Roh
Publisher School of Visual Arts
School School of Visual Arts
Country United States

WORLD
CHAMPIONSHIP 2010
DANKOOK UNIVERSITY
Poster or Billboard Advertisement

Designer Soonkyu Jang
School Dankook
University
Country
Republic of Korea

In 2010, we experienced
the biggest sports event
in the world. When I saw
last year's FIFA World
Cup 2010, it was my last
chance to enjoy a 24/7
sports event as a univer-
sity student. So I hoped
to enjoy my last chance
during the World Cup. I
started to make a design
with people cheering
during World Cup in front
of city hall. I had designed
each countries players
and coaches from 2009
to 2010. When I finished
designing all the players,
I made a banner showing
all the players, coaches
and countries cheering
and sharing information
before the 2010 event.
And I also made a pack-
age for talking about
prediction formation with
a friend. This design
was used during World
Cup 2010.

ELEPHANT
SCHOOL OF VISUAL ARTS
Miscellaneous

Illustrator Nina Carelli
Faculty Frances Jetter
Illustration/Cartooning
Department Chair
Thomas Woodruff
School
School of Visual Arts
Client
School of Visual Arts
Country United States

THEATER ONLINE GAME FOR XBOX
BADEN-WÜRTTEMBERG COOPERATIVE STATE UNIVERSITY, RAVENSBURG
Games | Hand-Held Game

Creative Director
Peer Draeger, Joschka Wolf
Designer Peer Draeger, Joschka Wolf
School
Baden-Württemberg Cooperative State University, Ravensburg
Country Germany

"Impresario" is a motion-controlled casual game with voice recognition for Xbox 360/Kinect. Players connect via Internet to tell stories through acting in a play on a virtual stage. The objective was to create a somewhat different gaming experience, without relying on typical genres. Using full capabilities of Kinect's motion tracking and voice recognition should ensure a deeply social, creative and expressive gaming experience. Especially challenging was creating a scalable, intuitive system which enables players to gradually discover their abilities to improvise and express themselves. Their movements are captured in real time and projected onto their customized 3-D avatars. The interface is completely gesture-based but nevertheless easy and fun to interact with. A karaoke-esque prompter suggests lines with keywords to recite, icons give stage directions. We used Kinect in a straightforward way without overburdening players. A cuddly visual design of a romantic, medieval world completes the experience. Break a leg!

VOICES FROM THE FIELD
ART CENTER COLLEGE OF DESIGN
Online Content | Non-Broadcast Media

Creative Director
John X. Carey
Art Director
John X. Carey
Copywriter John X. Carey
Editor John X. Carey
Cinematography
Kyle Murphy, Jeremy Jackson, John X. Carey
Producer Elisa Ruffino, Shawn Ruggeiro
Production Company Designmatters at Art Center College
School Art Center College of Design
Client Designmatters/Project Concern International
Country United States

In August 2010, two other film students and I went to Africa to make a film for the non-profit Project Concern International. I went through a lot making this film—it was a difficult first film, and a mesmerizing experience.

ACTIVE TRIBES
ART CENTER COLLEGE
OF DESIGN
Mobile | I-Reader Application
or Book

Designer Zhengxin Xi
Advisor Ricky Wong
Photography Advisor
Scott Liao
Composer Azhrak
School Art Center
College of Design
Client Active Tribes
Country United States

In a technology-driven digital environment, the identity of writers has shifted from someone who dedicates solely to the writing of a book, to someone who engages more actively or strategically with their readers using a variety of online media and who publishes their books without the help of publishing companies. Active Tribes is an exploratory solution addressing the emerging demand in digital writing and publishing. The service features a work-in-progress publishing style that fosters dynamic and interest-focused conversations between the writer and their readers, and bases the social mechanics on a credit system that encourages participatory and productive reading behaviors. It facilitates publishing of multi media and interactive content tailored to tablet devices and is capable of transforming the reading and note-taking patterns into visual forms to give the writer an immediate evaluation of the writings.

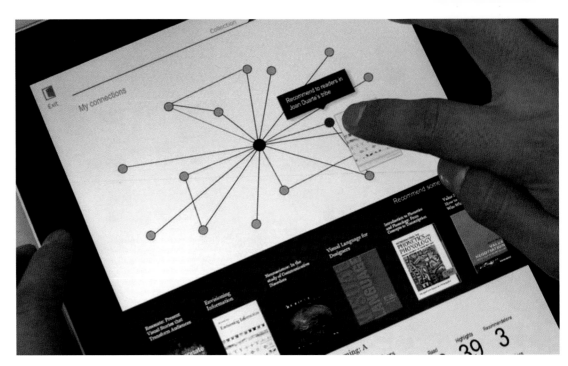

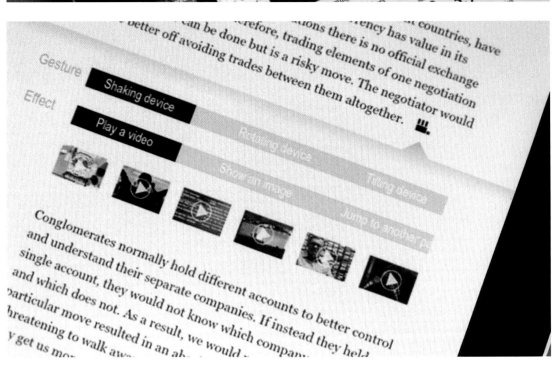

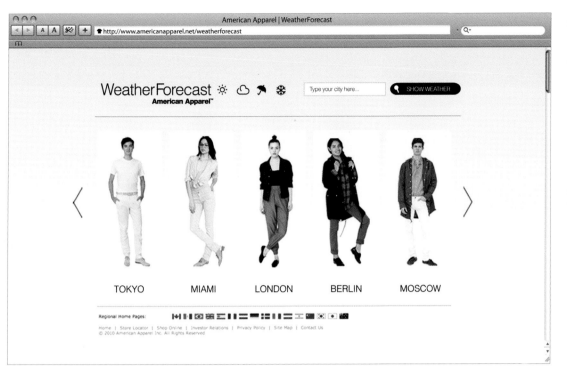

**AMERICAN APPAREL
WEATHER FORECAST**
MIAMI AD SCHOOL
EUROPE
Website | Campaign Site

Creative Director
Niklas Frings-Rupp
Art Director
Ilya Malyanov
Copywriter
Morgan Perrine
School
Miami Ad School Europe
Client American Apparel
Country Germany

NIKE+ GLOBERUNNER
MIAMI AD SCHOOL
EUROPE
Beyond The Web

Creative Director
Alvaro Sotomayor
Art Director
Andreas Rasmussen
Copywriter Pranay Suri
School
Miami Ad School Europe
Client Nike+
Country Germany

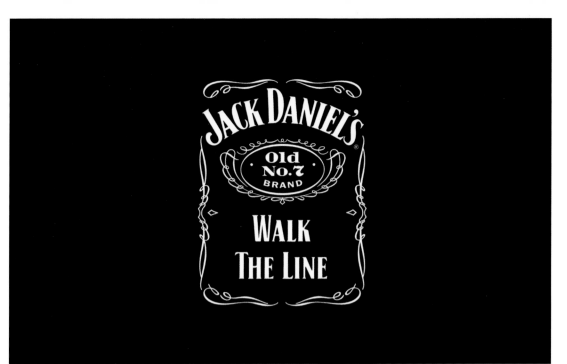

**JACK DANIEL'S
WALK THE LINE**
SCHOOL OF VISUAL ARTS
Mobile | Mobile Phone Application

Creative Director
Frank Anselmo
Art Director
Mark Forsman,
Vinny Garbellano
Copywriter Mark Forsman,
Vinny Garbellano
School School of
Visual Arts
Client Jack Daniel's
Country United States

THE MEMORYCLOUD
MIAMI AD SCHOOL
EUROPE
Social Networks | Social Network
Innovation

Creative Director
Niklas Frings-Rupp
Art Director Zoe Sys
Vogelius, Thomas Ilum
Copywriter
Duncan Munge
School Miami Ad School
Europe
Client Hallmark
Country Germany

ALWAYS FIRST
MIAMI AD SCHOOL
EUROPE
Poster or Billboard | Outdoor

Creative Director
Menno Kluin,
Graeme Hall
Art Director
Zoe Sys Vogelius,
Thomas Ilum
Copywriter Thomas Ilum,
Zoe Sys Vogelius
Director
Niklas Frings-Rupp
School Miami Ad
School Europe
Client FedEx
Country Germany

**GET OUT AND
EXPERIENCE
YOUR AMERICA**
UNIVERSITY OF
NORTH TEXAS
Poster or Billboard | Transit

Art Director Ryan Smith
Copywriter Ryan Smith
Photographer
Ryan Smith
School University
of North Texas
Client National Park
Service
Country United States

This campaign was
designed to encourage
people to get outside
and experience their
America. It's easy to like
the idea of being outside,
but with so many indoor
attractions, one's inner
adventurer is often
neglected. These large-
format posters would be
placed in airports and
other mass-transit areas
to encourage passersby
to consider a routine-
altering trip.

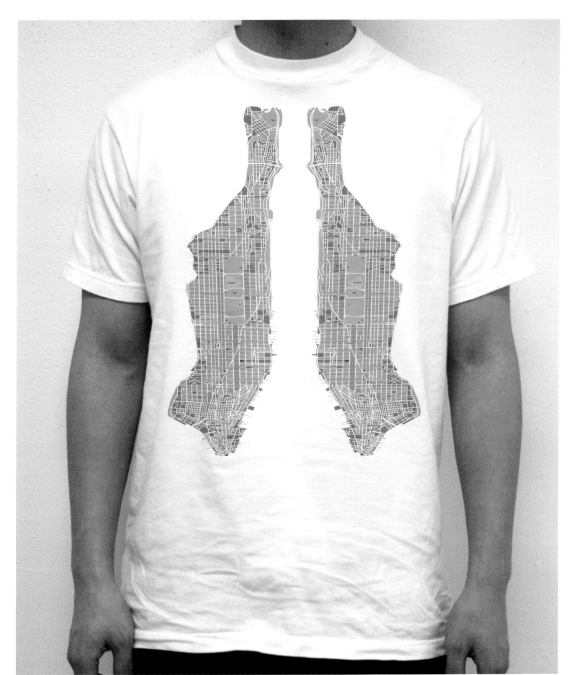

**MILLION TREES LUNG
MAP SHIRTS**
SCHOOL OF VISUAL ARTS
Collateral | Promotional

Creative Director
Frank Anselmo
Art Director Yoshie Asei,
Frankmy Olivo
Copywriter
Carlos Ochoa, Pablo Velez
Designer Yoshie Asei,
Frankmy Olivo
School
School of Visual Arts
Client Million Trees
Country United States

100 TREES REMOVE
1,000 LBS OF POLLUTANTS
FROM THE AIR ANNUALLY.

milliontrees**NYC**.org

COMING SOON
SCHOOL OF VISUAL ARTS
Poster or Billboard | Electronic

Art Director Jang Cho
Copywriter Jang Cho
Instructor Jack Mariucci,
Bob MacKall
School School of
Visual Arts
Client The Weather
Channel
Country United States

The electronic display
billboard plays the
weather forecast six
hours beforehand as a
video clip of the sky.

**THE MONEY ROLL
PROJECT**
MIAMI AD SCHOOL
EUROPE
Collateral | Unconventional /
Guerrilla

Creative Director
Niklas Frings-Rupp
Art Director
Zoe Sys Vogelius,
Thomas Ilum
Copywriter
Duncan Munge
School
Miami Ad School Europe
Client Nashua
Country Germany

SEE WHO YOU SAVE
MIAMI AD SCHOOL
EUROPE
Poster or Billboard | Electronic

Creative Director
Niklas Frings-Rupp
Art Director
Andreas Rasmussen
Copywriter Pranay Suri
School Miami Ad School
Europe
Client WWF
Country Germany

Student Brief: The global competition was open to students enrolled in graduate, undergraduate and continuing education programs in advertising, graphic design, photography, illustration and new media. This year's brief was for gourmet snack foods manufacturer Popcorn, Indiana, who challenged students to develop a marketing plan to make their popcorn products into household favorites. The ADC would like to congratulate all of the winners of the Student Brief. Creative thinking and risk taking are a tradition for the ADC and this year students proved to be wildly forward thinking with their entries.

SURPRISINGLY
HEALTHY
RIDICULOUSLY
TASTY

*We can neither confirm nor deny the use of the Flavor Fairy in the making of this product.

POPCORN FLAVOR FAIRY
MIAMI AD SCHOOL EUROPE
Advertising | Popcorn, Indiana Brief
Integrated

Art Director Andrea Aguilar, Andrew Bernstein
School Miami Ad School Europe
Client Popcorn, Indiana
Country Spain

Our objective was to create something that would transmit the jovial spirit we took from the brief, stick in people's minds, make them laugh, and explain how Popcorn, Indiana managed to achieve a delicious and healthy snacking experience. A seemingly impossible achievement deserves an equally impossible solution, so we created the Flavor Fairy and we came up with simple situations where the Flavor Fairy appears to champion his involvement in the making of the popcorn while informing the consumer about the product in an amusing manner. What helped us achieve our goal above all, was having as much fun producing the campaign as we wanted the audience to see.

ADD FLAVOR TO IT!

COLLEGE FOR
CREATIVE STUDIES

Interactive | Popcorn, Indiana Brief
Online Content

**Executive Creative
Director/Department
Chair** Mark Zapico
Creative Director
Danielle Cantin
Art Director Brandi Keeler
Copywriter Brandi Keeler
Designer Brandi Keeler
Editor Brandi Keeler
Music Doc Ellingsworth,
Jay North
School College for
Creative Studies
Client Popcorn, Indiana
Country United States

Seeking to build aware-
ness and desire for their
gourmet popcorn, Pop-
corn, Indiana describes
their target audience
(and biggest snackers)
as urban adults between
the ages of 18 and 24,
which leads to the ques-
tion, How do we make
Popcorn, Indiana relevant
to these heavy snackers?
We discovered that due
to the economy, young
adults are replacing going
to movies and clubs with
at-home movie nights
and house parties. "Add
Flavor to It!" is an idea to
turn fun nights at home
into poppin; parties with
Popcorn, Indiana! Launch-
ing with an original song
and music video, "Add Flavor to It!" introduces the
17 flavors in a fun and wild
way, and highlights each
with its own dance moves.
The spot went viral across
platforms and on social
content and networking
sites (YouTube, Facebook,
Twitter, Tosh.0, etc.)
showing viewers how
Popcorn, Indiana fans like
to get down and add fla-
vor to their party playlists.

WELCOME TO POPCORN, INDIANA
ACADEMY OF ART UNIVERSITY
Advertising | Popcorn, Indiana Brief
Integrated

Art Director Steve Lauria, Raza Ali Durrani
Copywriter Zack Browne
School Academy of Art University
Client Popcorn, Indiana
Country United States

"Welcome to Popcorn, Indiana" is an integrated campaign that promotes the idea that Popcorn, Indiana isn't a brand, it's a place where anything is possible. The campaign starts with teasers like air ads and outdoor boards that lead people to Facebook. By changing your current location to Popcorn, Indiana, a new world opens up. You become an official resident of Popcorn, Indiana, where membership has its privileges. We created interactive outdoor boards that serve as checkpoints. Current residents of Popcorn, Indiana get access to instant prizes and deals. Using social media, we gave our residents a chance to tell us what their wildest dreams are. We held elections where citizens could vote for their favorite community contribution. Those elected are featured on limited-edition packaging as "The Pride of Popcorn, Indiana." This campaign takes a unique product and builds a community around it. Welcome to Popcorn, Indiana.

DISGUISE
SCHOOL OF VISUAL ARTS
Advertising | Popcorn, Indiana Brief
Poster or Billboard

Creative Director
Frank Anselmo
Art Director Yong Jun Lee,
Sanggun Park
Copywriter Yong Jun Lee,
Sanggun Park
Designer Su Hyun Chung
School School of
Visual Arts
Client Popcorn, Indiana
Country United States

NATURALLY IRRESISTIBLE
SCHOOL OF VISUAL ARTS
Advertising | Popcorn, Indiana Brief
Broadcast

Creative Director
Frank Anselmo
Art Director Anna Kim,
Min Yeong Park
Copywriter Haehyun
Park, Hongjoon Jang
School School of
Visual Arts
Client Popcorn, Indiana
Country United States

LION
SCHOOL OF VISUAL ARTS
Advertising | Popcorn, Indiana Brief
Broadcast

Creative Director
Frank Anselmo
Art Director
Aksana Berdnikova,
Juan Pablo Gomez
Copywriter
Aksana Berdnikova,
Juan Pablo Gomez
School
School of Visual Arts
Client Popcorn, Indiana
Country United States

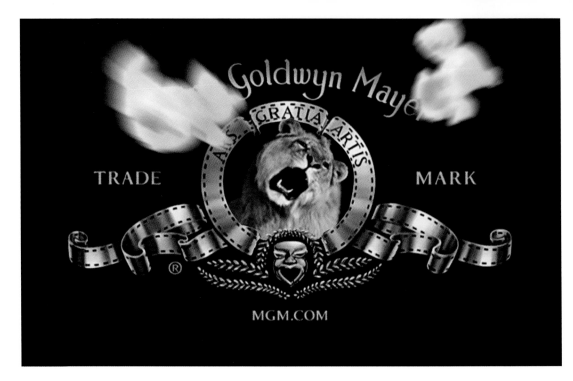

PERFUME
SCHOOL OF VISUAL ARTS
Advertising | Popcorn, Indiana Brief
Collateral

Creative Director
Frank Anselmo
Art Director
Jarwon Jamie Shin
Copywriter
Bryan Hyung Ahn,
Ruben Antonio Perez
School School of
Visual Arts
Client Popcorn, Indiana
Country United States

A bikini friendly snack

BODY BY CHIP'INS
FASHION INSTITUTE
OF TECHNOLOGY
Advertising | Popcorn, Indiana Brief
Poster or Billboard

Art Director Nicole Jordan
School Fashion Institute
of Technology
Client Popcorn, Indiana
Country United States

The purpose of this print
campaign for Popcorn,
Indiana's Chip'ins is to
show consumers how
wholesome and delicious
the product is. With so
many snacks on the mar-
ket today, the challenge
is to differentiate Chip'ins
from all other products,
including healthy yet
bland snacks, and snacks
with artificial ingredients.
In order to solve this problem, the physical Chip'ins
are used to create simple
imagery to establish the
product as a great choice
for the target consumer
of women interested in
maintaining a healthy
lifestyle. Showing the distinctive shape of Chip'ins
and creating visuals associated with a healthy body
and life reinforces the
product as a nutritious
option for snacking.

MAKES MOVIES HEALTHIER
SCHOOL OF VISUAL ARTS
Advertising | Popcorn, Indiana Brief
Poster or Billboard

Creative Director
Frank Anselmo
Art Director
Jae Sung Jung, Bomi Jo,
Dahee Song
Copywriter
Jae Sung Jung, Bomi Jo,
Dahee Song
School
School of Visual Arts
Client Popcorn, Indiana
Country United States

PUZZLE
SCHOOL OF VISUAL ARTS
Advertising | Popcorn, Indiana Brief
Poster or Billboard

Creative Director
Frank Anselmo
Art Director Stella Hye
Jung Na, Ian Liu
Copywriter Stella Hye
Jung Na, Ian Liu
School
School of Visual Arts
Client Popcorn, Indiana
Country United States

SHARE BAG
MIAMI AD SCHOOL
BROOKLYN
Design | Popcorn, Indiana Brief
Packaging

Art Director Ricky Anolik,
Andrew Tobin
Copywriter
Jacklyn Shelton
School Miami Ad School
Brooklyn
Client Popcorn, Indiana
Country United States

We wanted to make Popcorn, Indiana, stand out among popcorn brands as a fun, social, snacking brand. The playful design of the share bag, combined with the different "share sayings," on each bag, remind users to have fun with their snacking and position Popcorn, Indiana, as the brand to do so.

Popcorn, Indiana wanted to know, "How can we make our products synonymous with insanely delicious snacking." The campaign, "Tips for Maximum Enjoyment," reinforces the product's deliciousness. Television ads show situations that snackers may encounter while enjoying Popcorn, Indiana in theatres and other locations. Magazine ads give tips such as grow a beard to catch scrumptious tidbits for later or keep a decoy around to thwart others from stealing your delicious popcorn. Outdoor and out-of-home ads remind viewers that feeding Popcorn, Indiana to birds may cause them to swoop in and snatch it from your hands. Facebook fans are put into these situations to see how they react. React correctly and you may receive an awesome bird suit. React wrongly and you may find yourself with an empty bag. Ultimately, Popcorn, Indiana's, "Tips for Maximum Enjoyment," lets their audience know just how insanely delicious these snacks truly are.

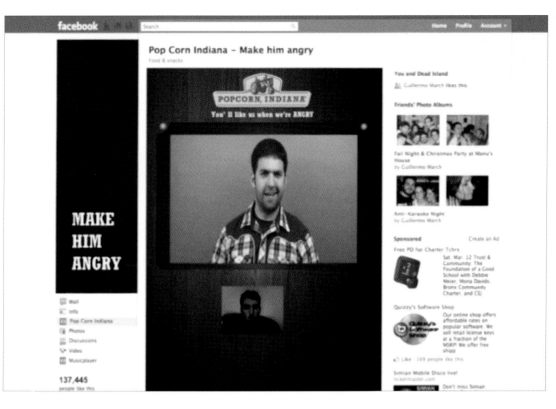

YOU'LL LOVE US WHEN WE'RE ANGRY
MIAMI AD SCHOOL BROOKLYN
Interactive | Popcorn, Indiana Brief
Online Content

Art Director
Jesus Reig Verdú,
Dominic Mattachione
Copywriter Duncan
Munge, Michael Ziman
School Miami Ad School
Brooklyn
Client Popcorn, Indiana
Country United States

People slinging insults at their computers. Subversion via social media platforms. Getting under people's skin. This is how the digital generation will receive some free popcorn. All in good fun.

POP!—WHAT EVERYONE WANTS
HTL1 BAU UND DESIGN, DEPARTMENT FOR ART AND DESIGN
Advertising | Popcorn, Indiana Brief
Poster or Billboard

Creative Director
Dominik Essletzbichler
Art Director
Dominik Essletzbichler,
Wolfgang Leitner
Copywriter
Dominik Essletzbichler,
Wolfgang Leitner
Illustrator
Wolfgang Leitner
School HTL1 Bau und
Design, Department for
Art and Design
Client Popcorn, Indiana
Country Austria

For this years, brief on
Popcorn, Indiana we were
excited about giving the
brand a pop feeling. On
the one hand we wanted
a subject dealing with
pop culture, idols and
stars. On the other hand
we were crazy about the
idea of showing the, "way
of a single corn". We did
it both ways and created
a campaign for the brand
itself without referring to
a product and a cam-
paign for different flavors.
Important was to trans-
port this certain feeling of
desire—the desire to be a
star. We kept it as simple
as possible: "I wanna be
a pop star". The product
had to be iconic and we
could not think of anyone
better to transport the
message than Marilyn
Monroe. With Bruce Lee
and John Wayne we found
two further idols, giving
the product the touch of
myth we were heading for.

That's what everyone wants.

NETFLIX
SCHOOL OF VISUAL ARTS
Advertising | Popcorn, Indiana Brief
Collateral

Creative Director
Frank Anselmo
Art Director Bryan Hyung
Ahn, Ruben Antonio Perez
Copywriter Amanda
Askea, Bona Jeong
Designer Jarwon Jamie
Shin, Hanso Lee
School
School of Visual Arts
Client Popcorn, Indiana
Country United States

Popcorn, Indiana bags
are printed on the
backs of Netflix DVD
envelops to communicate
how perfectly movies
go with popcorn.

90th Cube Project:

The Art Directors Club launched the celebration of its 90th year by inviting top creatives to give their own interpretation of the iconic ADC Cube image and bring their own vision to what ADC means today. The project was open exclusively to post–2000 winners of the ADC Cube award, who represent the best and brightest in international creative and design. This group of approximately 600 visionaries from around the world was contacted and granted access to a special ADC 90th Annual Awards Call for Entries website containing templates to follow. The ADC Awards Committee then selected five submissions to represent the upcoming awards season. In addition, 90 entries were reproduced and appeared in a special exhibition at the ADC 90th Annual Awards launch party at the ADC Gallery. ADC gratefully acknowledges René Clément, Marc Cozza, Paul Davis, Jeong Eun (Elle) Kim, Masashi Kawamura, and NOSIGNER, and thanks them for their tremendous support of the 90th Annual Awards.

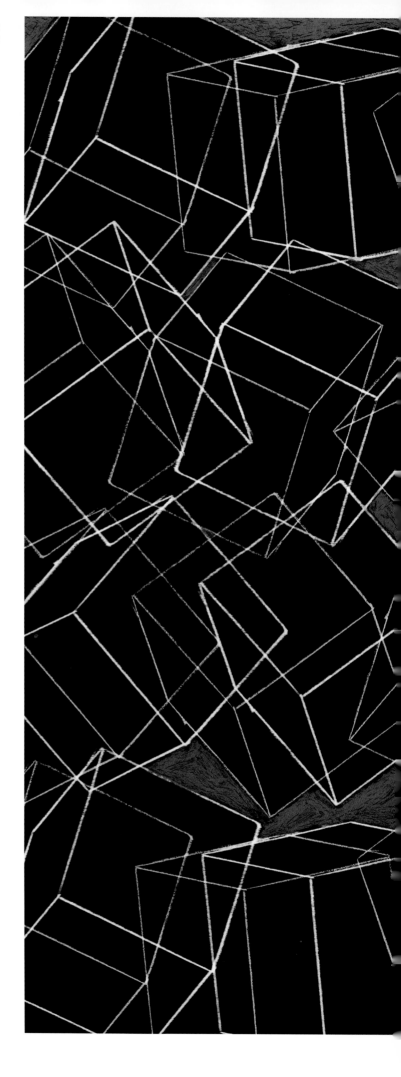

PAUL DAVIS
CFE Design
Title Illustrator
Country United States

MARC COZZA
CFE Design
Title Creative Director
Company
CO Design Agents
Website
www.co-hq.com
Country United States

RÉNE CLÉMENT
CFE Design
Title Art Director
Company Paprika
Website
www.paprika.com
Country Canada

NOSIGNER
Gala Design
Website
www.nosigner.com
Country Japan

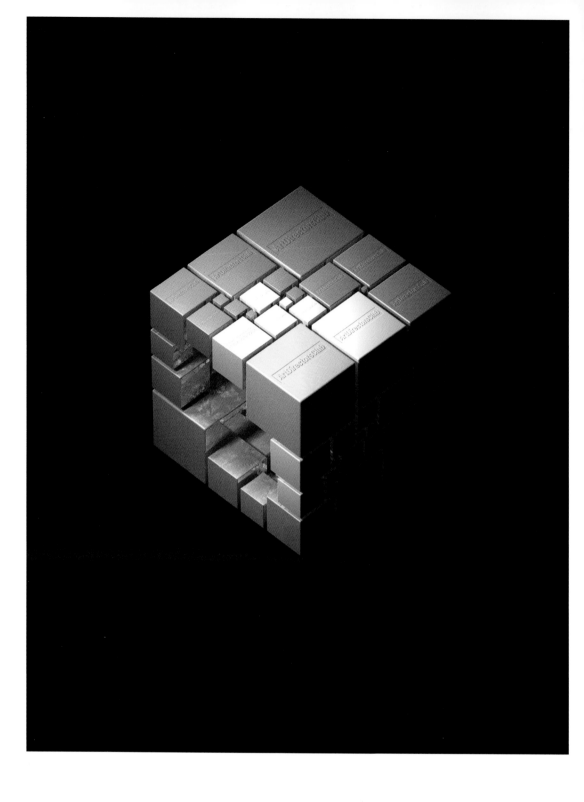

MASASHI KAWAMURA
CFE Design
Title Art Director
Website
www.masa-ka.com
Country United States

JEONG EUN (ELLE) KIM
CFE Design
Title Senior
Graphic Designer
Website
www.elle-kim.com
Country Republic of
Korea

Traveling Show: The Art Directors Club Traveling Exhibition is a way for our winners to go far beyond the Annual and the juries' inner deliberations. The visceral connection and participation people can have with the winning work is invaluable. The Traveling Show spreads ADC's mission to "Connect, Provoke, and Elevate" around the globe. The ADC 89th Traveling Exhibition traveled the world last year from Buenos Aires to Bangkok to Johannesburg. Far—reaching and impacting countless people, it is our honor to work with schools and major players in the field.

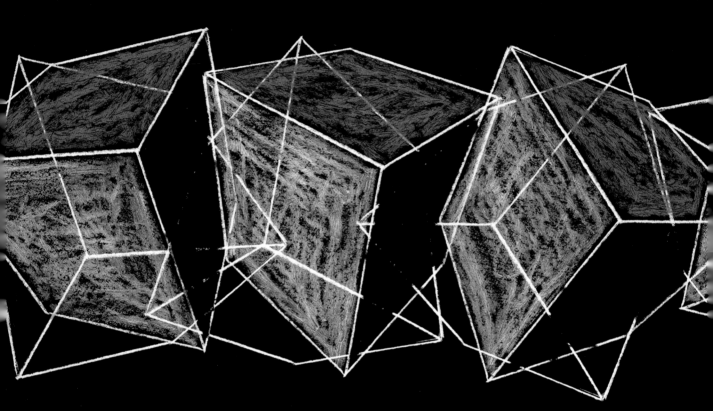

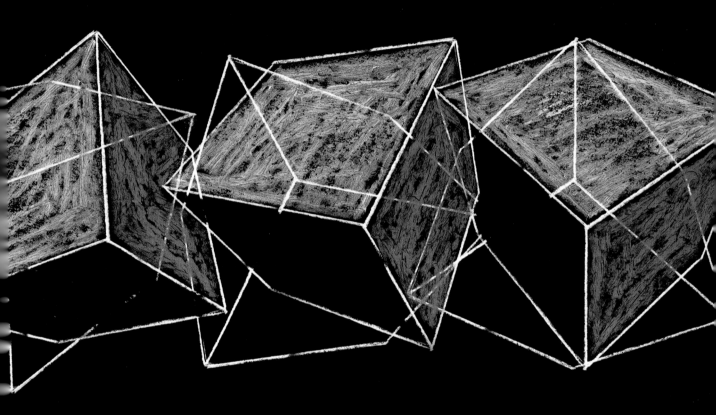

ADC's representative program is in its second year and has sought out individuals or organizations from around the globe engaged in advertising, design, interactive/digital arts, photography, illustration, media, education and communications that will help promote global awareness of the club as well as the prestigious honor of winning an ADC Cube.

The program offers representatives a unique and rewarding opportunity to be an integral part of the continued global success of the Art Directors Club.

ADC Representatives are instrumental in a number of areas: finding hosts for the annual traveling exhibition; suggesting key individuals to participate on the jury panel for the annual awards competition; acting as ADC's official exclusive representative in his/her country by distributing ADC press, Call for Entries, deadlines and jury information; and helping ADC connect with the advertising, design, education and visual communications industry in his/her country.

Guillermo Tragant, Argentina
Eduard Cehovin, Austria,Bosnia and Herzegovina, Croatia, Macedonia, Montenegro, Serbia, Slovenia
Pancho González, Bolivia, Chile, Colombia, Ecuador, Peru, Uruguay
Galefele Molema, Bostwana, South Africa
Pippa Seichrist, Sao Paulo, Brazil; Berlin, Germany; Madrid, Spain; Miami, Minneapolis and San Francisco, USA
Velina Mavrodinova, Bulgaria
Baohua Ren, China
Jiri Janoušek, Czech Republic
J. Margus Klaar, Estonia
Anne Saint–Dreux, France
Angela Ng, Hong Kong
Halasz Gyula, Hungary
Harmandar Singh, Indonesia, Malaysia
Kobi Barki, Israel
Claudia Neri, Italy
Minoru Morita, Japan
Tautvydas Kaltenis, Lithuania
Dominique Trudeau, Montreal, Canada
Bae Seog Bong, Republic of Korea
Alina Alexandrescu, Romania
Elena Artamonova, Russia
Ken Tsai Lee, Taiwan
Niwat Wongprompreeda, Thailand
Meera Sharath Chandra, United Kingdom

Slovenia

ADC ADMINISTRATION

Olga Grisaitis
Director

Brett Rollins
Director of Development

Jen Larkin Kuzler
Director of Awards
Programs

Jenny Synan
Director of Technology

Kim Hanzich
Information Manager

Chelsea Temkin
Annual Awards Manager

Erin Biggerstaff
ADC Young Guns
Manager

Flora Moir
Director of Education

Brooke Wood
Event Coordinator

Hugo Verdeguer
Facility Associate

Michael Waka
Awards Associate

Carol Arango
Design Intern

ADC BOARD OF DIRECTORS

Doug Jaeger
PRESIDENT
JaegerSloan Inc., Partner

Rei Inamoto
FIRST VICE PRESIDENT
AKQA, Global Creative
Director

Brian Collins
SECOND VICE
PRESIDENT
COLLINS,Chairman/Chief
Creative Officer

Steve Smith
TREASURER
Stephen M. Smith & Co.,
Partner

Chee Pearlman
SECRETARY
Chee Company,
Principal/Creative
Director

David Angelo
David&Goliath, Chair-
man/Chief Creative
Officer

Roger Baxter
RIM, VP of Marketing
Communications

Scott Belsky
Behance, Founder/CEO

Craig Dubitsky
KIND, Managing Partner

Rob Feakins
Publicis New York, Chief
Creative Officer/
President

Janet Froelich
Real Simple, Creative
Director

Ann Harakawa
Two Twelve Associates,
Principal/Creative
Director

Rick Kurnit
Frankfurt, Kurnit, Klein &
Selz, Partner

Noreen Morioka
AdamsMorioka, Partner

Benjamin Palmer
the barbarian group,
Co–Founder/CEO

Rob Rasmussen
Tribal DDB Worldwide, US
Chief Creative Officer/
NY Executive Creative
Director

Anthony Rhodes
School of Visual Arts,
Executive Vice President

Jakob Trollbäck
Trollbäck + Company,
President/Creative
Director

ADC PAST PRESIDENTS

Richard J. Walsh
1920–1921
Joseph Chapin 1921–1922
Heyworth Campbell
1922–1923
Fred Suhr 1923–1924
**Nathaniel Pousette–
Dart** 1924–1925
Walter Whitehead
1925–1926
Pierce Johnson 1926–1927
Arthur Munn 1927–1928
Stuart Campbell
1929–1930
Guy Gayler Clark
1930–1931
Edward F. Molyneux
1931–1933
Gordon C. Aymar
1933–1934
Mehemed Fehmy Agha
1934–1935
Joseph Platt 1935–1936
Deane Uptegrove
1936–1938
Walter B. Geoghegan
1938–1940
Lester Jay Loh 1940–1941
Loren B. Stone 1941–1942
William A. Adriance
1942–1943
William A. Irwin 1943–1945
Arthur Hawkins 1945–1946
Paul Smith 1946–1948

Lester Rondell 1948–1950
Harry O'Brien 1950–1951
Roy W. Tillotson 1951–1953
John Jamison 1953–1954
Julian Archer 1954–1955
Frank Baker 1955–1956
William Buckley 1956–1957
Walter R. Grotz 1957–1958
Garrett P. Orr 1958–1960
Robert H. Blattner
1960–1961
Edward B. Graham
1961–1962
Bert W. Littman 1962–1964
Robert Sherrich Smith
1964–1965
John A. Skidmore
1965–1967
John Peter 1967–1969
William P. Brockmeier
1969–1971
George Lois 1971–1973
Herbert Lubalin 1973–1974
Louis Dorfsman 1974–1975
Eileen Hedy Schultz
1975–1977
David Davidian 1977–1979
William Taubin 1979–1981
Walter Kaprielian
1981–1983
Andrew Kner 1983–1985
Ed Brodsky 1985–1987
Karl Steinbrenner
1987–1989
Henry Wolf 1989–1991
Kurt Haiman 1991–1993
Allan Beaver 1993–1995
Carl Fischer 1995–1997
Bill Oberlander 1997–2000
Richard Wilde 2000–2002
Robert Greenberg
2002–2005
Paul Lavoie 2005–2008

90TH ANNUAL AWARDS SPONSORS

sappi

Mother
Tongue

A world of
difference

bravedog
award entry services

Thank you to our
partners at Moleskine©,
who provided our print
invitation.

ADC MEMBERS

GOLD CORPORATE MEMBERS

Iggesund Paperboard
Leo Burnett Worldwide

SILVER CORPORATE MEMBERS

deviantART

CORPORATE MEMBERS

Alamy Inc
the barbarian group
Brave Dog
Condé Nast
Direct Source Packaging
Interbrand
Maude
The Partners
Pentagram Design
Pomegranate, Inc
Publicis
Real Simple Magazine
Two Twelve Associates

ACADEMIC MEMBERS

Fashion Institute of Technology

New York City College of Technology

Savannah College of Art & Design

School of Visual Arts

INDIVIDUAL MEMBERS

UNITED STATES

Hassan Abdul–Hameed
Andrio Abero
Katrina Ablacksingh
Leif Abraham
Ryan Adair
Gaylord Adams
Roanne Adams
Peter Adler
Charles S. Adorney
Shigeto Akiyama
Joe Alexander
Arpine Alexanian
Peter Alfano
Michelle Alvarez
Darrin Amellio
Julia Amirzadov
Alexandra Anderson
Jack Anderson
Aaryn Anderson
Andre Andreev
Gennaro Andreozzi
Astrid Andujar
David Angelo
Frank Anselmo
Kieran Antill
Tatsuya Aoki
Gil Arevalo
Gail Armstrong
David Arnold
Michelle Arrowood
Neslihan Arslan
Jayson Atienza
Matthew Atkatz

Kemp Attwood
Victoria Azarian
Robert O. Bach
Ronald Bacsa
Priscilla Baer
Damon Bakun
Lindsay Ballant
Giorgio Baravalle
Sarah Barclay
Thomas Barham
Don Barron
Robert Barthelmes
Orlando Bartolome
Yana Barysheva
Andre Basso
Liz Bauer
Allan Beaver
Rodger Belknap
Shannon Bellanca
Fernando Bellotti
Felix Beltran
Ann Benoit
John Berg
Barbara Berger
Michelle Berki
Jacob Berlow
Wayne Best
Candace Bexell–Oukacine
Tim Bierbaum
Michael Bierut
Tai Blanche
Robert H. Blend
K.C. Blinn
Nina Boesch
Laura Bonnetti
Andrew Bouchie
Jeroen Bours
Harold A. Bowman
Conor Brady
Lindsey Brand
Al Braverman
Patricia Brinkmann
Ed Brodsky
Ruth Brody
Robert E. Brothers
Craig Brown
Jason Brown
Bruno E. Brugnatelli
Victoria Bukowski
Christina Burcin
Anna Burns
Kendel Burton
Mikey Burton
Jack Butcher
Jordan Butcher
Iryna Butsko
SooJin Buzelli
David Byrd
Jamie Caliri
Molly Callaghan
Marsha Camera
Yi Cao
Wilson Capellan
Maria Carmanno
Thomas Carnase
Andreina Carrillo
Mike Carsten
James Carter
Vicente Casellas
Nicole Casper
Stephanie Casper
Michelle Cates
Katia Cerwin
Lisa Champ
Kari Chan
Tommy Chan
Natasha Chance
Andrew Chang
Chia–wei Chang

Jessi Chang
Anthony Chaplinsky Jr.
Carrie Chatterson
Jennifer Chen
Tiffany Chen
Ivan Chermayeff
Frank Chimero
Stephanie Chin
Luke Choi
Yon Joo Choi
Mary Choueiter
Hoover Chung
Shelly Chung
Stanley Church
Seymour Chwast
Maggie Ciavarella
Gerardo Cid
Elfe Cimicata
Herbert H. Clark
Kelly Clark
Noelle Clark
Thomas F. Clemente
Joann Coates
Bryan Coello
Kelsey Coffey
Alexa Cohen
Karen Cohn
Paul Collins
Nolan Constantino
Robert Cooney
Andrew Coppa
Sheldon Cotler
Niko Courtelis
G. Dan Covert
John Cowell
Lindsay Craig
Meg Crane
Kathleen Creighton
Crobin Crobin
Gregory Crossley
Renato D'Agostin
Keith D'Mello
Scott Dadich
Meghan Dailey
Jennifer Daniel
Flory Danish
Caitlin Finn Daoust
David Davidian
Myrna Davis
Paul Davis
Randi B. Davis
Jessica Dawson
Sheila Levrant de Bretteville
Enmibeth De La Cruz
Richard Degni
Joe Del Sorbo
Kaitlin Delcampo
Nazaury Delgado
Richard DeSimone
David Deutsch
John F. Dignam
Paul DiNovo
Jonathan Disegi
Ceil Diskin
Mary Jordan Djurasevic
Nate Dolce
James Donaldson
Gal Dor
Marc Dorian
Kay E. Douglas
Nina Dubin
Craig Dubitsky
Donald H. Duffy
Kristen Duffy
Joanne Dugan
Spring Dunn
Arem Duplessis
Tay Duran
Daniel Dyksen

Carla Echevarria
Bernard Eckstein
Geoffrey Edwards
Jai–Lee Egna
Stanley Fisenman
Trevor Eld
Eric Elms
David Epstein
Lee Epstein
Gabriel Escobar
Assaf Eshet
Jason Falk
Corinna Falusi
Jeff Faust
Pete Favat
Rob Feakins
Daniel Federman
Jeffrey Felmus
Michael Fenga
Lauren Festine
Mikell Fine Iles
Blanche Fiorenza
Carl Fischer
Bernadette Fitzpatrick
Nicole Fleisher
Donald P. Flock
Sarah Foley
Brady Fontenot
Raymond Forbes
Stephen Frankfurt
Mike Freeland
Carl Adam Freiholtz
Michael Freimuth
Christina Freyss
Fidel Frias
S. Neil Fujita
Leonard W. Fury
Raanan Gabriel
Danielle Gallo
Ryan Ganley
Brian Ganton Jr.
Kenneth Garcia
Gino Garlanda
MC Garofalo
Mike Geiger
Steff Geissbuhler
Thibault Gerard
Michael Gericke
Christine Gignac
Monica Gil
Lisa Gilardi
Steven Gilliatt
Frank C. Ginsberg
Sara Giovanitti
Bob Giraldi
Milton Glaser
Felipe Godinez
Rachel Gogel
Bill Gold
Ryan Goldberg
Kayla Gomez
Ana Gomez Bernaus
Natalia Gonzalez
Heloise Goodman
Timothy Goodman
Derek Gordon
Michele Gorham
Jason Gorman
Mariana Gorn
Shaun Gough
Cybele Grandjean
Hayley Grassetti
Kyle Grazia
Amanda Green
Geoff Green
Michael Greenberg
Jack Griffin
Christopher Griffith
Aaron Griffiths
Glenn Groglio

Raisa Grubshteyn
Matthew Guemple
Peter Gunther
Samantha Guzman
Robert Hack
Jordan Hadley
Kurt Haiman
Laurent Hainaut
Joe Hajek
Emily Hale
Graeme Hall
Carl Hammond
Tim Harms
Phil Harris
Keith Hart
Sarah Haun
Tom Hauser
Sagi Haviv
Molly Hawthorne
Luke Hayman
Elizabeth Haywood
Alexander Heil
Steve Heimann
Karl Heine
Nora Heo
Nancy Herrmann
Elana Hershman
Nessim Higson
Jonathan Hills
Andy Hirsch
Jessica Hische
Julia Hoffmann
Marilyn Hoffner
Janet Holmes
Linda Honan
Shiouwen Hong
Eric Hu
Cavan Huang
Mario Hugo
Tara Iannotti
Elisabetta Iannucci
Rei Inamoto
Brian Inatsuka
Itai Inselberg
Todd Irwin
Sabrina Italiano
Chris Italiano
Raisa Ivannikova
Consuelo Izquierdo
Nicole Jacek
Harry Jacobs
Doug Jaeger
Dannecker Jamie
John Jay
Lee Jensen
Rose Jensen
Patricia Jerina
Peninna Jeruzalmi
Mariah Jochai
Judy John
Jeff Johnson
Margaret Johnson
Sean Johnson
Jennica Johnstone
Jeremy Johnstone
Obamaniqua Jones
Spencer Jones
Hope Jordan
Nicole Jordan
Mirela Jurisic
Ardis Kadiu
Matthias Kaeding
Eric Kallman
Tim Kan
E Roon Kang
Walter Kaprielian
Amir Kassaei
Masashi Kawamura
Norman Kay
Felicity Keane

Stephen Kelleher
Terrence Kelleman
Nancy Kent
Inna Kern
Kelsey Kesko
Satohiro Kikutake
Andru Kim
Helen Kim
Hoon Kim
Jeong Eun (Elle) Kim
Christina King
Joey Kirkman
Marc Klatzko
Judith Klein
Chris Kline
Hilda Stanger Klyde
Katherine Knab
Mike Knaggs
Andrew Kner
Chris Knight
Henry O. Knoepfler
Nobuko Kobayashi
Gary Koepke
Lauren Kosteski
Dennis Koye
Sam Kramer
Crystal Krimpuri
Mike Krol
Ola Kudu
Anthony La Petri
Greg Lakloufi
Alina Landry
Jude Landry
Christopher Lane
George Lange
Alessandra Lariu
Diana Lau
Stefanie Lauria
Paul Lavoie
Amanda Lawrence
Leonardo Lawson
Sal Lazzarotti
Margaux Le Pierres
Michelle LeClerc
Caroline Lee
Gina Lee
Hang Hyun Lee
Jee-Eun Lee
Minki Lee
Seungyong Lee
SongHee Lee
Pum Lefebure
Tisa Lerner
Adam Levite
Taylor Levy
Mario Licato
Micah Lidberg
Brian Lightbody
Alex Lin
Ruy Lindenberg
John Peter Andreas
Lindstrom
Jen Little
Daniel Littlewood
Laura Ljungkvist
Rebecca Lloyd
George Lois
Bianca Londono
Patti Look
Francisco Lopez
Lihi Lothan
George Lott
Yi-Fan Lu
Alan Lum
Fredrik Lund-Hansen
Krisna MacDonald
Richard MacFarlane
David H. MacInnes
Jess Mackta
Lou Magnani

Lisa Maione
Dan Mall
John Maloney
Chetan Mangat
Jon Mannon
Alison Marana
Monica Marcil
Elena Margulis
Joe Marianek
Leo J. Marino, III
Alfred Marks
Chris Martin
Laurence Martin
Joseph Masci
Leonard Mazzone
William McCaffery
Sara McCarthy
Casey McClurg
Will McGinness
Tara McNulty
Meg McRae
Jens Mebes
Jeff Meier
Bryan Mendez
Scott Meola
Erin Mercurio
Ean Mering
Adele Merlo
Jack Messina
Jackie Merri Meyer
Alejandro Meza
Olga Mezhibovskaya
Andres Miguel
Abbott Miller
Kelli Miller
Michael Miranda
Miguel Miranda
Can Misirlioglu
Susan L. Mitchell
Michael Molloy
Sascha Mombartz
Karen Monahan
Sakol Mongkolkasetarin
Alex Mooney
Nick Moore
Tyler Moore
Ben Morahan
Benjamin Morejon
Noreen Morioka
Jean Morley
Deborah Morrison
William R. Morrison
Ahmed Mossobbir
Margaret Muhlfelder
Rachel Mui
N Silas Munro
Yoshichika Murakami
Erik Murillo
Monica Murphy
Sophie Murrell
Lisa Naftolin
Premanand Nankoo
Jessica Natches
Vera Naughton
Joel Nealy
Jose Jorge Netto
Sue Ng
Lauren Niebes
Lotta Nieminen
Chihiro Nishihara
Joseph Nissen
Seungkuk Noh
Roger Norris
David November
Jennifer Nunez
Jill Nussbaum
Gareth O'Brien
Kevin O'Callaghan
Nak Kyu Oh
Niall O'Kelly

John Okladek
Takashi Omura
Eddie Opara
Lysa Opfer
Thomas O'Quinn
Lauren Oswald
Andy Outis
Nina Ovryn
Onofrio Paccione
Majid Padellan
Michelle Padron
Tatiana Pages
Brad Pallas
Mitchell Paone
Cynthia Park
Hyewon Park
Shawn Park
Ilena Parker
Adam Parks
Karen Parry
David Paul
Juston Payne
Claudia Pearson
Steve Peck
Diana Pecoraro
Taylor Pemberton
Emely Perez
Daghan Perker
Harold A. Perry
Lexi Peters
Ben Peterson
Robert Petrocelli
Theodore D. Pettus
Allan A. Philiba
Jessica Philpott
Alma Phipps
Ernest Pioppo
Grant Piper
Carlos Pisco
Robert Pliskin
Emlyn Portillo
Jake Portman
Jonathan Posnett
Gavin Potenza
Ryan Potter
Mads Jakob Poulsen
Monika Pravs
Mcdonald Predelus
Michael Preston
Shelly Prisella
Abbey Prokell
Ivana Pulchan
James Quist
Christine Raniets
Idris Rashid
Robert Rasmussen
Robert Rasparini
Cynthia Ratsabouth
Anthony Reda
Daniel Redman
Samuel Reed
Herbert Reinke
Deirdre Reznik
Anthony Rhodes
David Rhodes
Stan Richards
Angela Riddlespurger
David Riedy
Christina Rinaldi
Jason Ring
Arthur Ritter
Brittany Rivera
Santiago Rivillas
Klajdi Robo
Luis Roca
Thomas Rockwell
Christoffer Rodemeyer
Lemuel Rodriguez
Peter Rodriguez
Dylan Rogers

Alan Roll
Andy Romano
Andrew Rosenthal
Vivian Rosenthal
Glenn Rosko
Charlie Rosner
Richard J. Ross
John Rothenberg
Michael Roznowski
Jaron Rubenstein
Randee Rubin
Renee Rupcich
Don Ruther
Stephen Rutterford
Thomas Ruzicka
Kathy Ryan
Jin Ryu
Puneet Sabharwal
Pia Sachleben
Elizabeth Sadkowski
Mai Sakai
Robert Saks
Nadia Saleh
Kimberly Sall
Zaid Salman
Robert Salpeter
James Salser
Laura Salvan
Floyd Sanchez
Monica Sanga
David Santana
Yolanda Santosa
Stanton Sarjeant
Robert Sawyer
Sam Scali
Ernest Scarfone
David Schaefer
Robb Scharetg
Paula Scher
David Schimmel
Elana Schlenker
Klaus F. Schmidt
Yuri Schneider
Michael Schrom
Eileen Hedy Schultz
Patti Schumann
William Seabrook III
Leslie Segal
Sheldon Seidler
Anna Sharp
Christy Sheppard
Ben Sherwood
Sangmin Shim
Michael Shirley
Joe Shouldice
Samantha Siegel
Jeff Sikaitis
Louis Silverstein
Todd Simmons
Milton Simpson
Steve Simpson
Abhilasha Sinha
Leonard Sirowitz
Kristin Sloan
Zach Slovin
Phil Smith
Bart Solenthaler
Cierra Sparta
James Spence
Brett Spiegel
Christopher Spohr
Chad Springer
Sandy St. Jacques
Joe Staluppi
Mark Alan Stamaty
Gary Stamps
Mindy Phelps Stanton
Matthew Starch
Elizabeth Stein
Doug Steinberg

Karl Steinbrenner
Fernanda Steinmann
Peter Stemmler
Heather Stephens
Lea Stepken
Daniel E. Stewart
Deborah Stewart
Jessica Stewart
Colleen Stokes
Bernard Stone
Jimmie Stone
Craig Stout
Rob Strasberg
Tina Strasberg
William Strosahl
Gerhard Stubi
Emily Suber
Baekkyu Suh
Samim Surel
Emily Susen
Orion Tait
James Talerico
Persia Tatar
Jack G. Tauss
Karen Tavares
Graham Taylor
Jarrod Taylor
Nichola Taylor
Robert Taylor
Mark Tekushan
Jim Temple
Simona Ternblom
Anne Thomas
Roland Tiangco
Casey Tierney
Ramona Todoca
John Torres
Damian Totman
Gael Towey
Dinah Tran
Victor Trasoff
Jakob Trollbäck
Ling Tsui
Rich Tu
Vinny Tulley
Mark Tutssel
Yuichi Uchida
Lauren Ullman
Robert Valentine
Maia Valenzuela
Darlene Van Uden
Laura Varacchi
Andrea Vargas
Marcos Vaz
Diane Painter Velletri
Amanda Vinci
Joseph Vinci
Frank A. Vitale
Jason Vogel
Andrew Vucinich
Kay Wakabayashi
Jennifer Walsh
Jessica Walsh
Justin Walsh
Tracy Walsh
Michael J Walsh Jr
Sean Wands
Barbara Warnke
Damion Waters
Jessica Weber
Lauren Webster
Jessica Wei
Stefanie Weigler
Susan Weil
Roy Weinstein
Craig Welsh
James West
Robert Shaw West
Delanie West Cheatam
Tim Wettstein

Richard Wilde
Benjamin Williams
Christopher Williams
Jason Winn
Ian Wishingrad
Bernd Wojtczack
Laury Wolfe
Connie Hoi Yin Wong
Jon Wyville
Betsy Yamazaki
James Kyungmo Yang
Efrat Yardeni
Phil Yarnall
Iee Ling Yee
Chieh Yen
Zen Yonkovig
Tony Yoo
You Jung Yoon
Danny Yount
Jessica Zadnik
Anthony Zambataro
Mark Zapico
Jeffrey Zeldman
Emily Zier
Jeff Zimmerman
Bernie Zlotnick
Andrew Zolty
Alan H. Zwiebel
Katarzyna Zyskowska

ARGENTINA

Camilo Barria Royer
Kellie Campbell
Juan Frontini
Lizi Hamer
Guillermo Tragant
Guillermo Vega

AUSTRALIA

Jay Benjamin
Chun Yi Chau
Nils Eberhardt
James Hancock
Horacio Lorente
Ricardo Ovelar Cuella
Adam Yazxhi

AUSTRIA

Tibor Barci
Mariusz Jan Demner
Stefan Müllner
Franz Merlicek

BELGIUM

Tuuli Sauren

BRAZIL

Joao Carlos Mosterio
Renata Zincone

CANADA

Marian Bantjes
Rob Carter
René Clément
John Gagné
Louis Gagnon
Jeremy Hall
Carlos Huezo
Diti Katona
Gracia Lam
Ric Riordon
Ross Rodgers
Jason Safir
Fernando Salvador

Dominique Trudeau
Ronaldo Vianna
Sabrina Wong
Josh Zak

CHINA

Han JiaYing
Kai Song
Zhiqiang Wang
Lixian Xu
Hei Yiyang
Nod Young
Shasha Zheng

COSTA RICA

Jose Antonio Ramirez

DENMARK

Lars Pryds

FRANCE

Ruff Benoit
Pierre Berget
Jeremie Fontana
Milan Janic
Mat Letellier

GERMANY

Frank Aldorf
Michael Eibes
Kahen Grace
Stefan Guzy
Harald Haas
Rudy Halek
Sascha Hanke
Oliver Hesse
Michael Hoinkes
Christoph Kirst
Claus Koch
Oliver Krippahl
Katharina Langer
Olaf Leu
Andreas Lueck
Sophia Martineck
Joel Micah Miller
Marko Prislin
Achim Riedel
Sven Ruhs
Eva Salzmann
Hans Dirk Schellnack
Tristan Schmitz
Joerg Schneider
Joerg Waldschuetz
Oliver Weiss
Joerg Zuber

GREECE

Yannis Konstantinidis

HONG KONG

Birdia Tak Wai Chan
David Chow
Iris Lo

ITALY

Robert Buganza
Jonathan Calugi
Andrea Castelletti
Moreno Chiacchiera
Dario Curatolo
Angela D'Amelio
Valerio de Berardinis

Alessandro Demicheli
Pasquale Diaferia
Davide Fissore
Debora Manetti
Gab Marcelli
Cristina Marcellini
Lorenzo Marini
Claudia Neri
Giorgio Rocco

JAPAN

Kan Akita
Masuteru Aoba
Katsumi Asaba
Norio Fujishiro
Toshiya Fukuda
Motoko Hada
Morihiro Harano
Keiko Hirata
Tomoyuki Hishiya
Takumi Inubushi
Masami Ishibashi
Mitsuyuki Ishibashi
Keiko Itakura
Genki Ito
Takao Ito
Yasuyuki Ito
Toshio Iwata
Takeshi Kagawa
Hideyuki Kaneko
Seijo Kawaguchi
Yasuhiko Kida
Pete Kobayashi
Ryota Kojima
Akiko Kuze
Kenichi Matsumoto
Kaoru Morimoto
Minoru Morita
Kentaro Nagai
Keisuke Nagatomo
Hideki Nakajima
Kazuto Nakamura
Shingo Noma
Sadanori Nomura
Yoshimi Oba
Kuniyasu Obata
Gaku Ohsugi
Yasumichi Oka
Hiroshi Saito
Hideo Saitoh
Michihito Sasaki
Hirotaka Suzuki
Zempaku Suzuki
Yutaka Takahama
Masakazu Tanabe
Soji George Tanaka
Yasuo Tanaka
Ryosuke Uehara
Katsunori Watanabe
Yoshiko Watanabe
Akihiro H. Yamamoto
Seitaro Yamazaki
Masaru Yokoi

KOREA, REPUBLIC OF

Kwang Kyu Kim
Han Lee
Kum-jun Park

MEXICO

Luis Ramirez

NETHERLANDS

Pieter Brattinga
Florian Mewes
Edwin van Gelder

NIGERIA

Oluseyi Frederick-Wey

PAKISTAN

Shahzad Nawaz

POLAND

Ryszard Sroka

REUNION

Pedro De Oliveira
Boutin Fabrice

SERBIA

Dejan Vukelic

SINGAPORE

Hal Suzuki

SLOVAKIA
(SLOVAK REPUBLIC)

Andrea Bánovská

SLOVENIA

Eduard Cehovin
Loni Jovanovic

SOUTH AFRICA

Ivan Johnson

SPAIN

Jaime Beltran
Miguel Bemfica
Oliver Haupt
Angel Montero Barro

SWEDEN

Kristin Bergem
Andreas Kittel
Mats W. Nilsson
Kari Palmqvist
Filip Redelius

SWITZERLAND

Florian Beck
Stephan Bundi
MC Casal
Bilal Dallenbach
Raymond Kaufmann
Conrad Malcher
Dominique Anne Schuetz
Rene V. Steiner
Philipp Welti

TAIWAN, PROVINCE
OF CHINA

Alain Fa-Hsiang Hu

TURKEY

Pinar Barutcu Fricke
Mete Gurgun

UNITED ARAB EMIRATES

Kalpesh Patankar

UNITED KINGDOM

Stella Ampatzi
Daryl Corps
Gemma Correll
Jeremy Craigen
John Hegarty
Geoff Linsell
Domenic Lippa
Martin Nicolausson
Ola Olowu
Sean Reynolds
Meera Sharath Chandra
Nik Studzinski
Ian Wharton

VIETNAM

Charles Valantin

STUDENT MEMBERS

Christine Aaron
Mikhail Abramov
Svetlana Akhmadieva
Sef Akins
Ahmad Al-Bataineh
Najeebah Al-Ghadban
Manuel Aleman
Darci Alexis
Amanda Aliperti
Rebecca Alvarez
Art Amaya
Paula Angarita
Fumiko Anspaugh
Brittany Antos
Michael Appuhn
Chris Arce
Ehab Aref
Jason Arias
Artem Artemov
Yoshie Asei
Rodger Austin
Ben Avny
Oluwafemi Awokoya
Kristie Bailey
Patrick Michael Baird
Erdenechimeg Bat-
Erdene
Eric Baum
Michelle Becker
Margot Belyea
Graciela Bernal
Jesse Bertolas
Katherine Bose
Justine Brilmyer
Nicolette Cantillo
Kimberly Capers
Richard Carbone
Andreina Carrillo
David Castillo
Justina Chang
Gin Chen
Jennifer Chen
Connie Cheng
Eva Cheung
Yooln Cho
Min Choi
Won Jin Choi
Youkyung Choi
Jailee Chung
Jayeon Chung
Joseph Cofone
Lindsey Cole
Alphons Conzen
Shannon Crabil
Lisa Cracchiolo

Kiara Dee Curbelo
Biliejean Curvan
Mary Dauterman
Kathryn Davenel
Dana Davis
Danielle De Biasio
Ramon De Los Santos
Xun Deng
Luke Derivan
Danielle DiCosimo
Vu Do
Michael D'ken Domondon
Pedro dos Santos
Lyanne Dubon
Ryan Duenas
Dominika Durtan
Nora Elbaz
Ariel Elias
Alison Eng
Sophie Erskine
Jin Fan
Shao-Ann Fang
Mia Feitel
Angelika Filinska
Anna Fine
Katherine Fisher
Mark Forsman
Kim Foster
David Freiman
Charles Gagneron
Vincent Garbellano
Roza Gazarian
Yong Geng
Donald George
Daniela Gill
Monika Golianek
Gabriel Gonzalez
Vera Gorbunova
Eric Goud
Marie Graboso
Adam Grabowski
Ben Grandgenett
Rose Greenstein
Chuck Griffith
Deborah Gruber
Tara Gupta
Sanjar Hakimi
Yu Kyong Han
Jaci Hays
Amanda Heil
Sooim Heo
Lauren Hom
Minji Hong
Seokmin Hong
Tiffany Hong
Sona Hovhannisyan
Genevieve Huba
Aimee Hunt
Jung Su Hwang
Jeffrey Iacoboni
Grace Ilori
Motoko Ishii
Gianna James
Kayla Jang
Yoon Deok Jang
Yi-Chieh Jen
Soobin Jeon
Bona Jeong
Rochelle Jiang
Byeolyi Jin
Connie Jun
Jae Sung Jung
Alla Kaba
Jamie Kakleas
Lilit Kalachyan
Aramazt Kalayjian
Callie Kant
Kie Kato
Chems Eddine Khiati
James Kiersted

Mara Kiggins
Anna Kim
HaYan Kim
Hyui Yong Kim
Jae Yeong Kim
Ji Won Kim
Minah Kim
Nari Kim
Woonji Kim
Won Young Kim
You Jin Kim
Ian Kirk
Erica Knauss
Eric Ko
Ai Kobayashi
Dominika Kramerova
James Kuczynski
John Michael Kuhn
Sherry Hsin-Ting Kuo
Christopher Kwon
Brandon Labbe
Margot Laborde
Zarina Rose Lagman
Irene Lau
Joyce Lau
Anna Laytham
Ella Laytham
Linh Le
Euikyung Lee
Heesang Lee
Hyun Hwa Lee
Jaedon Lee
Min Jung Lee
Narae Lee
Seo Jeong Lee
Seoyeon Lee
Tahui Lee
Sherry Leung
Philip Linnemann
Brittany Liszewski
Ian Liu
Ai-Lin Lo
Alicia Lo
Amy Love
Sandra Love
Yi-Wun Lu
Stephanie Macchione
Yasmin Rose Malki
Lance Marxen
Dianne Masse
Amanda Matelonek
Megan Matelonek
Khosi Makhosazana
Mbombo
Nicholas McMillan
Marvin Menke
Jacopo Miceli
Tal Midyan
Michael Miller
Whitney Miller
Christopher Mills
Timothy Min
Tyler Mintz
Hae Jun Moon
Jennifer Moore
Thomas Mori
Kerry Murdoch
Erin Murphy
Meaghan Murray
Hye Jung Na
Hamon Nasiri Honarvar
Christopher Nelson
Carmen Ng
Laura Ng
Justine Ngai
Paulina Niewinska
Wanqin Nong
Mariam Noureddin
Nathan Nowinowski
Jillian O'Brien

Hyangmi Oh
Kony Oh
Sol Oh
Jonathan Ong
Daniel Ortiz
Dylan Ostrow
Julia Pabiarezhnaia
Lisa Papa
Deva Pardue
Candice Park
Chan Young Park
Chei Jeong Yoon Park
Elaine Park
Guewon Park
Nari Park
Soo Bin Park
Kimberly Pasqualetto
Amie Paszel
Sonia Patel
Ruben Perez
Rheesa Persaud
Erica Peters
Jason Petersen
David Petrucco
Alex Place
Jacob Quigley
Jamie Raymond
Ren-Julius Reyes
Jose (Jay) Rivera
Jonathan Robbins
Audrey Rodriguez
Daniel Rodriguez
Denisse Rodriguez
Jessica Rodriguez
Naomie Ross
Samantha Russo
Yevgeniya Ryaboy
Fitgi Saint-Louis
Adrian Salajan
Diana Sanchez
Kate Sanders
Kira Yee Seul Sea
Heather Seksinsky
Megs Senk
Lydia Shacalo
Kelly Shami
Hilly Sharon
Aemin Shim
Thomas (Dong Hwi) Shim
Jarwon Shin
Tal Shub
Johanna Silfa
Abeer Sleiman
Catherine Small
Morgan Sobel
Hannah Song
Min Song
Aleanna Sonnylal
Scott Steidl
Yulsoo Ethan Sung
Magdalena Sztompka
Alicia Tagliasacchi
Junko Takano
Lingxiao Tan
Yu Ting Tan
Tonianne Tartaro
Andrew Teoh
Corel Theuma
Alexandra Thiel
Dana Tiel
Sloane Tittle
Matthew Tomboc
Eddy Tsai
Michael Ungano
Ashley Veltre
Bruce Viemeister
Elizabeth Villano
David Villouta
Jada Vogt
Tine Wahl

Deirdre Waski
Alan West
Matthew West
Arielle Wilkins
Rachel Willey
Katherine Willmann
Steve Winchell
Allen Wong
Youmin Woo
Peng Xu
Liz Yam
Aran Yeo
Svetlana Yershov
Samantha Yi
Erika Yost
Zipeng Zhu

INDEX

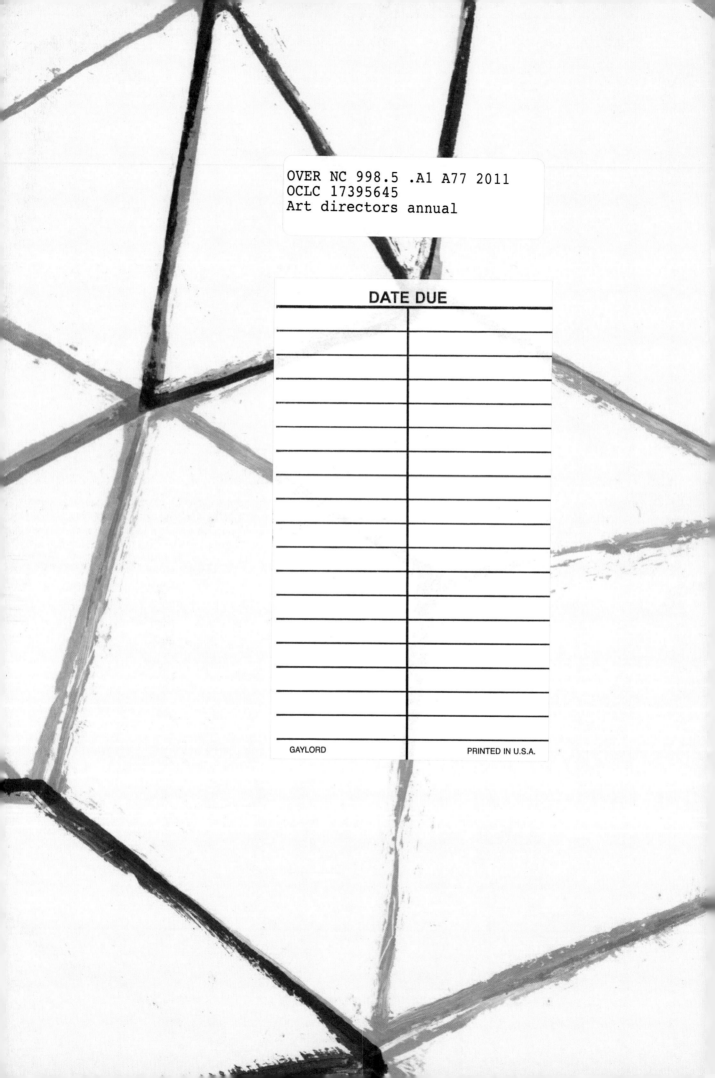